THE
GARLANDS
OF
REPOSE

Michael O'Loughlin

THE
GARLANDS
OF
REPOSE

THE LITERARY CELEBRATION OF CIVIC AND RETIRED LEISURE

THE TRADITIONS OF HOMER AND VERGIL, HORACE AND MONTAIGNE

THE UNIVERSITY OF CHICAGO PRESS

Chicago & London

The University of Chicago Press, Chicago 60637
The University of Chicago Press, Ltd., London

Library of Congress Cataloging in Publication Data
O'Loughlin, Michael, 1936–
   The garlands of repose.
   Bibliography: p.
   1. Leisure in literature. I. Title.
PN56.L404   809'.933'55   77–2206
ISBN 0–226–62657–1

For Maynard Mack

ut veni coram, singultim pauca locutus,
infans namque pudor prohibebat plura profari,
non ego me claro natum patre, non ego circum
me Satureiano vectari rura caballo,
sed quod eram narro. respondes, ut tuus est mos,
pauca: abeo; et revocas nono post mense iubesque
esse in amicorum numero.

CONTENTS

WORKS FREQUENTLY CITED

HORACE: Latin text and line numbers are to *Opera*, ed. C. Winkham and H. W. Garrod (Oxford, 1963). Translations, sometimes silently revised, are from the Loeb editions: *Satires*, *Epistles*, and *Ars Poetica*, trans. H. R. Fairclough (London, 1955); *Odes and Epodes*, trans. C. E. Bennett (London, 1952).

MONTAIGNE: French text and page numbers are to the Pléiade edition of the *Essais*, ed. Albert Thibaudet (Paris, 1950). The translation is from Donald Frame's admirable version, *The Complete Works of Montaigne* (Stanford, 1957).

VERGIL: Latin text and line numbers are to *Opera*, ed. R. A. B. Mynors (Oxford, 1969). Translations are from the version of C. Day Lewis, *The Eclogues and Georgics of Vergil* (Garden City, 1964).

Because of their accessibility, I have used the Loeb Classical Library texts in citing most classical authors.

PREFACE:
A POET'S DIGNITY AND EASE

Today the question "What do you do?" means "How do you earn your living?" On my passport I am described as a "Writer"; this is not embarrassing for me in dealing with the authorities, because immigration and customs officials know that some kinds of writers make lots of money. But if a stranger in the train asks me my occupation, I never answer "writer" for fear that he may go on to ask me what I write, and to answer "poetry" would embarrass us both, for we both know that nobody can earn a living simply by writing poetry. (The most satisfactory answer I have discovered, satisfactory because it withers curiosity, is to say *Medieval Historian*.)

> W. H. Auden, "The Poet and the City"

Essentially, Marx is saying that in the fullness of socialism, all men will work like artists. . . . By now we have become so accustomed to the regimen of compulsory (in an economic sense) labor that we have lost even the memory of the precapitalist period, when leisure was more common. In the Middle Ages the working year was only 150 to 200 days.

> Michael Harrington, *Socialism*

During the last decade of his life, in the retired leisure of his Twickenham grotto, Alexander Pope gave himself to "imitating" Horace in a group of poems which, despite their depth of vision and coherence of form, were to remain for two centuries the most neglected aspect of his achievement. Among these the "Epistle to Dr. Arbuthnot" is the one poem that does happen to be exceptionally well known, and its distinction may serve to introduce the preoccupation that characterizes others in its mode: not merely the imitation of a particular Horatian model, but the even more essentially Horatian transfiguration of those everyday occasions that we do not, every day, think of as unforgettable. Among such reminiscences the most evocative may be the poet's closing meditation on the secluded life and quiet death of his father and on his own filial piety in caring for his mother in her last days; yet there is a similar poignancy in the Horatian apologia, earlier in the poem, that concludes his recollection of the life and death of John Gay:

> O let me live my own! and die so too
> ("To live and die is all I have to do")
> Maintain a Poet's dignity and Ease
> And see what friends and read what books I please.
> (ll. 261–64)

In these lines, as so often in the later poetry of Pope, one begins to rediscover the existential as well as etymological origins of privacy in privation. For readers of a later century, however, the most troubling privation would seem to be that which prefigures the fate of these very imitations—the current impoverishment, not to say oblivion, of the very tradition of retired leisure they commemorate so movingly. There is already an elegiac accent in Pope's prayerful wish for content which is not to be found, for example, in the poem (Denham's "Of Prudence") which he quotes as a melancholy aside. If there is a heroic ring to the second couplet, its very assertiveness seems to admit that "maintaining" a poet's "dignity and ease" may be even more difficult than enjoying it, for some precious essence of it can be lost in the very insistence that it be "maintained."

In the century before Pope "dignity and ease" had often enough been the subject of a distinctive kind of English poetry, inspired by the Latin classics and articulated in poems like Ben Jonson's "To Penshurst." There they had been celebrated not as a private privilege but as the expression of an entire cultural order, a public context that had its consummate emblem in the festive free time of a great house and an organic society. In this tradition the "dignity" of "ease" enjoyed a civic sanction which today we would probably be more likely to accord to the "dignity" of labor. Indeed, though it has escaped the notice of Pope's editors, the very phrase "dignity and ease" might once have evoked a Ciceronian formula that seemed to epitomize to this older tradition the goal of a civilization in a schoolboy tag: *otium cum dignitate.*[1] We have lost much more here than a once familiar phrase.

In the near future I hope to complete a study of this tradition in English literature of the seventeenth and eighteenth centuries, with special attention to the achievement of Pope. I began the present essay years ago as an introductory chapter to such a study, designed to contain a few reflections on classical sources such as Horace and on Renaissance analogues such as Montaigne; but it soon became apparent to me that, however important—and neglected—the English expression of this tradition might be, the larger inheritance we had received was even more so. The moral continuity and literary complexity of the earlier ways of celebrating free time had never received anything like the critical attention they deserved and seemed especially to deserve in our time.

Without claiming finally to have answered that need, I hope that this book may at least call attention to certain primary issues: first, to the significance of leisure as a characteristic theme in certain representative works whose literary value is, I feel, better appreciated by considering them together; next, to the importance of discriminating what I call a civic from a private vision of leisure in the expression of that theme; and, finally, to the self-reflective character of the (leisurely) reader's reading (about leisure). Without adducing the infinite regress of writing and reading about such writing and reading, I must admit that these issues still have not received here the subtlety or thoroughness of investigation that they deserve. But to have glimpsed them together from afar, to have suggested a certain novel critical vocabulary for dealing with them, to have invited other readers critically to reconsider the works they inform— this is all that I can hope to have done. This is not a survey of all writers from Homer to Montaigne who have celebrated free time. Many such have been entirely or relatively neglected; they await reappraisal and may, in the meantime, I like to think, receive a degree of illumination from the categories I have suggested. Those I have chosen for extended comment have been selected for both their historical significance and literary complexity—especially the complexity that celebrates leisure where we least expect it.

ACKNOWLEDGMENTS

My primary concern has been with the careful reading of texts in their cultural contexts. My great privilege has been the challenge of a wide range of critical specialization to which a few footnotes will never do justice. Let me at least acknowledge a few debts close to home. *Causa fuit pater his*; this book began years ago when an artist gave his son his first liberal education, traditionally making him feel *chez nous* in Greece and Rome, provocatively making him find his own place in religion and politics. Among early teachers let me mention two from his school and mine, the late Joseph Ahearne and the late Henry Bean, Jesuits who embodied the best of Holy Cross College's classical tradition and who, without ever thinking of themselves as "new" critics, taught me to read Greek and Latin with close attention and with complex concern for the ultimate questions. At Yale, where for too many years this essay was in the writing as a dissertation or as a potential book, I enjoyed the encouragement of the best teachers, colleagues, and friends one could want at a time when "working on leisure" was, to a beginning teacher, no longer a whimsical contradiction. Among many, let me at least thank those whose thinking has most influenced me, even in ways that may surprise them: Professors Bloom, Brooks, Culler, Feidelson, Hartman, Kernan, Martz, Pope, and the late Professor Wimsatt. When I reflect that there is scarcely an English text in the following pages, I trust that they will understand how, merely by taking such breadth for granted, they tempered my desire to transfer to comparative literature. In a yet more immediate way this is true of the three readers of the original manuscript: Thomas M. Greene, whose intellectual scope and depth, stylistic finesse, and humane magnanimity set a standard for any study of this kind; George deF. Lord, who generously shared his own insights on a book that he had thought of writing; Martin Price (*o et praesidium et dulce decus meum!*), who, while creating a major new syllabus with a young instructor, encouraged me to enlarge my scope at the same time that he sought to keep me from being pretentious by persuading me that he took me seriously.

Among those who, happily, did not always take me seriously I am grateful to the colleagues of my generation teaching at Yale in the sixties: Michael and Susan Holahan; C. Earle Ramsey and Howard Weinbrot, for their sense of English analogues; and Cyrus Hamlin and Michael Simpson, for keeping me alive in the classics. *Et in Arcadia ego*: Stanley Fish has been from a golden age of the guild at Yale my guide, philosopher, and friend; despite our evident differences in method and perspective, my reflections on the leisurely reader's response to reading about leisure owe an obvious debt to more than a few conversations with him. More generous than he would admit to being, he has been more critically stimulating than he deserves to be told. While designing courses or considering the past—and the future—of the West, A. Bartlett Giamatti has sustained me with the depth of his commitment to comparative literature; his wit, never separable from his integrity, has been my moral support. His own work on a similar topic from a different perspective has provided me from the start with an example to which I might repair.

While I have been teaching, my contemplative quest has enjoyed the gift of leisure, first when this book's original form was awarded the John Addison Porter Prize in New Haven, and later, when a generous university gave an instructor a Morse Fellowship for a year in which to write and think. In my short time at the College at Purchase, the State University of New York bestowed a research grant for study and travel. Indeed, that splendid young college has managed to blend life with art in a way that is the theme of this book. Talking with Peter Bell, Bell Chevigny, Albert Fried, Myra Jehlen, Hélène Moglen, Robert Neville, Kathleen Paradiso, and Frank Wadsworth, I have come to a deeper grasp of what I presume to call civic leisure. More specifically, at Purchase I have enjoyed the advice of Seth Schein in the classics and of Naomi Holoch and Richard Stack on Montaigne. Finally, the gift of free time was vouchsafed to me as a fellow of the National Humanities Institute in New Haven. There, in the best kind of symposium, it was my luck to be able to discuss the implicit social issues of this book with Peter Berger, George Graham, Clyde Griffen, and Irving Howe, to benefit from Harry Berger and William Bouwsma on the Renaissance, and to be reminded by William Barrett, Wayne Fields, Carol Kyle, Richard Rubenstein, Patricia Spacks, and Marilyn Stokstad that myth and cosmos have claims not dreamt of in the world of historical action.

In realms of practice and research, let me thank the two Yale students who served as my Bursary Aides: Gregory Coleman, whose work on Montaigne is a book in itself, and Thomas Hanlon, precise on the Greek middle voice, indefatigable over miles of Migne. Through many copies, foul and fair, Rosanne C. O'Loughlin typed this manuscript with the shrewd sense of a good editor and the incredible kindness of a superb helpmate. In arduous circumstances Ellen Thayer O'Loughlin helped to sort pages and discovered footnotes in the fifth grade. In the last hours Carol Kyle painstakingly helped check the languages and somehow persuaded me that my English could be made comprehensible.

My largest debt blends with my first acknowledgment and is indicated in the dedication. Years ago Maynard Mack made the mistake of telling a student on his first paper that it was good to find someone who could read Horace. To him I have simply come to owe what Ben Jonson owed to his humanist teacher: "All that I am in arts, all that I know." Over the years, inside and outside the Scaean gate (and sometimes around and around), he has inspired me beyond description: those sprung from kings have known less joy than I.

1

INTRODUCTION:
THE GARLANDS OF REPOSE

How vainly men themselves amaze
To win the Palm, the Oke, or Bayes
And their uncessant Labours see
Crown'd from some single Herb or Tree,
Whose short and narrow verged Shade
Does prudently their Toyles upbraid;
While all Flow'rs and all Trees do close
To weave the Garlands of repose.
>> Andrew Marvell, "The Garden"

It was not by vile loitering in ease
That Greece obtained the brighter palm of art;
That soft yet ardent Athens learned to please,
To keen the wit, and to sublime the heart—
In all supreme! complete in every part!
It was not long thence majestic Rome arose,
And o'er the nations shook her conquering dart:
For sluggard's brow the laurel never grows;
Renown is not the child of indolent repose.
>> James Thomson, "The Castle of Indolence"

"To apprehend the point of intersection of the timeless with time," writes T. S. Eliot in "The Dry Salvages," is "an occupation for the saint." This book is about the literary celebration of "free" time within time as it was variously apprehended in two perennial kinds of imaginative structure. One of these was indeed conceived as an occupation for saints but also, and earlier, for citizens of the secular city. The other was the discovery of those who, like Horace or Montaigne, found it explicitly in retirement from the occupations of citizens and saints. The title is drawn from Marvell's "Garden," but the subject is as complex as that superb poet's lifelong deliberation of these alternatives. "The Palm, the Oke or Bayes," emblems of what I term "civic leisure," will flourish here alongside the garlands of "retired" leisure, for an awareness of each tradition enriches, and is enriched by, an awareness of its contrary. What the title does acknowledge, of course, is that to think of leisure today is to think of it not as the consummation of civic engagement but as the consequence of withdrawal. And assuming that retired leisure best introduces this complex of issues to a contemporary reader, let us turn immediately to our usual conception of Horace and Montaigne.

They are names that seem to belong together. Though they have not been previously studied together, they have long been associated in an appreciative but uncritical way, and that very phenomenon may serve to define what this book is about. More than most authors, Horace and Montaigne have been preserved in cozy reputations as pleasant, idle dabblers at life. Theirs are preeminently the books to be read by the fireside—bedside books to be culled at random. They do not, we are told, keep the reader awake—a reader, typically, like the bourgeois Pacome portrayed in Sartre's *Nausea*, who, without looking very far into the self, was content every evening to read over a few pages of "his old Montaigne or one of Horace's Odes in the Latin text."[1]

"The best men in the best ages," wrote Matthew Arnold, "have never been thoroughly satisfied with Horace," and, given this reputation, it is not hard to see why Arnold dismissed him as exquisite but not interpretative or fortifying.[2] And one suspects that the same might apply to Montaigne. But, as a matter of fact, Arnold relished Montaigne for the free play of his mind on all subjects, his sense of life as *divers et ondoyant*.[3] And yet, if Montaigne shares that sense of life with anyone, he shares it with Horace. Even more significantly, he shares a way of dramatizing the self in search of itself which saves that attitude from the insouciance of a M. Pacome and recalls Nietzsche's hope that men might someday take up Montaigne and Horace "as pioneers and guides for the understanding of Socrates."[4]

The divergence of these responses is instructive, for there does seem to be some quality of Horace and Montaigne that gives rise to their reputations for genial irrelevance and that distracts us from the very considerable claims on our attention that they can and should make. Now, in dealing with the familiar literary genres or modes, most readers generally take it for granted that they are supposed to bring a certain view of reality to a particular kind of structure. We do not, for example, blame *As You Like It* for not answering the questions of *King Lear*. Accepting the limitation of the form, our imaginations are liberated in other ways. In this sense, to accuse Horace or Montaigne of being "idle dabblers" or "irrelevant" is simply to accuse them of playing the fictive roles or *personae* they cast for themselves in the worlds of their creation. What then prevents us from accepting that characterization as we might accept, say, the apparent "misanthropy" of satiric fiction? The answer, I suspect, lies in our failure to respond to what seems like "idle dabbling" or "irrelevance" as the distinctive expression of a generic expectation that has long exercised the Western imagination: the myth of leisure—a vision that could not only inspire retirement but also sanction political or religious involvement. If today it is mainly associated with "retirement," the current status of that term is a significant commentary on its imaginative appeal.

"Retirement," as most of us use the word in the mid-twentieth century, means withdrawal from work because of disability or old age, an unwelcome process that often requires "adjustment." At the same time, at the opposite end of the spectrum, a similar predicament is involved in "dropping out," "turning on," "doing one's own thing." These two versions of retirement—especially in their mutual exclusiveness—attest to a profound cultural crisis in this age of technological revolution: the challenge of leisure time, the need for a redefinition of the value of work and the purpose of play or "unalienated" work. What Thorstein Veblen scorned as the privilege of the few is increasingly the predicament of the many: the time has come, writes Robert Lee, for a Theory of the Leisure "Masses."[5] In the language of social psychology, this is the crisis of Riesman's lonely crowd, of Marcuse's one-dimensional man, or, more optimistically, of Fromm's revolution of hope. Paradoxically, the very unfamiliarity in our time of the value system we are to discuss seems to give "the irrelevant" a novel relevance.

What we mean by leisure today is essentially and negatively "un-business." "Free time" connotes only time free *from* the world of affairs; like a day "off" in the work week, the meaning depends on, and the value is restricted by, a temporal frame of reference. We have "time on our hands" and "time to kill," but we have no locution to indicate time free for its own sake, time in another dimension from that of the busy world, free time not as escape but as fulfillment. "For that is the only true Time which a man can properly call his own, that which he has all to himself; the rest, though in some sense he may be said to live it, is other people's Time, not his."[6] So, at least, Charles Lamb writes in praise of a superannuated man's retirement from work. The blessings he cites, however, are those long associated with an older sense of the word, what Milton means in "Il Penseroso" when he speaks of "retired Leisure / That in trim Gardens takes his pleasure." In that sense of the word at least, "retirement" requires little "adjustment": "It was like passing out of Time into Eternity—for it is a sort of Eternity for a man to have his Time all to himself."[7]

The Greeks had a word for it: *scholē*. Their word for leisure is the root of our word "school." What they had in mind as "free" time survives in what we still appropriately call the "liberal" arts. Significantly, it is business that the Greeks defined negatively, calling it "un-leisure" (*a-scholia*), just as the Romans opposed *otium* to *neg-otium*. The emphasis is more than an etymological curiosity: "We do without leisure [*ascholoumetha*]," writes Aristotle in a famous formulation of priorities, "only to give ourselves leisure [*gar hina scholazomen*]."[8] In contrast, as Bertrand Russell put it in a witty example, modern man feels that it is virtuous to cook food but frivolous to eat it.[9] There is more than one feast evoked in the present book, and all of them, I hope, can be consumed as ends in themselves.

Now, just as it is in "Il Penseroso," the most ambitious justification of the condition of leisure is its religious translation into a state of mystical rapture: "Dissolve me into ecstasies / And bring all Heaven before mine eyes" (ll. 165–66). Indeed, that vision might best be described as a recreation of the self through participation in an ultimate reality that is itself essentially playful, as divine wisdom was at the creation of the world, according to the Book of Proverbs:

> I was with him forming all things; and was delighted every
>   day, playing before him at all times;
> Playing in the world. And my delights were to be with the
>   children of men.
>   (Proverbs 8:30–31, in the Vulgate text)

This text is familiar to many readers today from the conclusion of Huizinga's classic *Homo Ludens*,[10] but it is interesting to find Aquinas citing it in a commentary on Ecclesiastes 32:15, in which he notes the aptness of "calling man home to play," because play, like wisdom, is not directed to some other end but is sought for its own sake; hence in Proverbs, he explains, eternal wisdom likens its joy to that of play.[11] Centuries earlier Gregory Nazianzen had compared the creativity of the divine word to the play of a child,[12] and, still earlier, Plato, and especially Heraclitus, had touched on the same analogy, to awaken in Nietzsche, for our time, the Dionysian vision of how, "just as the child and the artist play, the eternal living fire plays, builds up, and destroys in innocence—and this game the Aeon plays with himself."[13]

This integration of leisurely recreation and divine creativity is also involved in the mythical situation of the religious festival, where, according to Mircea Eliade, the participant encounters a liberation from profane time in "the eternal present" of sacred time, enacting the cosmogonic moment when the world came from the creator's hands.[14] In his complementary discussion of *Leisure: The Basis of Culture*, Josef Pieper has also urged the implications of the original German title, *Musse und Kult*: "There is no such thing as a festival without gods." Without the context of festive worship, Pieper says, work becomes inhuman and leisure becomes idleness. Idleness, he reminds us, is that least understood of the old seven sins, *acedia*, and the polar opposite of true contemplative-creative leisure.[15]

These are ultimate perspectives, and later chapters will owe much to them even as they also recognize another, more humanistic point of view, in which the condition of leisure is seen not as sanctioned by a playful god but as the ultimate aspiration of human play itself. After all, though he quotes Milton, Lamb's retired man envisions a far more mundane version of "the Cherub Contemplation" than that vouchsafed to "Il Penseroso," and Huizinga's survey is seldom as concerned with ultimates as the quotation from Proverbs suggests. Humanistic discussions of play have become more seriously anthropological and philosophical, following the lead of Huizinga's book and Caillois's *Les Jeux et les hommes*.[16] Thus, Eugen Fink's discussion of "the ontology of play" links it explicitly to the concerns of the present study: "In the autonomy of play action there appears a possibility of human timelessness in time. Time is then experienced, not as a precipitate rush of successive moments, but rather as the one full moment that is, so to speak, a glimpse of eternity."[17] It is amusing to recall that this is the same prospect, expressed in almost the very terms, that in his earlier, more whimsical version Lamb had promised us in the retired leisure of a superannuated man.

Those whose humane fulfillment lies in the higher play of literary art have, of course, long enjoyed certain self-reflective images of the reader's own leisurely game: a golden age, an earthly paradise, or, more popularly, a Land of Cockaigne, a Big Rock Candy Mountain, a Yellow Submarine, a Greening of America. Among literary forms this is surely the appeal of pastoral and romance, those two "play idealizations" par excellence—two "Golden Ages of Play," as Huizinga designated them to characterize the consummate playfulness of Renaissance culture.[18] In recent years, probably the most conspicuous achievement of the influential criticism of Northrop Frye has been the theoretical elaboration and rhetorical celebration of this imaginative possibility. In rehabilitating romance, in proclaiming the mythic resources of comedy, Frye beckons the reader beyond the ironic works favored by an earlier generation of critics— indeed, beyond what had seemed the reality principle—to "the central myth of art . . . the vision of an end of social effort, the innocent world of fulfilled desires, the free human society."[19]

Like Plato's, Frye's utopian vision would exist "in the present, not in the future, not as a dream to be realized in practice but as an informing power of the mind"—a city, indeed, like the city Socrates offers to Glaucon as a pattern laid up in heaven for the education of the imagination.[20] Later, in Frye's *The Modern Century* and other studies, this vision is articulated in an examination of true leisure and the authentically social dimension of the liberal arts.[21] One need not be an absolute votary of Frye to allow that his utopian interests arise opportunely in "the modern century." The challenge of leisure time is crucially a challenge to a continuing "liberal" education, a challenge to the creative imagination to celebrate such gods as make possible our feast or as our feast makes possible. Whether or not the enjoyment of leisure can be called the central myth of art, the means to that end surely lie in that artistic transformation of life which might be called the central myth of leisure, one in which the centrifugal business of the busy world (which we like to call the real world) has been

imaginatively reordered around the radically human center of
a man cultivating his garden and recreating his soul.

The specific concern of this book is with the dramatization
of this myth, not only as something "given" in sacred contemplation or liberal education, pastoral play, or romance enchantment, but as something earned amid the urgencies of profane
time and exigent history—indeed, often in civil war. Typically,
the imagined world to be considered here is a quotidian one
that seems to resist the irradiations of myth; its authors' positive distrust of fancy is one of their major themes. To adopt
Frye's term, it is often "low mimetic," a world which seems
much closer to satire than to romance or pastoral. Indeed, it is
significant that these latter two visions of delight will finally
be seen in the following pages, if not ironically, at least as a
prelude to that domestication of the fabulous which marks the
achievement I hope to define. It is perhaps the achievement
which Sainte-Beuve had in mind when, discussing "what is a
classic," he cunningly introduced Montaigne, *ce vrai poète*,
into Horace's corner of the sociable poets. He did so, he said,
to deprive them of the air of a literary school. But in his medi-
tations on Horace and Montaigne, the one prosaically conversational in poetry and the other truly poetical in conversational
prose, he did in fact suggest a way of integrating the concrete
and the ideal which is shared more deeply by these authors
than the apparent difference of one medium from another
would suggest.[22] The world of Horace and Montaigne is not
the escapist reverie of Sartre's Pacome, but it has its own answer
to nausea in the existence they share with his Roquentin.

If the retired leisure of Horace and Montaigne has introduced some of today's implications of our subject, those implications have also gradually and variously suggested another
way of conceiving leisure that transcends privacy and that
might begin to account for the presence here of such works as
the *Odyssey* and the *Georgics* and for my opening reference
to the occupations of citizens and saints. "Retirement," after
all, need not be synonymous with leisure; it can mean idleness,

escapism, and solipsistic fantasy. This is what Freud means in his indictment of "the hermit" in *Civilization and Its Discontents,* and we remember that in an earlier time Dante put a saintly pope outside hell for his "great refusal" in abdicating a seat of power for the security of contemplative peace. Privacy can be literally a state of privation, and the world retired "from" may be either the busy world of action or even a world in which leisure is regarded as the fruition of civic involvement. Indeed, the condition of leisure which today we think of as a private privilege would seem to originate in, and be first sanctioned by, a suprapersonal awareness, an allegiance to the classical *polis,* for example, or to the Christian kingdom of God. This vision of what I call "civic" leisure has its most interesting and complex articulation in those imaginative works, like the *Odyssey* and the *Georgics,* in which the life of active service is somehow affirmed in time and history and yet transcended in the larger context of a public goal of free time.

The achievement of Horace and Montaigne is thus doubly distinctive, since it involves not only a vision of leisure but one in which retired, moderate human content is endowed with something like the mythic and civic significance formerly derived from public contexts. Here privacy is not escapist, nor is it transcended. It is transfigured.

The next chapter is a survey of some early and tentative versions of these two traditions within the Greek legacy, useful as an introduction to Vergil and Horace but important too for their own complication of the themes and images which will engage us. In what literary form did the life of leisure first emerge as a cultural ideal? How was the life of withdrawal or privacy first depicted? For although it became, as for Horace, the peculiar promise of "retirement" to invest privacy with the virtues of a higher life, it is important to see that the condition and its consequence were not always so creatively related. The story of their conjunction makes an interesting chapter in the history of ideas and literary forms.

2

THE DREAM OF EASE: IMAGES OF LEISURE FROM HOMER TO THEOCRITUS

Mere dreams, mere dreams! Yet Homer had not sung
Had he not found it certain beyond dreams
That out of life's own self-delight had sprung
The abounding glittering jet . . .
             W. B. Yeats, "Meditations in Time of Civil
                          War: Ancestral Houses"

The Public Context

The Example of the Odyssey: *Phaeacia and Ithaca*

The gods, according to the Homeric formula, are those who
live at ease (*rheia zōontes*).[1] In the schoolboy's translation, they
are the "happy" gods, the "blessed" gods, and their bliss is the
special kind of happiness we call leisure. The discovery of how
this condition might be man's as well is the central drama of
the literature dealt with in this chapter, as we seek to trace
from Homer to Theocritus the imaginative quest for that festive island, removed from the flux of time, that would seem to
be the governing image of the human version of divine ease.
It will not, for reasons touched on in the previous chapter, be
a simple quest, just as the ease of the gods is not unequivocally
attractive if taken literally. Given the nature of the human
condition, as Hannah Arendt has eloquently argued, such an
existence for mortals would be "a lifeless life."[2] And yet, lifeless, too, in another way, would be the human condition if
deprived of the ease of the gods as a metaphoric or mythic
inspiration for the vision of leisure. To Aristotle it offered an
illustration of the civic primacy of contemplation, and Epicurus
might have found in it the prototype of his own retirement.[3]
The myth is relevant, too, to the issues of the previous chapter.
Schiller evoked the ease of the gods to justify play as the
distinctively human and humanely fulfilling activity: "The
Greeks," he lamented, "transferred to Olympus what they
should have realized on earth."[4] And finally, translating the
myth into Christian terms, Virginia Woolf speculates on how
it might be realized on earth in those pleasures that are ends
in themselves—like reading. At the Day of Judgment, she muses,
when the men of affairs come to receive their rewards, "the
Almighty will turn to Peter and will say, not without a certain
envy when He sees us coming with our books under our arms,
'Look, these need no reward. We have nothing to give them.
They have loved reading.' "[5]

It is tempting to postpone that divine reaction until our concluding discussion of Montaigne's transformation of Christian contemplation, but it is also irresistible here to introduce the *Odyssey*, the first work not only to offer the leisurely enjoyment we expect in all art but to have as a subject the validity and complexity of such ease. In contrast, we might take for example the lines from the *Iliad* in which Andromache comes to hear of Hector's death. She was weaving a robe, we are told, and preparing hot water for his bath; but when the brute fact penetrates from outside the wall, the shuttle drops from her hand, and in her shock we feel the civilizing art of her inner room crushed as irrelevant. Hector's body lies stripped and mutilated, far from the folded robe and the inwrought figures she was weaving, far from the hot baths prepared for it (*Iliad* 22. 437–48).[6] "Nearly all of the *Iliad*," writes Simone Weil, "takes place far from hot baths."[7] When we turn to the *Odyssey*, on the other hand, it seems that the quality of life depicted there—even including the slaughter of the suitors—is never too far from hot baths. What Alcinous tells Odysseus of the Phaeacian way of life is but one conspicuous expression of the cultural ideal that seems to irradiate the poem:

> and all our days we set great store by feasting,
> harpers, and the grace of dancing choirs,
> changes of dress, warm baths, and downy beds
> (*Od.* 8. 249–51)

To stress the *Odyssey* as a celebration of civilized leisure is not to deny but to complement a current school of interpretation that might be called the *"Iliad* critic's" emphasis on the tragic or existential aspect of the poem.[8] The name of Odysseus, for example, does mean pain, and, actively and passively, the "Odysseusing" of the hero defines his identity.[9] In the following pages, however, this process will be seen, not as an end in itself, but as the means of realizing a goal of leisurely values, like those of Alcinous' island—only in human terms, in Ithaca. In Ithaca, too, unlike the tragic world of Andromache's dropped shuttle, Penelope's weaving will have preserved her

inner freedom from the deadlines of the suitors—but only because she unweaves her artifact every night. "Unweaving," like
"Odysseusing," is a means to the fulfillment of the leisurely
ideal variously reflected in the first half of the poem and realized in its still neglected and significantly less exotic second
half. Such an account of the poem might be epitomized in two
feasts: first, the hospitality which Odysseus enjoys on the happy
island of Phaeacia; second, the inhospitable reception which
he suffers from the suitors at Ithaca, which ends with his handling the murderous bow like a harper and, later, commanding
the music to play on so that passers-by may take the slaughter
for a wedding feast (21. 406–9; 23. 129–40).

In the first half of the poem, the landing at Phaeacia is of
course but the grandest instance of that governing image—the
calm harbor sought from the sea's flux—that continually informs the narrative. If these books ask us how a man defines
his identity, it is a question that arises from the searching exploration of this image in a variety of contexts. What—if anything—we are asked, again and again, will make a harbor fit
for man, whose condition is so much affected by the tides and
tempests of the flux of time? In the *Iliad* there is no such
prospect, save for the inhuman ease of the gods. That some
measure of that ease might be man's, and might not deny but
fulfill his humanity, seems to me the emergent issue of the
Odyssey's quest. At the same time, we must bear in mind that
the discovery of such ease can also be seen as an emergent issue
in the reader's experience of the poem, since in reading the
Odyssey we enjoy the very leisure it is in the process of defining. This self-reflective aspect will enrich the reader's experience of the literature in this book, but it is especially relevant
here because of the poem's originally oral character and consequently more festive relationship to the free time of its audience.

Our earliest version of the timeless harbor as a human possibility is found, appropriately enough, in a description of the
afterlife, the Isles of the Blest. This myth, which might have
come to the Greeks from Egypt, was not as widespread as the

legend of Hades.[10] Unlike that gloomy underworld, these islands offer what Homer matter-of-factly calls the "life which
is easiest for men," *rhēistē biotē pelei anthrōpoisin* (*Od.* 4.
565). In the haunting phrase of a modern translation, this is
where "all existence is a dream of ease"; but the integration
of dream and reality had already begun in the original. These
islands of calm, apart from the flux of the world, are a classic
instance of the governing metaphor of the opening books of
the *Odyssey*; and the freedom from time experienced by those
who dwell there is especially suggested by the details of the
weather:

> Snowfall is never known there, neither long
> frost of winter, nor torrential rain,
> but only mild and lulling airs from Ocean
> bearing refreshment for the souls of men—
> the West Wind always blowing.
>
> (4. 563–68)

Significantly, this freedom from the tempest is the very aspect
which the poet chooses to emphasize in his description of
Mount Olympus, "where the happy gods spend all their days
in pleasure" (6. 46): "Never a tremor of wind, or a splash of
rain / no errant snowflake comes to stain that heaven" (6. 42–
45).

It is in the postwar world of Menelaus (whose afterlife is
destined for those islands) that we have our first hint of godlike
free time within human life. We cannot imagine the characters
of the *Iliad* living in peace, said Werner Jaeger,[11] but as we
come to it in the fourth book of the *Odyssey*, with Telemachus,
the luxurious Spartan court is superbly festive and graciously
hospitable. "This is the way the court of Zeus on Olympus
must be," says Telemachus (4. 74). Yet his response is not likely
to be that of today's reader, who may prefer to contrast the
corresponding details of the other place Telemachus visits,
the less luxurious home of Nestor in Pylos. Here there is worship outdoors; in Sparta, there is nuptial festivity indoors (3.
5–6, 32–33; 4. 3–4); and we note the differing welcomes to

Telemachus (3. 34–35; 4. 20–36), the differing character of the wives of each king and the number of his children (3. 402–3; 4. 121–22), and, indeed, what would seem to be differing attitudes even to bedtime (3. 329–37; 4. 294–95). We might even begin to conclude that in the simpler home in Pylos Homer is suggesting a norm by which to indict the good life at Sparta.

There is, I think, no better introduction to the leisurely *ēthos* of the *Odyssey* than to entertain this conjecture. For what the reader soon discovers is not only the absence of any disvaluation of the wealth of Menelaus as such but indeed the positive pride of Nestor in his own portion of the good life, his wealth and his artifacts. This is delightfully apparent when Telemachus presumes to spend the night on his ship instead of imposing on Nestor's hospitality. He is no pauper, Nestor insists—he too can offer blankets and deep-piled rugs (3. 353–58). Meanwhile, the reader may also have begun to discover not only the value of such artifacts as blankets and deep-piled rugs but also the value of the very artifact he at present happens to have the leisure to be reading.

But all this seems to be contradicted when, in book 5, we meet Odysseus on Calypso's island, yearning to leave an immortal existence of voluptuous ease that seems so much like the life celebrated in the recurrent imagery of the previous excerpt. Certainly it seems so when Hermes lingers on his mission from Zeus to contemplate the luscious details of the enchanted isle (5. 55–75): "Even a god who chanced to come here," we are told, "would gaze and marvel and feel his heart beat with delight" (5. 73–74). Even the rhetorical effect of the survey has aptly been called leisurely. "You feel," writes Thomas Greene, "that the poet is a man who can afford to take his time, to linger, even, over the scenes he most enjoys."[12] But if the reader is momentarily beguiled by the desultory style, he will soon begin to understand, as Odysseus has, that this easeful existence will still leave one homesick for an authentically human repose. Though his wife is doomed to die and is, he admits, less beautiful than Calypso, something permanent seems to abide in time at Ithaca that makes the deathless nymph seem curiously ephemeral. To be homesick for Calypso would be unimaginable. Hers is the bliss of nostalgic fantasy that turns to ennui. Within time, at the poem's end, with a wife growing old, Odysseus will achieve a leisurely content he never enjoyed in the arms of Calypso. He leaves her island not because he restlessly prefers activity for its own sake but because he seeks to realize the dream of ease not as an otherworldly gift but on his own terms, as husband, father, and king. Unlike Menelaus, Odysseus need not look forward to the Isles of the Blest for the perfection of this life in the afterlife. He need only look homeward, as in fact he soon does, from the happy island of Phaeacia.

In the present reading of the poem, Odysseus' sojourn among the Phaeacians will be much more than an epic interlude providing the hero with an occasion to retell his adventures, plunging his hearers *in medias res*. Here, in the richest exfoliation of our parent metaphor of the calm harbor, the poem's quest is not so much interrupted as, in a deeper, proleptic way, it is fulfilled when the hero and the reader stand back from the tides of time to contemplate the urgencies of the past from the vantage of a civilization enjoying the fruits of leisure, where life is shaped by art.

We remember how Odysseus comes to this happy island after his raft has been battered and he himself has nearly drowned in the worst storm of his career (5. 365–440). Then, gradually, the narrative shifts from this turbulent scene to a windless calm, in which the shipwrecked wanderer swims to the smooth stones of a natural harbor (5. 441–53). There, in a protective grove, he finds repose in the shelter of two bushes. Above him the intertwining branches are so closely interwoven as to be impenetrable by the elements. Covered with their fallen leaves, he sleeps (5. 475–93).

As if a dream were coming true, the shining Nausicaa comes to the shore, playing and singing. What she means to Odysseus and to the reader is evident in his first words to her. Having praised her virginal beauty and tactfully entreated for her succor, he prays the gods to grant her heart's desire, a husband and a happy home. Then follows a famous declaration that nothing in the world is finer than when husband and wife share a house in one accord, a grief to their foes, a joy to their friends—"but they know this best themselves" (6. 149–85). The speech, of course, is contrived to appeal to a young girl, but this should remind us of what in fact this young girl is: not a Calypso, tempting to escapism, but the incarnation of those values which gain added poignancy in the light of Odysseus' struggle to renew them.[13]

These values are manifest as the panorama of the Phaeacian way of life unfolds at the court of Alcinous. Once oppressed by the aggressive Cyclopes, these people have founded a new world on this distant island, "far from men who live by toil" (6. 4–8). There, as Alcinous tells Odysseus, in the lines already quoted to introduce the poem, they cultivate the arts of peace and the good life (8. 248–49). For, as was intimated in the figure of Nausicaa, this island is more than a quiet harbor, far from a turbulent world; the timeless calm has been transformed into the favorable climate for a special kind of human animation.

This transformation is superbly evident in the famous description of the gardens of Alcinous, where the symbols of the Isles of the Blest come to fruition among men:

> Fruit never failed upon these trees: winter
> and summer time they bore, for through the year
> the breathing Westwind ripened all in turn—
> (7. 117–19)

The passage is famous as one of the poem's detachable "beauties" or *topoi*, but we miss its profoundly humanistic significance if we ignore the relation of the garden to the rest of the story, especially to the expanding vision of Phaeacian life which it may be said to symbolize. For if leisure here, in Pieper's phrase, is truly "the basis of culture," it is because cultivation, culture, and cult are all aspects of the same experience. Just as the perpetual fair weather nurtures the ever-fruitful garden, so the garden sustains and, as it were, invites us to the festivals which are the characteristic activity of this happy folk, and in which Odysseus now joins. What M. I. Finley tells us about Homer's feasts is nowhere more vivaciously manifest than in

the holidays of this island. Through the sharing of food and
drink, in a substantial, not merely symbolic fashion, he writes,
a bond was instituted or renewed, "tying men and gods, the
living and dead, into an ordered universe of existence."[14] It
is more than a coincidence that, having surveyed "the glorious gifts of the gods" in the gardens (7. 132), Odysseus should
next come upon the Phaeacian leaders pouring a last libation
to Hermes (7. 136–37). Nor are we surprised to learn that here,
as in all Hellas, strangers are welcomed because they are sacred
to Zeus (6. 207–8) or that the gods themselves often come to
visit these celebrations (7. 201–3).[15] For what we contemplate
here not only epitomizes the pattern we have discussed in the
first half of the poem; it is also the grandest early manifestation
of that vision of civic leisure which was so long to exercise the
classical imagination. Centuries later, for example, we read in
Plato's *Laws* a defense of public festivals which could be a
commentary on Odysseus' Phaeacian experience. The gods sanction these occasions, Plato says, in compassion for the hard-
ships and fatigue of the human condition, "besides giving us
the Muses, their leader Apollo, and Dionysus to share these
festivals with us and keep them right, with all the spiritual
sustenance these deities bring to the feast."[16]

As Odysseus himself says at the high point of the Phaeacian
festival, addressing not only his fictive audience but the early
hearers of the poem in a similar situation and even the later
reader in a comparable moment of free time:

> Alkinoos, King and admiration of men,
> how beautiful this is, to hear a minstrel
> gifted as yours: a god he might be, singing.
> There is no boon in life more sweet, I say,
> than when a summer joy holds all the realm,
> and banqueters sit listening to a harper
> in a great hall, by rows of tables heaped
> with bread and roast meat, while a steward goes
> to dip up wine and brim your cups again.
> Here is the flower of life, it seems to me.
>
>   (9. 2–11)

The "flower of life" (like "a summer joy") beautifully captures
for a modern reader that convergence of calm, garden, and festival which reaches its center in the leisurely experience of this
moment. For what Homer simply but immensely calls "the
fairest thing there is" (9. 11) is the climactic—and untranslatable—enactment of all that the Phaeacian way of life has promised. It is also the fulfillment in more human terms of that
otherworldly "dream of ease" whose adumbrations we have
observed in the Isles of the Blest, Mount Olympus, and even
the Isle of Calypso. It looks back to the comforts of Menelaus'
court, but it is achieved without the cost which experience has
exacted there. It looks ahead to the final blessings of Odysseus'
restoration—the regeneration of peace and virtue and their fruition in the life of leisure. The Phaeacian episode is not so
much a temptation to unearned ease for Odysseus as a fabulous
stimulus to the earning of free time in his own world, the recreation there of what he so admires here.

Because Phaeacia is such a stimulus, Odysseus will compli-
cate the superlative affirmation, just quoted, before concluding
his speech. As he gives his name and rather poignantly describes the unpicturesque landscape of his homeland, we are
brought back to the world across which he must toil and travel,
a world where time is anything but free (9. 19–28). He recalls
the sensuous delights of Calypso's captivity, but again this only
deepens his longing for the domestic values he has gone so long
without (9. 29–33). Soon, with another superlative, he seems
to deny his praise of the joys of the feast. Now nothing is
sweeter than the sight of homeland and parents; even a house
of gold in far lands is no compensation (9. 33–36). The "flower
of life" has thus evoked its own dismissal. Here, as in the encounter with Nausicaa, the Phaeacian way of life appeals to
Odysseus by virtue of qualities which turn his mind (and that
of the poem's audience) to how things might be in Ithaca (or
outside the poem). The leisurely festival is eclipsed by a sense
of the journey's urgency; yet, paradoxically, the journey is
urgent only because its end is the reconstitution of the good
life such as Odysseus has found it, here on this peaceful isle.

This paradox is nicely dramatized in the course of the next day's festival. Odysseus has finished his narration and his ship has been outfitted. The feast is, we gather, much like the feast of the previous night. Odysseus, however, is no longer able to share in the delights he praised the day before. Now he is acutely conscious of their true significance as a symbol of the goal he must reach. While all around him make merry, and Demodocus the minstrel sings again, he alone is distracted by his consciousness of time, his commitment to a future action. So he keeps looking at the sun, waiting for it to set, eager for the voyage home. The tension between the joys of the feast and the longing for Ithaca is then condensed in this remarkable simile:

> Just as a farmer's hunger grows, behind
> the bolted plow and share, all day afield,
> drawn by his team of winedark oxen: sundown
> is benison for him, sending him homeward
> stiff in the knees from weariness, to dine;
> just so the light on the sea rim gladdened Odysseus.
>   (13. 31–35)

It is an extraordinary analogy, for the tenor of the comparison seems to contradict its vehicle: the lines say, in effect, that in leisure Odysseus longs for work, just as the worker longs for free time. Just as Odysseus is simultaneously aware of the summons of the setting sun and the joys of the feast, the simile holds the opposed attitudes of action and repose in solution; it presents the burdens of time as pressing, but it reminds us that we take up these burdens only to be able to put them down. Like the action which it describes, it suggests that we do without leisure to have leisure; and like the episode which it concludes, it insists that leisure is worth having.

The same complex relationship of means and ends informs the action of the second half of the poem, in which Odysseus moves to realize the joys of the Phaeacian holiday by the kind of tactics that culminate in the slaughter of Penelope's suitors. That there is, potentially, a leisurely goal to be achieved is manifest the next day, when, ferried over the waves, Odysseus awakens to contemplate a harbor so lovely in its fusion of nature with art as to convince him that once again he has been deceived in his destination:

> There on the inmost shore an olive tree
> throws wide its boughs over the bay; nearby
> a cave of dusky light is hidden
> for those immortal girls, the Naiades.
> Within are winebowls hollowed in the rock
> and amphorai; bees bring their honey here;
> and there are looms of stone, great looms, whereon
> the weaving nymphs make tissues, richly dyed
> as the deep sea is; and clear springs in the cavern
> flow forever.
>
> (13. 102–9)

More than just the climax of all the happy islands in the poem's quest, the scene also anticipates the restored and transfigured Ithaca, whose perfect symbol will be the olive tree, which Odysseus identifies to Penelope as the stock of his bedpost and the organic foundation in which his whole house is literally rooted (23. 177–208). Indeed it is worth noting that, following the revelation of the bed in book 23, Odysseus will embrace Penelope in a fashion which not only is the best dramatic explication of the symbol of the bedpost but also returns us to a scene recalling Odysseus' arrival here in Ithaca or, shortly before, in Phaeacia:

> As the sun-warmed earth is longed for by a swimmer
> spent in rough water where his ship went down
> under Poseidon's blows, gale winds and tons of sea.
> Few men can keep alive through a big surf
> to crawl, clotted with brine, on kindly beaches
> in joy, in joy, knowing the abyss behind,
> and so she too rejoiced, her gaze upon her husband,
> her white arms pressed as though forever.
>
> (23. 233–40)

Eventually we shall recall this scene and discuss the final meaning of its duration as Athena lengthens the night and holds back the dawn (23. 241–46), but let us first examine the

means of its accomplishment, the tactic by which the promise
of a harbor that seems like a dream is fulfilled in a rooted Ithacan reality. The tactic has a special interest here; for even as
Odysseus first awakens to a similarly lovely scene on his native
shore, the reader discovers that an outraged Poseidon has turned
the Phaeacian ship into an island of stone, forcing the hospitable Alcinous to vow to welcome no more castaways in the
future (13. 169–83). The Phaeacians suffer the perennial vexa-
tion of the life of art and leisure in a world of flux and action
that does not play by the rules of their feast.

How then will Odysseus realize in time a vision of leisure
like the one he enjoyed on their island? It is a question that
will recur in the major texts of this book, and the often unlikely answer, be it in the civic labor of Vergil's farmers or
Benedict's monks or the homely self-description of a Horace
or Montaigne, may well remind us of the special tactic of this
homecoming, which, like the unweaving of Penelope, achieves
its liberation through an artful imperfection. We recall how
Odysseus, when he landed on Phaeacia, was transformed by
Athena into a veritable work of art fit for such hosts, his hair
"like gold infused on silver by a craftsman" (6. 229–35). Place
beside this what happens on the beach at Ithaca, when Athena
reveals herself to him as a woman "tall and beautiful and no
doubt skilled at weaving splendid things" (12. 288–89). Significantly, the effect of her art this time is to undo the very qualities she had heightened on Phaeacia:

> Speaking no more, she touched him with her wand,
> shriveled the clear skin of his arms and legs,
> made all his hair fall out, cast over him
> the wrinkled hide of an old man, and bleared
> both his eyes, that were so bright. Then she
> clapped an old tunic, a foul cloak, upon him,
> tattered, filthy, stained by greasy smoke,
> and over that a mangy big buck skin.
> A staff she gave him, and a leaky knapsack
> with no staff but a loop of string.
>
> (13. 429–38)

How far this transformation seems from the first one, so much more suited to a world of calm harbors, gardens, and festivals; and yet the fascination of the second half of the poem lies precisely in how the more down-to-earth fiction is related to the earlier, more fabulous archetypes of leisure, how indeed it makes them come true with a special kind of irony. Irony usually involves letting the voice of affirmation or even over-statement have its way while the author and the reader share a negative or more "realistic" secret perception, as we do, for example, when, for various reasons, we sense that Odysseus will not rest in any of the prior islands, however attractive they may seem. In the conclusion of the *Odyssey*, however, as in so many of the later Western celebrations of free time *in* time, we shall find that an ironic realism, assured of its homecoming secret, will expose the vaunted realism of the busy world as centrifugal and illusory. Unlike the irony that serves a certain kind of re-alism, this authenticates what might otherwise seem too fabu-lous to be true. Melanthius and Irus can see only a loutish-looking idler, just as the suitors scorn a "beggar's" handling of the bow ("Maybe he has one like it at home," 21. 398). So too, when Odysseus enlists the practical involvement of his outnum-bered supporters, we are struck by how different this self-portrayal is from the festive contemplation of fantastic adven-tures that had regaled the leisurely Phaeacians. At the same time, the rising comic expectation of the poem's conclusion springs from *our* knowledge that the joys of such a feast have been in fact experienced and indeed are beginning to come true here. For his Ithacan host, the swineherd Eumaeus, Odys-seus contrives the plausible, prosaic fiction of a Cretan exile moving through a fallen world of restlessness, greed, and be-trayal; but it is, ironically, the only true part of his guest's grim history—the promise of Odysseus' return—that Eumaeus rejects as unrealistic: "Why must you lie, being the man you are?" (14. 364–65).

Assured of our homecoming secret, we learn to see the un-heroic activity, even the degradation, of Odysseus as but a means to an end which transforms drudgery. Hence Telemachus, who has tasted the good life at Pylos and Sparta, will now be taught by his father to endure the opposite of such hospitality in order to realize it in Ithaca (16. 274–80). Indeed, one of the most entertaining aspects of this part of the poem is just the way in which the newly instructed Telemachus, employing the language of hard-headed realism, leaves the reader only more convinced of the values that are busily being denied: "Why should I care for this beggar?" he inhospitably protests to Eumaeus. "I have my own problems and can't take care of everyone that comes along" (17. 6–15). Similarly, later, he matter-of-factly reports to Penelope only that he learned in Sparta that Odysseus is still on Calypso's island (17. 108–49).

Penelope will soon be reassured by Theoclymenus of the truth of Odysseus' homecoming, but it is hard to resist the impression that she, who most embodies the domestication of the fabulous, did not need the interpretation of omens to prompt her interest in the beggarly stranger who has just arrived.[17] Her response is worthy of her husband's ironic tactics. While she allows herself to be seen by the suitors as a glamorous artifact (18. 158–280) and even entertains their proposals (281–83), she maneuvers to expose the emptiness of their festivity by proposing the down-to-earth test of stringing the bow.

The subsequent slaughter of the suitors provides a climactic instance of the ironic tactic of "realistic" disfigurement that has been evident since Odysseus first arrived at Ithaca, the paradoxical means of realizing through unromantic action the festive leisure praised at the feast of Alcinous. Appropriately, the suitors had even been enjoying a holiday of sorts: as Antinous tells Eurymachus, this is "no day to sweat over a bowstring" (21. 258–59). And a holiday it will continue to be—not for these idlers, but for him who slowly turns over the old bow in his hands, checking for wormholes, and who then, having strung the bow "like a harper" and having won the contest, proclaims how he will achieve, for Ithaca, leisure of another kind. He did not miss the mark or waste time in stringing the bow, he reminds them, but now it is time to give the suitors the feast they deserve while there is still light. Other entertainment will follow—songs of the lyre, for these are consecrated to festivity (21. 425–30).

In contrast to Odysseus' awareness of the setting sun at the close of the Phaeacian banquet, there is a curiously leisurely and detached quality to our contemplation of the violent elimination of this idle party. Take the way we see them running from Athena's aegis:

> like stung cattle by a river
> when the dread shimmering gadfly strikes in summer,
> in the flowering season, in the long-drawn days.
> After them the attackers wheeled as terrible as falcons
> from eyries in the mountains veering over and diving down
> with talons wide unsheathed on flights of birds,
> who cower down the sky in chutes and bursts along the valley—
> but the pouncing falcons grip their prey, no frantic wing avails,
> and farmers love to watch those beaked hunters.
>
> (22. 296–306)

Similes like these, especially in the *Iliad*, often point up the contrast between life in the countryside and the uprooted struggle on the plains of Troy; but the effect of the rural evocation here is to suggest a deeper and more complex consonance with the action described. Not only does the vengeance of Odysseus profoundly resemble the simile in its blend of violence and ease; it is also the only possible instrument for restoring to Ithaca the georgic vision that Odysseus had already prefigured when he praised Penelope's fame as being like a just king's, whose countryside is the emblem of his rule:

> his black lands bear
> both wheat and barley, fruit trees laden bright,
> new lambs at lambing time—and the deep sea
> gives great hauls of fish by his good strategy,
> so that his folk fare well.
>
> (19. 111–14)

Now that prospect of civic leisure has begun to come true—not in a fabulous locale but here at home in rocky Ithaca, and by tactics suited to the place.

We can now appreciate the full significance of the passage
in which Odysseus identifies his bed made of the olive tree and
embraces Penelope like a castaway saved from the tempest.
Here, in their own kind of harbor, they will enjoy a leisurely
transcendence of clock time as Athena slows the night and
keeps back the dawn (23. 241–44). And yet, even this expanded
moment must, we know, be lost. Penelope will rest only when
Odysseus tells her that he will finally propitiate Poseidon only
after he has traveled overland to a place where men take his
oar for a winnowing fan. This reference will become a major
source of the legend of a restless Odysseus, but in the poem's
own economy such an inconclusive motif is also peculiarly con-
clusive, deepening our apprehension of free time, not as "happiness ever after," but as the transfigured moment of repose
within time. It is therefore profoundly appropriate that, in the
next line, after having told Penelope of his propitiation of the
"deathless" gods, Odysseus should emphatically introduce his
own death (23. 280–81). Yet even this is shaped by a context
of homecoming and civic leisure. Death will come to him from
seaward, he predicts, an easy death, the discomfort of a com-
fortable old age, while his people around him enjoy prosperity
(23. 281–84).

Nothing better illustrates the existential urgency of the
Western quest for leisure, from Odysseus to Montaigne, than
its confrontation with the fact of death. In the passage just
cited, the vision traced earlier, in the imagery of the festive
island, comes to fruition even as it yields to the flux of time.
Significantly, Odysseus will soon tell Penelope how he could
not rest with Calypso even though she would make him ageless
and immortal (23. 335–36). Such immortality, as we have seen,
would have meant a kind of death-in-idleness, the opposite of
leisure. Here, where death's reality principle looms as the culmination of all the ironic disfigurements, unweavings, and
slaughters that have characterized Odysseus' Ithacan experience, there also emerges the possibility in time of that festive
leisure he had praised at the feast of Alcinous.

When we recall how that feast offered the reader an image of his own leisurely enjoyment of the poem, we can also contemplate how, from the sundown departure from Phaeacia through the events of Ithaca, the reader has been prepared by the narrative structure of the poem for the experience of its conclusion. All poems, of course, must end; but here, as later, the closure of works devoted to leisure is of special consequence to the reader who has self-reflectively participated in them. To close the *Odyssey* is to experience its theme. We close the poem, as once we might have left the feast of its singing, to land on our own Ithaca, disfigured and doomed to die, mindful that, like Odysseus, we shall not stay forever on any happy island but mindful too, like him, that there are civic orders worth working for which have their consummation in a human version of the dream of ease and that, for us, this includes the very contemplation of the *Odyssey* itself. The poem tells us that we close our *Odyssey*s in order to reopen them, that leisurely experience is what we do without in order that we may have it more abundantly.

Civic Leisure

When, centuries later, Aristotle argued in his *Politics* that we do without leisure only in order to give ourselves leisure, he was proposing an essentially civic conception of *scholē*, such as we have just seen first emerging in the *Odyssey*. In Lewis Mumford's words, "Beginning as a representation of the cosmos, a means of bringing heaven down to earth, the city became a symbol of the possible. Utopia was an integral part of its original constitution." As he goes on to say, it was also the source of its tension.[18] Certainly, in the Greek tradition we are considering, the defense of leisure was an issue of social value, not private privilege. This is why Odysseus' praise of "the fairest thing there is" at the feast of Alcinous was taken so seriously as a definition of the end of the good society. Because the passage seemed irresponsibly to endorse tippling on a state-

wide scale, Socrates condemns it in the *Republic* as an example
of the bad influence of poetry.[19] On the other hand, in discussing Odysseus' praise of that feast, we have already encountered
Plato's great defense of civic and religious festivals in the *Laws*.
In this affirmative tradition, too, while discussing the ends of
the good society in his *Politics*, Aristotle cites these same lines
from the *Odyssey* as proof of the importance of music in train-
ing the young, evidence that "there is a sort of education in
which parents should train their sons, not as being useful or
necessary, but because it is liberal or noble."[20] Just as the civilized ethos of the *Odyssey* supplants the martial code of the
Iliad, so in the *Politics* Aristotle envisions a community opposed to the warlike state of the Spartans. "So long as they were
at war," he says, "their power was preserved, but when they
had attained empire, they fell, for of the arts of peace they knew
nothing, and had never engaged in any employment higher
than war."[21] But the end of war, he argues, is peace, just as the
reason for work (or unleisure) is leisure.[22] That is why, as in
the above defense of music as a liberal art, the *Politics* concludes (books 7–8) with an extensive discussion of the educational goals appropriate to a state at peace: the inculcation of
those virtues of philosophy, temperance, and justice necessary
to a leisurely society—necessary even, he insists, on the Isles
of the Blest[23]—and the cultivation of those leisurely activities,
such as music and contemplation, which are "superior" to all
others because they are enjoyed, not as means to an end, but
as ends in themselves.[24] For, as he put it in the *Ethics*, it is in
the intrinsic satisfactions of contemplative leisure that men
most approach the happiness of the gods.[25] And since, for Aristotle, men are essentially political animals, the furtherance of
their pursuit of that happiness is the objective of the state. To
use the terms of a contemporary political scientist who is in
this respect a votary of Aristotle, "If a man is at leisure anywhere he is free, the good state must exist to give him leisure."[26]
In the terms of our Homeric example, Aristotle preserves a
sense of the journey's urgency (the active life, the practical
necessities of statecraft)[27] but subordinates these means to the

leisurely values of the journey's end (the joys of the feast, music, and contemplation).[28] "The dream of ease," which began as an otherworldly idyll, had become the first principle of a treatise in political science.

In the late twentieth century, Aristotle's account seems even more humanistically convincing as technology replaces the slave labor that he took for granted as a condition for the leisure of his citizens. When Hannah Arendt summons readers beyond the merely biological or worldly spheres of "labor" or "work" to the truly human condition of political "action," perhaps the last sphere might be better understood by what I call "civic leisure."[29] Such a designation, at least, would enable us to understand and transform the notion that political action is a "waste of time," whether it be our contemplation of it in print or television or our actual (if often ironic) participation in its versions of the festive process or, at best, our enjoyment of its consummation in the form of "public happiness," to borrow the title of August Hecksher's book vindicating civic encouragement of the arts. Civic leisure is political "action" conceived as the contemplation, realization, and celebration of humanistic values that are ends in themselves.

THE PRIVATE FOCUS

Personal Poetry: Satiric and Lyric Dimensions

In or out of his time, Aristotle's integration of *scholē* and *polis* remains a high point of Hellenic culture and a continuing critique, as in the works of Arendt or de Grazia, of whatever culture happens to be contemporary. Yet the very inclusiveness of this synthesis reminds us of an alternate vision, more congenial to a later age than to his but significant for its emergence even then. We must now turn to the shift in focus which tended to divorce the life of leisure from the aims of the community—to detach the peace of the garden and the joys of the feast from the necessity of resuming the journey and restoring a fallen kingdom. For the scholiast records a curious anecdote

at the conclusion of our emblematic scene from the court of
Alcinous: it was in reading Odysseus' praise of the fairest thing
there is, we are told, that Epicurus was led to his philosophy
of pleasure.[30]

The line of thought which we are to discuss culminated in
the Gardens of Epicurus, and its characteristic precept was that
philosopher's unpolitical injunction: "Live retired."[31] It would
be hard to conceive a state of mind more opposed to the earlier
Homeric or Aristotelian view of leisure; for it was the traditional conception of the *polis* as the center of gravity which
prompted Pericles to boast in his Funeral Oration of Athens'
contempt for the unpolitical man,[32] and today our word "idiot"
preserves this scorn for the "private" man—the original meaning of the Greek root.[33] Thus, the commendation of withdrawal
did not come early or easily to the Greek mind; and to describe, however cursorily, the conditions which eventuated in
its acceptance is to trace the curve of a civilization. In his mon-
umental study of Greek culture Werner Jaeger has proposed
that the evolution of the city-state coincides with a shift of the
source of value (*aretē*) from the social ideal of the political
community to a more personal and spiritual kingdom "within,"
such as we find in Plato.[34] Later, with the disintegration of the
polis in the Hellenistic age, this tendency culminated in codes
of radical individualism, such as Stoicism or Epicureanism.[35]

To return to the *Odyssey*, Laertes, who is probably the first
"retired" man in Western literature, is a rather abject figure.
Ravaged by experience and with his son apparently lost, the
old man lives apart, with no sense of a transformation of his
condition. When Odysseus meets him, he is poorly dressed and
unkempt; his head is bowed, and he is digging about a plant
(24. 242–43). Only by a return to the exigencies of experience
and the problems of the community, at the side of his heroic
son, will Laertes earn the peace and leisure which he could not
find in retirement. What we must now consider is how these
values came to be regarded as incompatible with the means
Laertes and Odysseus used to achieve them. For by the time of
Epicurus, retirement had become the sole means of rediscov-
ering a leisurely innocence which was unavailable elsewhere.

In the Gardens of Epicurus, to use our Homeric examples, the isolation of Laertes' retirement would be transformed into something like the affirmation of Alcinous' feast.

The poetic discovery of the private focus begins as a slight motif, one which we hear in counterpoint below the historically dominant theme of public responsibility. Indeed, we hear its first literary expression at about the same time that the idealization of the political community occurred, when the old heroic code was being converted into a civic ethic.[36] In the fragments of Archilochus, the Ionian precursor of the Horace of the *Satires* and the *Epistles*, we read, for example, that an anxiety over public reputation deprives one of many delights,[37] or that the poet did happen to lose his shield in battle but suffered no shame at the disgrace, since he escaped with his life,[38] or, more somberly, that a dead hero's glory is soon forgotten.[39] As in the last example, Archilochus' detachment from the values of the community really amounts to a questioning of commonly accepted appearances. His centripetal concentration is really an effort to reach a core of reality which, in their centrifugal striving, public men never reach. Thus, in what is probably the most famous fragment, Archilochus turns away from the perennial goals of man's busyness:

> I care not for the wealth of golden Gyges, nor
>   ever have envied him.
> I am not jealous of the works of the gods.
> And I have no desire for lofty despotism.
> For such things are beyond my ken.[40]

What gives even this brief passage its force is the intensity with which the retiring poet repudiates men's aspirations in several dimensions at once: the yearning for wealth is linked to a crude titanism and then to grandiose political ambition. The poet dismisses them all peremptorily with the same negative shrug and for the same reason: they all seek to expand what is seen as man's limited condition, to transcend the contracted vision artlessly confessed in the last line.

The conclusion is notable, too, because its seemingly naive stance is to become an ever deeper feature of the retired man's characterization. According to Aristotle, the lines in Archilochus' poem are supposedly spoken by one Charon, a carpenter —a good instance, he says, of using a fictional character, or *persona*, to express views too provocative for personal attribution.[41] But there is also an intrinsic significance in such a mask, and eventually the identity of the humble carpenter will shape the confessional fictions of a Horace or a Montaigne. Indeed, the best witness to the achievement that begins with Archilochus is the last page of Montaigne's *Essais*, where our study of the tradition will end. There, in the spirit of the fragment we have just read, Montaigne will repudiate the public aspirations of his time, warning against those transcendental humours that would turn men into angels, reminding us that even on the loftiest throne we sit on "nostre cul," and insisting that the loveliest lives are those of the common mold, "sans miracle et sans extravagance."

But the contracted focus alone will not be the final vision of the *Essais* or its tradition. Montaigne's next sentence, and his last, is a prayer to Apollo for health and wisdom, "mais gaye et sociale." That is why Montaigne will close the essay quoting from Horace's *Odes* 1. 31, a prayer to Apollo for content, for health in body and mind, for an old age without shame, but also, significantly, not without the songs of the lyre ("nec turpam senectam . . . nec cithara carentem"). If Horace was able to transmit to Montaigne a gay and sociable lyrical transformation of Archilochean withdrawal, it was because he was also the legatee of the two Greek poets whose work so anticipates his *Odes*, Sappho and Alcaeus. In their works the private focus had become the product not so much of a centripetal movement away from the ambitious world of affairs as of a new celebration, where one came to realize, in Bruno Snell's words, that "though the individual who detaches himself from his environment severs many old bonds, his discovery of the dimension of the soul once more joins him in company with those who have fought their way to the same insight. The isolation of the individual is by the same token the forging of new bonds."[42] The new bonds, of course, were often erotic. This is quite manifest in the case of Sappho; it is less obvious, perhaps, but for our purposes more important, in Alcaeus' praise of the symposium, or drinking party, as in this fragment, which Horace probably used as a model for an ode we shall be reading:

The Sky-God bows himself;
There is a great storm in the heavens;
The streams of water are frozen fast . . . .
Defy the storm with a good fire and a bountiful
    mixing of honey-sweet wine:
And then put a soft cushion on either side of your brow.[43]

The informing metaphor of these lines draws, it will be noticed, from the *Odyssey*'s celebration of leisure.[44] A timeless place of calm, fruitfulness, and festivity is to be secluded from the foul—or changeable—weather of a world of flux and violence. In this case the leisurely feast has become a harbor of warmth in a wintry storm, but it could just as readily be described as an oasis of cool refreshment during the heat of the dog days.[45] Whatever the seasonal extreme, the imaginative venture of the sympotic lyric is to transform the outer fair weather of Olympus or the Isles of the Blest into the inner climate of a gay and sociable island of free time.

As with time, so with politics; as with foul weather, so with the stormy exigencies of public responsibility. The ship of state, Alcaeus sings in another fragment, is beaten by the roaring waves; indeed, so battered is she by the tempest that she would willingly strike a reef and sink to the bottom. "That is her plight; but as for me, dear comrades, I would forget these things and make merry with you and with Bacchus."[46] In such a passage the delights which Odysseus praised at the feast of Alcinous are cut free of their social context and free, too, of Odysseus' awareness that the setting sun renews the journey's urgency, back to the storm, to return the sinking ship of state to harbor.

But however they might enjoy the prospect of abdicating from politics, Archilochus and Alcaeus still had their stake in the common weal, and both in fact led strenuously public lives. More deeply felt is the reactionary alienation of Theognis from the regime of "rich plebeians" that has taken over in Meg-

ara and left his own landholding aristocracy relatively des-
titute.[47] For the aristocratic remnant, the poet's "Sayings to
Cyrnus" prescribe a kind of Stoic ethic, insisting on the priority of virtue over wealth and the acceptance of one's lot,
however tragic.[48] Yet—and this is what interests us—not all the
maxims have this negative cast; the joys which for Alcaeus were
a momentary relief from the occasions of his political poems
are for Theognis a continuing transformation of his isolation
from politics. The sympotic themes show a singularity and an
intensity that reflect the absence of the hymns, war songs, political songs, and encomia one also finds in Alcaeus. Wine strips
off appearances as fire reveals true gold or silver,[49] and the
carpe diem theme of our selections from Alcaeus is now charged
with an overpowering sense of the temporal flux that surrounds
the feast.[50] In the afterlife, Theognis ruefully remarks, no lyre
sounds in the house of Persephone or Erebus, nor do the gifts
of Dionysus flow in that gloomy region.[51] That is why, in this
life, the poet invites us to

> Drink the wine which came to me of the vines that
> were planted in the mountain dells 'neath topmost
> Taygetus by that friend of the Gods, old Theotimus,
> who led cool water for them from Platanistus' spring.
> If thou drink of this, thou'lt scatter troublous cares,
> and when thou hast well drunken be greatly light-
> ened.[52]

To the extent that feasts like this embody Snell's "discovery
of the dimensions of the soul," the sympotic lyric transforms
the satiric, unpolitical shrug of an Archilochus into the festive
affirmation of a higher reality in a lower one, perfectly symbolized here in this wine from vines planted in a dell beneath
high mountains, but planted by an old friend of the gods who
found water for them springing up from below.

Contemplation and Retirement

With the feast at the core of the private focus, we have our
first glimpse of the transformation of withdrawal into contemplative leisure; but the evolution of the contemplative tradi-

tion itself, the *bios theōrētikos*, "the life devoted to seeing," has an equally significant function in the revaluation of the free time of the unpolitical man. After all, from the time of Thales' proposals for Ionian unity to Plato's ill-fated efforts at Syracuse to convert theory into practice, the social responsibility of the contemplative man was a paramount concern of the Greeks.[53] Ideally, as in the *Republic*, he was to turn from the vision of ideal truth (which Plato compares to life on the Isles of the Blest) to serve those who dwell in the darkness of the cave.[54] Having already touched on "civic leisure," we shall be less concerned in the coming pages with such a synthesis than with the tension between contemplative isolation and public action which gives a special poignancy to some of the Platonic dialogues. How did the *bios theōrētikos*, the philosophic life, come to be more and more necessarily the *bios idiōtou*, the life of the retired man? And we shall end with the example of Epicurus.

In one sense, the relationship between philosophical detachment and public responsibility would seem to be as old as the very notion of the philosopher or scientist as the unworldly inhabitant of an "ivory tower."[55] The story was told, for example, of how Thales was so intent on observing the heavens that he fell into a well, or of how Democritus lived so withdrawn in a garden house that he spent a day oblivious to the presence of an ox in his quarters.[56] A more serious political question is raised, however, by the anecdote of Anaxagoras, who, accused of not caring for his country, declared that he cared greatly for *his* country and, so the story goes, pointed to the heavens.[57] Similarly, in the allegory of the three lives attributed to Pythagoras, life is compared to the Olympic games, and the role of the spectator is exalted as a type of the leisurely contemplative; that role is not only distinguished from the busyness and pleasure-seeking of the mob but is also described as superior to the activity of the participants, who, representing political leaders, seek to win the wreath.[58]

In a society where such games were, in fact, held to honor heroic achievement and where ethics was almost synonymous with politics, the tradition reflected in these anecdotes was

bound to meet resistance; certainly it did in the thought of
Plato, who gave "science and philosophy a new subject, namely,
the state."[59] Plato, as A. E. Taylor insisted, was "no champion of a mere *via contemplativa* divorced from practical social
activity."[60] One wishes the matter were that simple. The fact
is, however, that from the execution of Socrates (who was conspicuously unpolitical) to the failure of his own venture with
Dion of Syracuse, Plato's experience enforced a different conclusion regarding the possibility of the philosopher's successful
participation in the active life of his society.[61] The admission
of the concrete difficulty (or even the impossibility) of realizing
the ideal will always be one of the most exciting features of the
Platonic dialogue, and we discount the complexity of the *Republic* if we forget that the ideal of the philosophic ruler is
introduced by what is probably Plato's most stinging account
of the necessary retirement of the contemplative man from
actual society. There is a small remnant of serious philosophers,
Socrates tells Adeimantus, who have discovered that there is
nothing of value in any present political process. Such a philosopher will mind his own affairs and stand aside from the law-
lessness of others like a man who has found shelter under a
wall from the dust and sleet of the storm.[62]

This undercurrent of isolation pulls strongly against what is
ostensibly the main theme of the book, and it wells up at the
conclusion in a way that is curiously subversive of the social
ideal of the philosophic ruler when Socrates relates to Glaucon
a fable of reincarnation, the Vision of Er. Er, so the story goes,
returned miraculously from death to tell how he had seen the
souls of men and living things come to select what would be
their next mode of existence. The first man to choose selects
immediately the life of maximum public power, but it proves
to be a miserable destiny. A typical example, remarks Socrates,
of one who had lived in a well-ordered state and whose virtue
was merely the product of habitual acceptance. The most experienced man present, Odysseus, is the last one to choose.
Disenchanted of heroic ambition by the recollection of former
toils, he seeks out the one existence which all other men have

ignored but which, he says, he would have chosen had he been first instead of last, "the life of a private man who has no cares."[63]

If our reading of the *Odyssey* has had any validity, it would be hard to conceive of a less characteristic choice for Homer's hero, but it is a singularly prophetic one for the predicament Plato represents. Like his Odysseus, Plato became "disenchanted of ambition with the recollection of former toils"; and with his followers in the grove of the original Academia, his old age was devoted to purely theoretic study.[64] There, to judge by the humorous account of their behavior in the *Theaetetus*, these first academics were willing to match the pre-Socratics in the extremity and eccentricity of their withdrawal into privacy.[65]

The retirement of the philosopher to the garden need not, however, be seen only as a privation of the opportunity for civic leisure. In a perceptive study of "Landscape in Greek Poetry," Adam Parry has suggested that we can find in Plato's disillusion with society an early expression of the pastoral impulse.[66] Thus, if we turn from the *Republic*, with its isolated philosopher in the storm or its Odysseus, choosing privacy, to the opening of the *Phaedrus*, we find, as in the lyric poets, a transformation of negative withdrawal into leisurely affirmation of a new, though private, situation. Phaedrus, fresh from hearing the rhetoric of Lysias, encounters Socrates outside the city. They stroll by the Ilissus and rest beneath a shady plane tree, where they discuss the speech. It is, claims Socrates, not usual for him to leave the city, for "the men in the city are my teachers and not the trees or the country."[67] As Parry points out, however, the irony of the lines, in view of the forthcoming discussion, is precisely how little there is to be learned in the urban milieu of the rhetorician,[68] and this gives a special significance to the sounds and sights of the opposed setting:

> . . . a delightful resting place, with this tall, spreading plane, and a lovely shade from the high branches of the *agnos*. Now that it's in full flower, it will make a place ever so fragrant. And what a lovely stream under the plane tree, and how cool to the feet! Judg-

ing by the statuettes and images I should say it's
consecrated to Achelous and some of the nymphs.
And then too, isn't the freshness of the air most welcome and pleasant, and the shrill summery music of
the cicada choir! And as crowning delight, the grass,
thick enough on a gentle slope to rest your head on
most comfortably.[69]

Expansive in size and sunlit with grapes laid out to dry, the
gardens of Alcinous were nevertheless in the heart of the city,
the consummation of a culture which welcomed the gods to its
feasts. In this intimate and shady suburban scene we manage
to see the images of the gods, but the very seclusion of the place
makes the perception a private experience, even as the other
senses seem enlivened by the shade itself. With the cool touch
of the stream to the feet, the fragrance of the air, the music of
the cicadas, the lushness of the grass to the dozing head, it is as
if Plato had taken the festive action of a sympotic lyric and
moved it outdoors. Like those lyrics, and unlike the gardens
and feasts of Alcinous, this leisurely scene is not an emblem
of a civic culture; it is an alternative to it.

From the death of Aristotle until the establishment of Christianity, the enterprise of philosophy became more and more
the quest for that alternative, the constitution, in one way or
another, of a new (private) sort of *paideia*. Anaxagoras' fabled
loyalty to *his* country was no longer felt to be in tension with
other commitments; the center of gravity had shifted from the
polis to the garden. For the Stoic and the Epicurean (and, one
might add, for the Skeptic and the Neo-Platonic mystic) the
isolation of the contemplative man became not implicit and
conjectural but explicit and radical. To read in the maxims
of the Stoics or Epicureans, or to peruse Alberto Grilli's remarkable *indice dei termini*, is to discover an underlying metaphoric configuration which knits together the conceptual
language of self-sufficiency (*autarkeia*) and imperturbability
(*ataraxia*) with the imagery of the calm sea, the clear sky, and
the quiet port.[70]

To trace this pattern would be to collect an anthology of Stoic and Epicurean writings; it would also be to discover how the *Odyssey*'s metaphor of the quest for the calm island is now rendered austerely personal and radically interior. "Do you not revere a man," writes Seneca, "unterrified in the midst of dangers, untouched by desires, happy in adversity, peaceful amid the storm, who looks down on men from a higher plane and views the gods on a footing of equality?"[71] "Sweet it is," writes Lucretius, "when on the great sea the winds are buffeting the waters, to gaze from the land on another's great struggles; not because it is pleasure or joy that any one should be distressed, but because it is sweet to perceive from what misfortune you yourself are free."[72]

Appealing as this image of detachment and calm is, one must acknowledge a certain impoverishment in its symbolism. We miss those possibilities of creative leisure suggested by the garden and the feast. I have referred to the negative or satiric shrug of Archilochus, but here, especially among the Stoics, the repudiation of the great world partakes of a heroic and tragic isolation. It is hardly accidental that, for the Stoic solitary, the acceptance of death seems to be predicated on viewing it as the ultimate retirement, the final port after stormy seas.[73] *Verum gaudium*, writes Seneca, *res severa est.*[74]

But philosophy, to revise Montaigne's dictum, as he himself did, should do more than teach us how to die; it should teach us how to live. The *nil admirari* of the detached sage must always come to terms with Byron's protest that, "had none admired / Would Pope have sung or Horace been inspired?" The fascinating question once again is how, given the exclusions of the private focus, there could be generated a vision to transfigure it. We turn, then, to the philosopher of the garden. Epicurus is, of course, the preeminent representative of the retired life; to Grilli it is "la contemplativa assoluta."[75] The Stoic ultimately still finds himself committed to a political ethic; his retirement (one thinks of Cicero's or Seneca's) is more a state of mind than a way of life. But in Epicurus the state of mind and the way of life are inseparable; in him we see the triumph of "the life of a private man who has no cares." "The world of politics," he declares, is "a prison."[76] "Live retired."[77] "The greatest fruit of self-sufficiency is freedom."[78]

One might wish that the last maxim were as well known as the preceding ones. To understand it is perhaps to see what inspires those who have committed themselves to not admiring. For self-sufficiency here is not conceived as an end in itself but as a creative situation, literally, a fruitful condition; and the freedom which is so generated, we should add, is not only freedom *from* the cares of the world but *for* something in another dimension. "Freedom from trouble in the mind and from pain in the body are static pleasures, but joy and exultation are considered as active pleasures involving motion."[79]

Perhaps the most engaging manifestation of this redefinition of self-sufficiency is the dynamic Epicurean view of friendship, "which goes dancing round the world proclaiming to us all to awake to the praise of a happy life,"[80] and its symbolic enactment in the feast in the garden. Thus, to return to our quotation from Lucretius, the serene detachment from the storm on the sea (*De Rer. Nat.* 2. 1–22) or from the desire to emulate the Roman equivalents of Archilochus' "Golden Gyges" (2. 23–28) is but the preliminary condition for a festive and pastoral vision of free time:

> And yet, for all this, men lie in friendly groups on
> the soft grass near some stream of water under the
> branches of a tall tree, and at no great cost delight-
> fully refresh their bodies, above all when the weather
> smiles on them, and the season of the year bestrews
> the green grass with flowers.[81]

It is, as Santayana remarks, a passage which invites us to look forward to Horace's "less cursory" treatment of the same theme;[82] but in an equally significant way, this Epicurean idyll should also turn our thoughts back to a tradition which preceded Horace.

*Pastoral Poetry and Personal Recreation: The Example
of Theocritus' Seventh Idyll*

Long before Lucretius but soon enough after Epicurus, and
probably influenced by him, the tendency to retirement which
we have discussed in the lyric poets and contemplative philosophers received new expression in a nascent literary mode, the
pastoral idyll of Theocritus. In the historical situation of the
Hellenistic Age the notion of withdrawal from the city had
gained impetus from the decline of the *polis* as an imaginative
center of gravity and its replacement by the metropolitan ideal
of a worldwide culture. Not until Vergil would the new conception elicit its own image of civic leisure. For though Theocritus wrote encomiastic tributes to Alexandrian patrons, his
notable poetry is not civic but urbane. That distinction also
illuminates the paradoxical genesis of pastoral poetry as a metropolitan phenomenon (a paradox best exemplified to a twentieth-century reader by the simple settings and simple-minded
folk of advertising's fictive world). "As civilization becomes
more complex and sophisticated," writes Renato Poggioli in
his classic discussion of the mode, "it tires man's heart, although it sharpens his wit."[83] In the pastoral poetry of Theocritus, the celebration of artless innocence becomes the typical
amusement of urbane artifice. Though its world is manifestly
that of shepherds and the naturalness we think of as peculiar
to the countryside, it is also uniquely and self-consciously fictive and playful, peopled by unrealistic shepherds whose typical activity is singing, often in ritual competition and for the
sake of artifacts lovingly described; its natural details are in
fact "unnaturally" sympathetic and humanized. The attractions
of the fabulous islands of Odysseus' voyage have been transplanted to Sicily and the isle of Cos and are fancifully recol-
lected by a city-dweller for his fellow sophisticates.

The relation of such poetry to the tradition that stems from
Archilochus and ends with Horace is a more complex one than
it may seem at first; for example, though we have had the land-

scape used as an emblem of private festivity, we have not encountered, nor shall we, singing shepherds among the speakers.
The achievement of Horace, speaking through a more personal
persona, will be to domesticate the fanciful nature which the
singing shepherd creates and enjoys. The Horatian process is
to realize the pastoral dream of ease in a private way, just as,
in a more public way, in Ithaca, Odysseus realized the delights
of Phaeacian hospitality. This process is, however, to some
degree anticipated in Theocritus' finest poem, the Seventh
Idyll, or "Harvest Festival." The poem, as A. S. F. Gow notes,
"has a personal tone quite absent from the other bucolic
idylls."[84] Some of the characters seem to stand for real people,
and the narrator, Simichidas, is presumably Theocritus himself. Whatever their actual identities, they clearly come from a
world unlike the one wholly created, in the typical idyll, by a
shepherd's song. Indeed, such songs will be but one facet of
a three-part narrative, in which three friends depart from the
city, then encounter a goatherd, and finally arrive at the harvest
festival, which is the climax of the poem. In that climax we
shall find, not only a shift from the opening public sense of
festival to a private one, but also the personal assimilation and
transformation of the fabulous world of the goatherd's songs.

It is significant, as the poem begins, that Simichidas and his
friends receive rather summary attention. What interests the
poet first is the public and legendary aspect of their destination: the family background of their hosts, who come from
good old Coan stock, going all the way back to a certain Chal-
con, who struck his knee against a rock and brought the fountains of Bourina gushing at his feet, while the nearby trees
wove green arches and shaded the place (ll. 6–9). In contrast,
the friends set out on their quest from the city hurriedly, kick-
ing pebbles in the road, while in the lifeless vacancy of noon
even the sun-loving lizard sleeps in the wall. This, at least, is
what the goatherd, Lycidas, smiling invitingly and clad in skins
still reeking of rennet, notices when the travelers meet him
(ll. 21–26). After expatiating on their holiday goal, Simichidas

convivially challenges him to a singing match, "for perhaps we can learn something from each other."[85] Lycidas elicits something important in Simichidas, and Simichidas will be more like him for having stopped to confront him.[86] We soon learn that the two already share a distaste for the epic aspirations of those who, like Apollonius, would rival Homer (ll. 45–48).[87] What kind of poetry is then available? We soon discover that Lycidas can take for granted a world now unaccessible to the worldly-wise Simichidas; it is a world which Simichidas will first parody but will eventually absorb.

The song which Lycidas "made one day on a hill" is technically a *propemptikon*, wishing his beloved Ageanax safe voyage. With its contrasting imagery of potential sea turbulence and longed-for calm, the goatherd's song is as universal as it is occasional, celebrating in a sympotic lyric enriched with rustic detail—the intimate equivalent of a Homeric feast—the voyager's safe arrival. On that day, sings Lycidas, he'll bind his head with flowers and drink wine by the fire while he roasts beans, and his bed will be piled to the elbow with fleabane and asphodel and crinkled parsley (ll. 63–68). Indeed, the celebration is also to be enriched by including the very genre the singer himself inhabits: it is a song about a festival of similar songs. Two shepherds will pipe while Tityrus sings two songs (ll. 69–73), the first telling how Daphnis wasted away for love, causing the hills to grieve and the oaks to sing dirges; the second, how once an evil king imprisoned the goatherd Comatas in a chest and how the bees came to feed him with honey because his mouth had been filled with nectar by the Muses (ll. 69–73).

If by this time—like the three travelers too, perhaps—we have lost sight of the original destination, it is because, in being led through these songs within songs, we have continually had to readjust our perspective as, again and again, the real world became the ideal landscape of a poetically humanized natural order: halcyons calm the waves for Ageanax, hills and oaks weep for Daphnis, bees feed the poet Comatas. Fulfilling this pattern, the inmost revelation at the core of the concentric design is the Orphic power of pastoral play to transform the rustic world: goats are lovely and work is song.[88] If only you had lived in my time, the singer concludes, I'd graze your lovely goats while you lay singing in the shade, godlike Comatas (ll. 86–89). And if we in the audience share his wistful yearning, it is because we have just heard that same kind of song. If, as Pater says, all art aspires to the condition of music, one might muse over the sense in which all literature aspires to the condition of pastoral.

But only an incurably idealistic reader would not laugh at this very reverie when it is interrupted by another kind of song from Simichidas, who, chuckling to himself, not only deflates love's young dream but mocks the idealism of Lycidas' final vision of the godlike poet-shepherd ordering nature. He tells how the lovers sneezed for Simichidas as a sign of good luck (for he loves Myrto as goats love the spring) and how his friend Aratus loves a boy and is getting nowhere (ll. 96–98). Thereupon, most of the song is taken up with a lengthy imprecation and deflation of the erotic pastoral figures invoked in behalf of ardent Aratus: Pan is threatened with beating and banishment, and a very pretty prayer to the Loves is juxtaposed to a reminder that by now the boy is rather like an overripe pear. Having demolished our pastoral expectations, Simichidas then proposes a worldly-wise alternative to the realm of Pan and the rosy Loves. Come on, he concludes, let's stop hanging around the door. Let someone else be shivering in the dew when the cock crows. Let's settle for peace of mind (ll. 122–27).

The singing match is over, and the reader, drawn to both the pastoral mythopoeia of Lycidas and the droll common sense of Simichidas, is left distrusting the former, for all his appeal, yet wanting more than the latter, for all his wit. It is the perfect preparation for the superb climax of the poem, when, in the harvest festival, the mundane narrator resolves this tension by personally recreating the festive leisure previously accessible only to the shepherd-poet or, as in the opening of the poem, in a public myth.

> but Eukritos
> and handsome Amyntas and I
> turned off at Phrasidamos's
> and happily laid ourselves down
> on beds of sweet grass and vine-leaves
> freshly picked. Overhead, many elms
> and poplars rustled, and nearby
> the sacred waters splashed down
> from the Nymphs' cave. Brown cicadas
> shrilled from the shady branches,
> and far off the tree-frog whined
> in the heavy underbrush.
> Larks and finches sang, doves crooned,
> and bees hummed about the spring.
>
> (ll. 131–42)

The conditions of leisure here are seclusion and privacy, as the depth and fragrance of beds of grass and leaves are accentuated by the rustling elm and poplar overhead. It is as if the scene were an emblem of the narrator's inner transformation of the public and pastoral myth of the first two parts of the poem. Regeneration here springs from within, from the recesses and shades of the landscape and from the consciousness that absorbs it and gives it significance. Within the shaded seclusion, the waters splash from the cave and blend with the rustle of the shading branches, just as the sounds of the darker creatures whom the shadows obscure blend with those of the birds and the bees that the springs reveal.

Within this symbolic context the poet proceeds to an evocation of all the senses, as festive as it is private:

> Everything smelled of rich summer
> and rich fruits. Pears lay at our feet,
> apples in plenty rolled beside us,
> and branches loaded down with plums
> bent to the ground.
>
> (ll. 143–46)

When they break the four-year seals on the wine jars, the speaker (and the reader) experiences the consummate example

of the private equivalent of the gardens and feasts of Alcinous,
the recreation, on Simichidas' own terms, of the idyll's earlier
references to a mythical past or a pastoral landscape. Nor is the
poet content only with the sensual delights of this earthly paradise. His mind withdraws into its own happiness, into the
realm of myth. Grateful for the wine, he addresses, not his
Coan hosts, but the Castalian nymphs who preside over the
Parnassian fountain of poetic inspiration. Was it a cup like
this, he asks the nymphs, that Chiron offered Heracles? Was it
such a drink that set Polyphemus dancing (ll. 148–53)? One
should not, of course, be too solemn with the introduction
of myth into this personal moment of saturnalian misrule. In
fact, only the comic elements—a hospitable centaur and a tipsy
cyclops—are selected from legends that had more grisly consequences. Nevertheless, something Dionysian that is more than
bibulous whimsy does seem to have taken hold of the mundane
narrator. In his conclusion there is an anagogic quality that
transfigures his earlier self-declared limitation of vision, and,
in the final celebration of the wine, banter yields to awe when
Demeter is evoked. The sympotic and the theoretic here become one: feasting is shown to be a way of seeing.

> such nectar as you mixed for us,
> you Nymphs, that day by the altar
> of Demeter of the Harvest.
> May I plant the great winnowing-fan
> another time in her grain-heaps,
> while she stands and smiles at us
> with wheat-sheaves and poppies in her hands.
>
> (ll. 154–57)

Demeter is depicted with her two characteristic emblems, the
stalk of seed pods left from the poppies that flower in April
and the sheaves saved from the winnowing at harvest time. So
designed, her statue would in fact be located on the harvest
floor, and at the conclusion of the winnowing the workers
would place their fans in the heaps of grain before taking their
leisure. Such a scene invites us also to meditate on the fact that
this is, especially, a harvest, for this feast is not simply a private

and internal version of the civic celebration of an Alcinous. Because it is a harvest, it also enacts a personal and symbolic equivalent of the way, in the disfigurements of time, Odysseus realized the leisurely delights of serene islands far from seasonal extremes. A harvest implies, if not seasonal change, at least temporal process, even though the product is incommensurate with the process. It is a whole that is more than the sum of its antecedent parts, and yet, as the cognate relationship of "ripe" and "reap" reminds us, its very plenitude defines its dissolution. When a poem of increasingly internal quest ends this way, the consciousness of the character in the poem, like the experience of its reader, enjoys a leisurely fulfillment, both as a harvest and as something to be harvested. For in an important sense the festival which was the destination of the poem's quest is over before the poem's end, when, in a personal reverie, the speaker yearns for the next time he can plant his winnowing fan here. And yet, and this is the poem's supreme achievement, the reader is left not with a sense of inconclusiveness and expectation but, in the last two lines, with the image of the goddess holding the sheaves and stalks, her emblems of the past, and smiling in something like the eternal "now" of Eliade's sacred time—eternally "now" at least while the narrator contemplates that image and the reader contemplates the poem. And when, finally, the crop, the feast, and the poem are harvested, the reader, again like the narrator, may return to time still liberated from time in the private realm of his recollection—and anticipation—of the holiday which will be his next reading of the poem, which, if it must always be reaped, will always be ripe.

3

Hoc erat in votis:
CIVIC AND RETIRED LEISURE
IN VERGIL AND HORACE

—Call it, wait, the professor said, opening his
long lips wide to reflect. Call it, let me see. Call
it: *deus nobis haec otia fecit.*
—No, Stephen said, I call it *A Pisgah Sight of
Palestine or the Parable of the Plums.*

James Joyce, *Ulysses*

"Ah!" said I, pressing him, for I thought I saw
him near a loophole here; "but would that be
your opinion at Walworth?"

"Mr. Pip," he replied with gravity, "Walworth
is one place, and this office is another. Much
as the Aged is one person, and Mr. Jaggers is
another. They must not be confounded together.
My Walworth sentiments must be taken at
Walworth; none but my official sentiments can
be taken in this office."

"Very well," said I, much relieved, "then I
shall look you up at Walworth, you may depend
upon it."

"Mr. Pip," he returned, "you will be welcome
there, in a private and personal capacity."

Charles Dickens, *Great Expectations*

Two Quests for the Golden Age, One without, One within, History (Epodes 16; Eclogues 1 and 4)

The quest for the happy island informs and distinguishes the characteristic myth of the two greatest Roman poets in a way that reflects the preceding chapter's distinction between a public and a private vision of leisure, but that vision is deepened now by an awareness of the promise and the burden of history. In Vergil's *Eclogues* and *Georgics* we shall find the old "dream of ease" restated in history as the consummation of civic order, as the fruition of Octavian's, later Augustus', triumph in the civil wars. To introduce that civic vision, however, let us first consider a poem to which Vergil might in fact have been responding in his *Eclogues* and which, in any case, represents the prior, Hellenistic kind of sensibility, which we have just glimpsed in pastoral's urbane dismissal of the city and which, if it was the achievement of Vergil to transform, it was the achievement of Horace to authenticate. In his Sixteenth Epode, which Eduard Fraenkel has termed "probably the noblest" among his early works,[1] Horace summons the citizens of Rome to sail off to the Isles of the Blest, using the very isolation of the place to underscore, not the urbane detachment of pastoral play, but a profound alienation from the course of Roman history. In the manner of an impassioned address to the populace, the poem swells from the forensic to the prophetic. To discover the good life, good men must leave the city and sail off to the West.

In the civil wars, the poet proclaims, Roman history has reached a point of apocalyptic crisis. The city which has withstood the onslaughts of outsiders, from Porsena to Hannibal, is now destroying itself (*Epodes* 16. 1–8). The poet's denunciation draws from primordial resources: this impious generation is doomed; its very bloodline is accursed, *impia perdemus devoti sanguinis aetas* (1. 9).[2] Then the poet-orator turns to his proposal for the deliverance of a righteous remnant, a proposal

couched in the language not of escape but of heroic commitment: *vos quibus est virtus, muliebrem tollite luctum,* "you
who are men, put away womanish sorrow" (l. 39). This is
heroic in the way that Odysseus' *nostos* was heroic, in seeking
a homeland where peace has its issue in leisure.

Horace's description of his *arva beata* looks back to many of
the early motifs that we encountered in chapter 2, and it
charges them with his own sense of historical urgency, even
with personal poignancy. Unploughed, the land yields grain;
unpruned, the vines and olive trees produce their fruits. Figs,
honey, splashing fountains—the rural plenitude is instinct with
a natural generosity fulfilled in man's happiness. Unbidden
the goats and cows come to be milked, absent is the prowling
bear at evening and the swelling viper underfoot, and absent
too are the extremes of rain and sun, for the king of the gods
tempers all excesses of seasonal change, *utrumque rege tem-
perante caelitum* (ll. 41–56). Thus the poet, now calling himself *vatis,* the prophet, recalls to an impious generation in an
iron age the golden time, the *tempus aureum* vouchsafed to
the god-fearing, the *piae genti,* if they will but heed his prophecy (ll. 63–66).

We have touched on the visionary power of this "happy escape for the righteous," but one cannot finally overlook the
quotient of personal frustration which must have charged this
fabulous image with a peculiar intensity for this particular
poet. His childhood was spent in the aftermath of Sulla's victory and in the shadow of that dictator's centurions.[3] While a
student at Athens, he had enlisted in the losing cause of Brutus.[4] Returning to Italy after Philippi, he saw the climax of his
alienation from history in the expropriation of his father's
property.[5] In relative poverty, he served as a minor civil servant
for about ten years, during which time he came to accept the
regime of Augustus and won the patronage of Maecenas.[6] At
what point in this career Horace composed the Sixteenth Epode
is of less importance here than the drama with which it enacts
the disinheritance of all those years and the luster with which
it first reveals a dream which Horace never forgot and which

finally found its realization, not in a legendary western isle, but on a Sabine farm.

For most Roman citizens, however, the golden age after the civil war was to be inaugurated in neither of these places but in that impious city whence Horace would have set sail and under the aegis of the very emperor he had once opposed. Nowhere in world literature is the prospect of what I have called "civic leisure" so celebrated as in those poems of Vergil which, using the Roman countryside as an emblem of Augustan order, announce this renewal.

Si canimus silvas, silvae sint consule dignae—"If we sing of the woodland, let the woodland be worthy of a consul": these lines from the Fourth Eclogue epitomize that assimilation of history into the pastoral mode which is the distinctive mark of Vergil's transformation of Theocritus.[7] Indeed, the subject of the Fourth Eclogue is precisely this assimilation or idealization of history, the theme of the very next lines, which herald the advent of a new golden age. The poem's immediate occasion was probably the birth of a son to C. Asinius Pollio, the friend in power who may have introduced Vergil to Maecenas and to whose consulship the earlier lines allude; but in a larger sense they declare what will become Vergil's characteristic allegiance to the ultimate fulfillment of national destiny under the Augustan regime:

> *Ultima Cumaei venit iam carminis aetas;*
> *magnus ab integro saeclorum nascitur ordo.*
> *iam redit et virgo, redeunt Saturnia regna . . . .*
> (*Eclogues* 4. 4–6)
> Ours is the crowning era foretold in prophecy:
> Born of Time, a great new cycle of centuries
> Begins. Justice returns to earth, the Golden Age
> Returns.

In this golden age, the earth untilled will bring forth fruit, the goats will come home unbidden, no huge lions, no serpents, will threaten, and so on (ll. 18–25), as if in reply to Horace's *arva beata*. "Do not seek the Golden Age elsewhere," Vergil seems to be saying. "It is dawning here in Italy, where our guilt shall be absolved, the earth released from continual anxiety" (ll. 13–14).[8]

The contrast with Horace is enforced by other aspects of Vergil's early life mirrored in the *Eclogues*, especially in the First. After Philippi, his home, too, was threatened with expropriation to reward Octavian's veterans: his fate was not unlike Horace's. Though Vergil's estate was spared, probably through the influence of the governor, Pollio, or his successor, Varus, the tensions generated by the threat survive in the First Eclogue. Poignantly dramatizing the expropriation of farms in his native Mantua, Vergil's poem is a dialogue between Meliboeus, who has been dispossessed, and Tityrus, who enjoys the favor of the higher-ups. It is customary to read Tityrus here as a mask of Vergil, acknowledging his own benefactions from Augustus at Rome; yet surely Meliboeus also expresses the anxiety which the poet might have felt, if only by anticipation. Here let us consider the eclogue, not biographically, but as a kind of parable for two attitudes to history, both of which may indeed have been present in Vergil's mind, though one was to become his own characteristic theme, while the other was to be associated more with Horace and would be transformed by him.

At the very start of the poem, Meliboeus contrasts the disinheritance he has suffered to the pastoral delights available to men like Tityrus: lolling in this shade, piping to the woodland muse (*Eclogues* 1. 1–2). As the exiled Meliboeus points out, it is alienation like his from the historical order which renders the pastoral mode inaccessible. Those like Tityrus, who are at one with the former, can find its emblem in the latter:

> *nos patriae finis et dulcia linquimus arva.*
> *nos patriam fugimus; tu, Tityre, lentus in umbra*
> *formosam resonare doces Amaryllida silvas.*
>
> (ll. 3–5)

While I must leave my home place, the fields so dear to me.
I'm driven from my home place: but you can take it easy
In shade and teach the woods to repeat "Fair Amaryllis."

To explain his happy state, Tityrus invokes the context of his culture. It is a *locus classicus* for the Vergilian vision of civic leisure: *O Meliboee, deus nobis haec otia fecit. / namque erit ille mihi semper deus* (O Meliboeus, a god has given us this ease—One who will always be a god to me) (ll. 6–7). Significantly, this shepherd's god (Augustus) dwells in the city; it was at Rome that Tityrus heard the promise of restoration: *hic mihi responsum primus dedit ille petenti; / "pascite ut ante boves, pueri: summittite tauros"* (I made my petition to him, and he granted it readily, saying, "My lads, pasture your cattle, breed from your bulls, as you did of old") (ll. 44–45). Thus the pastoral leisure of Tityrus gives symbolic life to the historical aspiration of urban, Augustan, order. As Meliboeus exclaims in an iterative lyric outburst, "Happy old man, your land will still be yours—happy here among streams you know, you'll enjoy the cool shade the way it used to be" (ll. 46, 51–53). Variously but repeatedly the poet has insisted on the larger themes of social harmony and historical continuity which give this exchange a temporal context of public importance: Pascite *ut ante* boves . . . tua rura *manebunt . . . non insueta . . .* pabula . . . flumina *nota* . . . hinc tibi, *quae semper.* Tityrus, we may note finally, has now forgotten about the (Theocritean) attractions of Amaryllis and Galatea; sooner shall the Parthian drink from the river Arar or the German from the Tigris than Augustus' image shall leave his heart (ll. 59–63).

As for Meliboeus, his lines are fraught with that peculiarly Vergilian compassion which makes their author something more than an imperial propagandist. Sadly he ponders the destinations of the outcasts: Africa, Scythia, Crete, Britain, "wholly separated from all the world." Like Horace's proposal to seek the *arva beata,* emigration here dramatizes (though here reluctantly) an alienation from the course of history. Some impious soldier will take over his land, Meliboeus complains; a foreigner will harvest his crops. To be so alienated from history is to lose not only land but the possibility of the new kind of pastoral bestowed by the god who gave ease to Tityrus. "Car-

mina nulla canam," Meliboeus concludes: I can sing no more
songs (ll. 75–77).

While it is true that Horace's early disenchantment never
reached this extreme of alienation, it is significant that his
characteristic vision of rural leisure was still quite different
from the pastoral mode accessible to a Tityrus or a Vergil. To
anticipate Horace's position, we might put the First Eclogue
to one last use as a parable about attitudes to history. In his
final lines Tityrus suggests that the outcast might have relaxed
with him for one last night:

> *Hic tamen hanc mecum poteras requiescere noctem*
> *fronde super viridi: sunt nobis mitia poma,*
> *castaneae molles et pressi copia lactis,*
> *et iam summa procul villarum culmina fumant*
> *maioresque cadunt altis de montibus umbrae.*
>
> (ll. 79–83)

Yet surely you could rest with me tonight and sleep
On a bed of green leaves here? You're welcome to taste
  my mellow
Apples, my floury chestnuts, my ample stock of cheese.
Look over there—smoke rises already from the rooftops,
And longer fall the shadows cast by the mountain heights.

Delicately poised between historical integration and alienation
as between day and night, Tityrus' invitation absorbs the poignancy of Meliboeus' dispossession and mutes the buoyancy of
his own optimism. In his description of the private repast we
forget for a moment that "a god has created this leisure" and
wonder if there may not be gods that leisure creates. It is a
singularly private, Horatian interlude; and though it lasts for
but a moment, it allows us to see the larger process of the public integration of history and leisure from a different, critical,
and possibly more humane perspective. It was not to be the
characteristic perspective of Vergil, but it is a measure of his
genius that here, as in his great epic of national destiny, he
could, with such sensitivity, include the private focus.[9]

The Public Context

Vergil's Georgics: *Rural Work and Civic Leisure*

To discover Vergil's more typical vein, our survey of Roman "civic leisure" turns to the *Georgics,* that massive effort to transform natural process and rural labor into an emblem, indeed a means, of achieving civic leisure. The poem's public urgency strikes us long before its practical advice on tilling the soil.[10] Consider, for example, the opening invocation of the rustic deities: Bacchus, Ceres, Neptune, Aristaeus, Pan, Minerva, Triptolemus, Silvanus, and especially Caesar, "overseer of cities," "warden of earth," "promoter of harvest and puissant lord of the seasons" (*Georgics* 1. 7–28).

We have met something like this identification of cult, culture, and cultivation already in the *Odyssey,* but nowhere in world literature are these aspects of *cultus* so memorably fused as in the poem before us. To measure the depth of its conception, one must turn, it seems to me, not to the superficially comparable treatises of Cato or Varro but to Shakespeare's history plays and their emergent vision of historical force conceived as organic rhythm, reshaping and reordering a sea-walled garden where the blood of Englishmen has manured the ground.

The first book of the *Georgics* is charged with the author's response to the horrors of civil war. In a way which recalls the system of correspondences available to Shakespeare in his treatment of the same theme, Vergil projects this disorder onto the various levels of human experience, drawing together images of decay and darkness. The keynote is sounded early in the book in the famous account of man's fall from a golden to an iron age (ll. 119–47). It is a theme which pervades the book, penetrating, for example, some homely advice on the degeneration of seeds and the flux of all things: "for a law of nature / Makes all things go to the bad, lose ground, and fall away" (*Sic omnia fatis / in peius ruere ac retro sublapsa referri*) (ll.

199–200). The climactic description of the storm enlarges these
hints with a terrifying reference to civic disorder. After some
reassuring advice on predicting the weather, we are led to a
recollection of those signs that forerun the death or fall of
kings: at the assassination of Julius Caesar, for instance, there
were portents of earth and sea, of dogs and birds, Mount Etna
erupting, the Alps trembling with shock, strange voices, dried
rivers, earthquake, weeping statuary, flood, threatening augu-
ries, blood from wells, wolves' cries through the city at night,
unprecedented lightning and comets, and, finally, the Battle of
Philippi (ll. 461–97).

And yet the true climax of this book is signaled by an almost
bathetic change of place. Abruptly Vergil shifts from the whirl
of natural and public disaster to dwell on the things that abide,
to remind us that someday, even at Philippi, a farmer, some old
Adam's likeness, will turn up with his plow old rusted spears,
useless helmets, heroes' bones (ll. 493–97). The lines are followed by an eloquent plea to the *Di Patrii, Indigetes*, the gods
of the fatherland, not to deter the young Augustus from restoring to order a world turned upside down. This prayer for renewal touches on Rome's mythic heritage of guilt and expiation
and charges the whole utterance with a sense of national destiny prophetic of the *Aeneid*: "long enough have we atoned
with blood for the promise Laomedon broke at Troy" (ll.
498–502).[11] The prayer crowns the structure of the first book,
fusing the aspirations of culture and the values of cultivation,
turning to the promise of Augustus as the natural conclusion
of a meditation on the stability of the farmer's world. Thus,
when he concludes with a prophetic indictment of his culture's
reversal of right and wrong, the poet sums up his indignation
by pointing to the negation of agrarian values: the plow is no
longer honored, the fields are untended, the curved sickles are
forged into stiff swords (ll. 505–8).

The *Georgics* is about nothing more than the reassertion of
these agrarian values, the exaltation of cultivation as the consummate emblem of culture, the return of dignity to the plow,

of men to the fields, the beating of swords into plowshares. We can now perhaps appreciate the poet's tact in building toward this conclusion by deploying martial imagery subtly and variously throughout the first book. For if that book underscores degeneration and decay, it does so to enlist resistance to these onslaughts, to summon us to man's noblest and most elemental combat: *exercetque frequens tellurem atque imperat arvis* (l. 99) . . . *ante Iovem nulli subigebant arva coloni* (l. 125) . . . *labor omnia vicit* (l. 145) . . . *adsiduis herbam insectabere rastris* (l. 155) . . . *Dicendum et quae sint duris agrestibus arma* (l. 160).

Beginning with the hard-earned victories of the farmer's war with nature in book 1, the *Georgics* symbolically enacts the raising of a civilization as the three remaining books lead us up ascending stages of the more and more humane agrarian arts. From the cultivation of the soil, book 2 turns to the culture of trees—from warfare, so to speak, to peace. In book 3 we find some primitive aspects of man's condition reflected in the description of livestock, their "loves" and their mortality; finally, in book 4's account of beekeeping, we see a miniature civilization, a model of the body politic.

To turn, however, from the demonstrable civic context of the work to its vision of leisure is to confront the rather commonly held opinion that its vision is nothing of the sort, that the poem asserts "the dignity of manual labor." *Labor omnia vicit.* Unlike the *Eclogues,* so the argument runs, the *Georgics* bears the stamp of a poet who "has moved from Arcadia into a world closer to reality, that of agriculture and hard work."[12] There is a certain truth in these impressions, just as, to recall our earliest consideration of civic leisure, there are in the *Odyssey* grounds for a reading that stresses only the journey's urgency, the necessity for action. But just as the dynamic urgencies of that poem have as their final cause the attainment of a goal, the restoration of the leisurely life of civilization, so in reading the *Georgics* one must perceive ends as well as means. One can agree with Mr. Eliot that by removing the stigma from banausic occupations Vergil does somewhat redefine the

Greek conception of the dignity of leisure. The essential question, however, would seem to be Does "the dignity of manual labor" in the *Georgics* spring from the fact that it is manual or labor, or does it come rather from the quality of life which labor makes possible, that is, ultimately, from the dignity of leisure?[13] Of course there is an obvious difference between the *Eclogues* and the *Georgics*, but the affinity of the works is even more interesting. In the *Eclogues* we have discussed, a good deal of historical reality is assimilated into the ideal world of poetry, and in the poem before us there will be an impressive degree of timeless pastoral "unreality," conceived in time as crowning history and hard work. As Sir Kenneth Clark remarks, the *Georgics'* "element of realism is combined with the most enchanting dream which has ever consoled mankind, the myth of a Golden Age."[14] Vergil's view of work, it seems to me, closely parallels his attitude to that other historical necessity, warfare. Both are necessary as a means of realizing the ideal—which is their opposite. The *Georgics* shudders at the horrors of civil war yet celebrates imperial conquest as a means to world stability, and, too, as noted above, it celebrates man's proper combat against the elements. We make war only to have peace; the same applies to the agrarian "warfare" of cultivation.

What then of man's degeneration from the carefree reign of Saturn, of the triumph of *labor improbus et duris urgens in rebus egestas* (1. 145–46)? Here, as certain perceptive critics have suggested, it is most important to see the difference between the original Hesiodic legend and Vergil's account: between Hesiod's justifying, however bitterly, the farmer's toil as a necessity for survival, and Vergil's glorifying of agrarian art as a means toward restoring the golden age.[15] It is a difference which is rooted in divergent ideas of the original "fall." In Hesiod's story Zeus's anger at Prometheus' theft of fire is essentially a condemnation of man's dreams of progress and perfectibility.[16] In Vergil's hands it becomes a kind of "happy fault," a means of stimulating human creativity to achieve a new golden age, more meaningful for having been earned:

Pater ipse colendi
haud facilem esse viam voluit, primusque per artem
movit agros, curis acuens mortalia corda
nec torpere gravi passus sua regna veterno.[17]

(1. 121–24)

For the Father of agriculture
Gave us a hard calling: he first decreed it an art
To work the fields, sent worries to sharpen our mortal wits
And would not allow his realm to grow listless from lethargy.

As Wilkinson remarks, Vergil has invested "father" Zeus with the role of Prometheus as educator of mankind: "But he is an educator who, instead of giving men fire, hides it so that they must bestir themselves to find it."[18] To see how hopeful is Vergil's presentation of the genesis of human craft, one might compare it with Tibullus' treatment of the same golden-age myth and his pessimistic condemnation, for example, of ship-building and commerce.[19] In Vergil's hands the same enter-prise becomes not an impious violation of limits but an excit-ing expansion of human possibilities, like Whitman's "passage to more than India." Hollowed tree trunks are pushed out to sea, and their navigators discover the stars, group them into constellations, and name them (ll. 136–38). This is, of course, a practical necessity in navigation, but it also partakes of the intrinsic delight of contemplative leisure, since it originates in gazing at the stars. So too in man's dominion over the earth: in hunting, fishing, and building, toil is transformed by inge-nuity and imagination into art, or at least into a kind of play (ll. 139–45). Another kind of achievement is envisioned in the very lines that acknowledge the triumph of *labor improbus*, the adjective itself set off emphatically to introduce a chiastic reflection of the inhuman side of work: *tum variae venere artes.* *Labor omnia vicit / improbus et duris urgens in rebus egestas* (ll. 146–47).[20] The true motto of the *Georgics*, it seems to me, is thus not *Labor omnia vicit* as an endorsement of the work ethic for its own sake;[21] rather, it is something like *Labor la-borem vicit* or, more precisely, *Ars laborem vicit*: labor elicits

ingenuity as a means to an imaginative end, that end being the
elimination of "labor," and that elimination—that transformation of work into art, contemplation, and leisure—is the source
of its dignity.[22]

Distinguished critics of the poem, especially Brooks Otis,
have pointed out that here, as in Vergil's other works, there
are contrasts and comparisons from book to book and within
each book.[23] But this "spatial" view of the poem needs to put
more emphasis on the dialectical relationship between the parts
of the poem that are means and the parts that are ends. Just as
Ithaca was not only contrasted to Phaeacia but was the means
of its human realization, so elements in book 1 of the *Georgics*
are not only contrasted to those in book 2 but represent a fallen
world that must be confronted in all its disfigurement and then
be imaginatively overcome in order for the reader to realize
the ironic truth that in fact a contrary is being generated by
the transformation of labor into art.[24] This is the affirmation
of man's leisurely happiness which irradiates the new golden
age of book 2. There is, first, the celebration of Italy with its
triumphant final salute, where the new Saturnian age of the
countryside is urged as the inspiration and the fulfillment of
civic myth:

> *salve, magna parens frugum, Saturnia tellus,*
> *magna virum: tibi res antiquae laudis et artis*
> *ingredior sanctos ausus recludere fontis,*
> *Ascraeumque cano Romana per oppida carmen.*
> (2. 173–76)

Hail, great mother of harvests! O land of Saturn, hail!
Mother of men! For you I take my stand on our ancient
Glories and arts, I dare to unseal the hallowed sources
And sing a rural theme throughout the cities of Rome.

Even more moving is the book's climactic praise of rural
beatitude and innocence, a magnificently orchestrated expansion of those key motifs we heard in the First Eclogue—*deus
nobis haec otia fecit . . . o fortunate senex*:

> *O fortunatos nimium, sua si bona norint,*
> *agricolas! quibus ipsa procul discordibus armis,*
> *fundit humo facilem victum iustissima tellus.*
>
> . . . .
>
> *fortunatus et ille, deos qui novit agrestis*
> *Panaque Silvanumque senem Nymphasque sorores*
>
> . . . .
>
> *aureus hanc vitam in terris Saturnus agebat;* . . .
>   (2. 458–60, 493–94, 538)

O, too lucky for words, if only he knew his luck,
Is the farmer, who far from the clash of armaments
Lives, and rewarding earth is lavish of all he needs!

. . . .

But fortunate too the man who is friends with the
    country gods—
Pan and old Silvanus and the sisterhood of nymphs:

. . . .

Such was the life that golden Saturn lived upon earth.

   These famous lines have probably been enjoyed detached
from their context more often than not, and their subjects are,
in fact, conventional rhetorical topics. In the poem's whole
context the lines deserve to be seen as neither "a purple patch
sewn on" nor simply as "the other side of the coin" in contrast
to book 1's fallen world.[25] Not only the presence of these divergent conditions but their dialectical interplay in books 1
and 2 attests to the structural consistency as well as the moral
complexity of the *Georgics*. This interplay is also a pattern
which penetrates the verbal texture of particular passages in so
artful a fashion as to confirm the old story that the poem was
painstakingly composed at the rate of seven lines a day. We
have already seen how the statement of original loss is charged
with an exuberant sense of man's potential; let us now consider
those passages which herald what Jackson Knight calls "the
golden age, but yet not quite the golden age,"[26] and see the
embodiment of such a double vision. For the affirmative lines
of book 2 assimilate meanings which weigh heavy upon our
sense of upward progress. They not only climax a regenerative

movement opposed to the decrescent movement of book 1, but
they also subtly repeat some of its stern injunctions precisely
because this is "yet not quite the golden age."

Like the happiness of the farmer, Vergil seems to be saying,
the blessings of history must be preserved by continual hus-
bandry. This blend of leisure with labor, of the golden with
the iron age, is most strikingly manifest in the last section before the final *salve . . . Saturnia tellus* in the account of the
Italian tribes. For what makes that panegyric more than a perfunctory ritual is the poet's historical sense, his insistence on
those very un-Saturnian virtues which make a golden age possible in the historical process: *haec genus acre virum* (2. 167)
. . . adsuetumque malo (168) *. . . verutos* (168) *. . . duros bello*
(170). We might call this the Ithacan aspect of Roman civic
leisure. It is most tellingly registered in the final tribute to
Augustus' might, which has kept the peaceful Indian, the
imbellem Indum, far from Rome. Augustus' power dominates
an unwarlike people; the end achieved by this unlikely means
is, ironically, a new Saturnian age of peace and plenty (ll.
170–74). Having used the sword, Rome can now fulfill the
hope of the *Di patrii* prayer: to restore dignity to the plow.

The same dialectical interplay of means and ends informs
the famous tribute to the happy leisure of the farmers, "if they
but knew their happiness." An instance of neither "hard" nor
"soft" primitivism, the sequence, like the *Georgics* as a whole,
is a subtle integration of work with leisure. It is of course the
leisure that first catches our attention as the condition of him
who "far from the clash of armaments / Lives, and rewarding
earth is lavish of all he needs" *(quibus ipsa, procul discordibus
armis, / fundit humo facilem victum iustissima tellus)* (ll.
459–60). It is not the leisure of civilized artifice, we are told
at some length (ll. 461–66), but one which is in fact richer and
more civilized: *at secura quies et nescia fallere vita, / dives
opum variarum, et latis otia fundis* (But calm security and a
life that will not cheat you, / Rich in its own rewards, are
here: the broad ease of the farmlands) (ll. 467–68). The following lines pleasantly lull the reader as the ease of broad domains
spreads over an increasingly inviting vista: caves, lakes, and

herds mooing and sleeping in the shade (ll. 469–71). But then, gently but insistently, the poet reminds us that this ideal landscape is rooted in the human condition, where youth must learn work and become inured to deprivation: *et patiens operum exiguoque adsueta iuventus* (l. 472).

For if the *O fortunatos nimium* passage is radiant with the last vestiges of original happiness, it is also darkened by the sterner realities of experience. This double vision of the importance of leisure and the necessity of the work which makes it possible is nicely condensed in the lines that bring this passage to a close: *extrema per illos / Iustitia excedens terris vestigia fecit* (When Justice / Left earth, her latest footprints were stamped on folk like these) (ll. 473–74). There is a twilight glow to this peculiarly haunting tribute, as evocative of original innocence as it is insistent on its loss. *Iustitia* is here, and yet she is not with us. We see her in the act of departure, as if in a present moment *(excedens)*, yet we know that she has gone *(fecit)*. The happiness of the farmer, like the civic leisure it epitomizes, is with us and yet not with us: it is something we do without only in order to have it. For the farmer, and for the nation, a youth *patiens operum exiguoque adsueta* leads to the mature enjoyment of *secura quies . . . latis otia fundis*. In the vestigial half-light of departed justice there gleams the dawn of Roman renewal in rural work and leisure.

The simultaneous presence and absence of *Iustitia* in the countryside is the perfect beginning for a meditation on books 3 and 4, or rather on why, after the praise of Augustus as the consummation of civic leisure in the temple at the start of book 3, we need books 3 and 4 at all; for book 3, on the breeding of livestock, soon slips into a falling movement, which begins with a reminder of the impermanence of things temporal and ends with a grisly plague scene, more expressive of degeneration than anything in book 1. Only by diligent cultivation, the poet reminds us, do the works of time, be they states or farms or even poems about farms, yield dialectically the free time which finds its symbol of culture in cultivation. The sense of flux reverberates throughout the discussion, organically imaged in the descriptions of the chariot horse (ll. 103–22) or the warhorse

(ll. 179–208). It is felt through all of creation in the meditation on love's frenzy, *in furias ignemque ruunt: amor omnibus
idem* (l. 244), and is especially exemplified in the storm and
stress of Leander's infatuation (ll. 258–63). Indeed, the sense
of flux hurries along the very pace of the narrator: *sed fugit
interea, fugit inreparabile tempus* (l. 284). A more ominous
note is sounded in the remarks on disease that bring the book
to a close, the reminiscence of that notorious epidemic which,
coming in a wretched season, aglow with the heat of autumn,
delivered to death all herds, tame or wild, by infecting the
lakes and pastureland (ll. 478–81). The horrible symptoms are
first recalled—sapless weakness, then too much blood, then violent self-destruction (ll. 482–514). Next comes the profoundly
moving vignette of the expiration of a faithful bull, which tells
first of the sadness of the plowman and the sympathy of the
yokefellow (ll. 515–24) and then the poet's protest at the tragic
futility of the faithful creature's labor, the pointlessness of his
simple life, so emblematic of rural values (ll. 525–28). It is a
cry that radically denies the expectations of the book we hold
in our hands. It challenges the end promised not only to the
means of rural labor but also to the enterprise of our reading
the poem. Its poignancy becomes more acute as we cast a last
glance at the fallen, indeed the infernal, world which is un-
veiled at the end of book 3: the plague-infested landscape,
filled with dead fishes, reptiles, and birds (ll. 541–47), and
then, from hell's darkness, the apocalyptic visitation of ghastly
Tisiphone, driving fear and disease before her, daily rearing
her head higher and more voraciously (ll. 552–55). Finally,
there is the particularly hideous detail of the putrescent sheep
carcass and hide that brings the book to a close:

> *ne tondere quidem morbo inluvieque peresa*
> *vellera nec telas possunt attingere putris;*
> *verum etiam invisos si quis temptarat amictus,*
> *ardentes papulae atque immundus olentia sudor*
> *membra sequebatur, nec longo deinde moranti*
> *tempore contactos artus sacer ignis edebat.*
>
> (3. 561–66)

You could not even shear the fleece, it was so corroded
With the foul pus, or work that rotten wool in the loom:
But if you were so foolhardy as to wear the hideous garment,
Inflamed pustules and a noxious-smelling sweat appeared
All over your limbs: not long then
Before the fiery curse ate up your tettered frame . . . .

The image of the putrid hide sears the mind that reads it as
it does the body it encloses. We shall soon see why the poet
chose this particular horror to bring his nightmare to a close.
As we turn to book 4, we find a shift from disorder to order,
from decay to regeneration, which parallels the earlier transition from book 1 to book 2. The change in tone and atmosphere is felt as soon as we read the opening lines' promise to
speak of that pattern of the good society devoted to "air-borne
honey, the heavenly gift" (4. 1). That this little state has as its
end the creation of "civic leisure" has already been suggested
inferentially; the view could be rooted more explicitly in certain texts which define the structure of the bees' polity, for
example the common blend of labor and free time, *omnibus
una quies operum, labor omnibus unus* (1. 184). As Otis has it,
"*Labor omnibus unus* is the answer to *amor omnibus idem* and
(*non*) *morti esse locum*, the divine immortal spirit (*esse apibus
partem divinae mentis et haustus aetherios*), to the *sacer ignis*
of the plague. Also the divine polity of the bees symbolizes the
kind of *labor* and *fides* which can cure the divided and corrupt
republic of the close of Book I and restore the golden-age co-
operation of man and nature in Book II."[27]
Yet on the deepest level book 4 conveys this theme in a less
restricted, even less discursive, way simply by underlining the
symbolic qualities of the bees' activity. It becomes a kind of
work which by its very nature—*tantus amor florum et generandi
gloria mellis* (1. 205)—transcends the laborious. Thus the opening remarks on the selection of a "settled home" for the community may well wake memories as old as the gardens of Alcinous, as fresh as "the golden age" of Vergil's *Eclogues* or the
second book of this poem. For here, similarly, the bees will
enjoy a location free from the turbulence of the winds or the

vexations of unfriendly creatures (ll. 10–12). As we might expect by now, the symbolic center of this landscape is the flow
of life-giving waters: clear fountains, moss-green pools, slight
rivulets slipping through the grass (ll. 18–19), combined with
a shade that offers to the young bees a place of cool repose from
their labor (ll. 20, 23–24). Soon, however, the poet's vision expands beyond this shady "capitol" to a sunlit domain, the ultimate georgic vista, where, as if Odysseus were once again beholding the Phaeacian way of life, the bees and their labors
become suffused with light and fragrance:

> *in medium, seu stabit iners seu profluet umor,*
> *transversas salices et grandia conice saxa,*
> *pontibus ut crebris possint consistere et alas*
> *pandere ad aestivum solem, si forte morantis*
> *sparserit aut praeceps Neptuno immerserit Eurus.*
> *haec circum casiae virides et olentia late*
> *serpylla et graviter spirantis copia thymbrae*
> *floreat, inriguumque bibant violaria fontem.*
>
> (4. 25–32)

Whether the water flows or is stagnant, fling in the middle
Willow boughs criss-cross and big stones,
That the bees may have plenty of bridges to stand on and dry
    their wings
At the summer sun, in case a shower has caught them loitering
Or a gust of east wind ducked them suddenly in the water
Green spurge-laurel should grow round about, wild thyme
    that perfumes
The air, masses of savory rich-breathing, and violet beds
Sucking the channelled stream.

This refulgent vein of imagery is seen again in the description
of a typical working day (ll. 51–56), and some of its glow lingers
even in the aftermath of a fight (ll. 98–99); but finally, and
most characteristically, the gleam and fragrance suffuse the
work at the hive (*fervet opus, redolentque thymo fragrantia
mella,* l. 169) and shine in the light, heat, and steam of the
Cyclopes, evoked as blacksmiths (ll. 170–73). So, in light and

fragrance, the scenes of the bees' activity glow and vaporize before our eyes, and, as nectar becomes honey, so labor itself seems to be distilled into a higher form of play. Surely, as Otis takes pains to remind us, the bees do not provide an accurate model for the human condition in its consciousness of mortality and morality,[28] but the very diminutiveness and even inconsequentiality of the "vehicle" here seem to expand and leaven and virtually become the author's "tenor" in a way not possible in the earlier and, as it were, weightier books. The cultural experience of reading the *Georgics* is not the chore of studying an agricultural manual precisely because, in reading it, our deepest cultivation is bee-like in its goals, seeking in the activity of gathering honey and wax the contemplation of what Swift and Arnold called those two best things: sweetness and light.

And yet, this is but the beginning of the end of the poem. If the bees' activity seems to deny the human condition, the poem itself will again subject its vision to time and history in a harvest that yields its final fruition. Beginning with advice on the regeneration of bees, in case a colony should be destroyed, the second half of book 4 is largely taken up with the legendary origins of this process in the interlocked stories of Aristaeus, the Arcadian beekeeper, and Orpheus and Eurydice. In its context (and despite its climactic situation) the section has been considered not as it is but as it might have been. This part of the poem many consider to have been composed originally as a tribute to Cornelius Gallus, governor of Egypt, who was later charged with disloyalty and took his own life in disgrace. Vergil replaced the praise of Gallus with at least the Orpheus story and, probably, with the whole Aristaeus sequence. Unfortunately, the scholarly awareness of this historical circumstance has not improved our appraisal of the poem's integrity;[29] and yet, rather than distract from our appreciation of the *Georgics'* conclusion, our sense of its historical circumstances should enhance our reading of it. For the achievement of this final sequence is to confront and resolve the tragic negations im-

plicit in the human struggle, be it the disease that besets cattle
or the disgrace of an eminent friend. In the "golden" passages
of book 2 and the opening of book 3 Vergil displayed the rewards of agrarian industry under the aspect of history. Now,
deepening that perception into something like Eliade's "eternal
now," he sees temporal loss and gain as the expression of a
timelessness rooted in the seasonal rhythm of nature.

This insight is movingly enacted in the instructions for the
generation of fresh bees from the blood of a slain bullock, a
sequence which is twice described: to introduce the Aristaeus
fable and to conclude it and the *Georgics*. Neither simply a
practical remedy for beekeepers deprived of their brood nor
a fantastically crude and superstitious business, the process in
Vergil's vision creates a sense of the holy at a center farther
from and deeper than these extremes. Toil has become ritual,
and, incorporating the meaningless, ritual has become meaningful. It is ritual of a sort that elicits our sensitivity to retic-
ulations of imagery and evokes a "correspondence" between
books 4 and 3 as compelling as any between books 2 and 1.
The lines' neglected import can readily be appreciated if the
reader pauses for a moment to recall the disgusting details of
the diseased hide, which closed book 3, and then sees how this
regenerative process looks back to that horror and transmutes
it into something rich and strange.

> *huic geminae nares et spiritus oris*
> *multa reluctanti obstruitur, plagisque perempto*
> *tunsa per integram solvuntur viscera pellem.*
> *sic positum in clauso linquunt et ramea costis*
> *subiciunt fragmenta, thymum casiasque recentis.*
>   (4. 300–304)

They stopper up, though he struggle wildly, his two
Nostrils and breathing mouth, and they beat him to death
    with blows
That pound his flesh to pulp but leave the hide intact.
Battered down in that narrow room they leave him,
    under his ribs
Laying fresh cassia and thyme and broken branches.

hoc geritur Zephyris primum impellentibus undas,
ante novis rubeant quam prata coloribus, ante
garrula quam tignis nidum suspendat hirundo.
interea teneris tepefactus in ossibus umor
aestuat, et visenda modis animalia miris,
trunca pedum primo, mox et stridentia pennis,
miscentur, tenuemque magis magis äera carpunt,
donec ut aestivis effusus nubibus imber
erupere, aut ut nervo pulsante sagittae,
prima leves ineunt si quando proelia Parthi.

(ll. 305–14)

This is done as soon as a west wind ruffles the water,
Before the meadows are flushed with vernal color, before
The talkative martin hangs her nest under the rafters.
Meanwhile, within the marrowy bones of the calf,
    the humours
Grow warm, ferment, till appear creatures miraculous—
Limbless at first, but soon they fidget, their wings vibrate,
And more, more they sip, they drink the delicate air:
At last they come pouring out, like a shower from
    summer clouds,
Or thick and fast as arrows
When Parthian archers, their bowstrings throbbing,
    advance to battle.

The same mystery informs the mythic account of Aristaeus' discovery of the regenerative process, a story artfully blended with the legend of Orpheus and Eurydice. Let us briefly consider the coordinate actions of each myth and then review the generative ritual as the climax of these stories and of the *Georgics* as a whole. Each myth originates as a response to tragic loss: Aristaeus' bees perish, killed by the sister nymphs of Eurydice, who died fleeing Aristaeus. Each dramatizes a common quest for restored life: Aristaeus descends to the underwater bower of his mother and thence to Proteus; Orpheus descends to the underworld. Finally, and most importantly, each demonstrates its hero's wit and industry: Aristaeus fetters Proteus (like Menelaus in the *Odyssey*), Orpheus enchants hell —instances interesting not only in themselves but as recollections of book 1's precept that suffering will stimulate human craft (1. 121–24). Indeed, when regarded in the context of the whole poem, the final meaning of the legends would seem to lie not so much in the difference between the success of Aristaeus and the *effusus labor* of Orpheus but in the convergence of these rising and falling movements in a common exaltation of *homo faber*, the identification of victor and vanquished in the opposed roles of suppliant and benefactor. The rites by which the "victor," Aristaeus, propitiates the "loser," Orpheus, thus enact the mystery at the heart of the *Georgics*. In the ritual of regenerating the bees there is celebrated, and sanctioned organically, a creative fusion of time the destroyer and time the preserver, whether we call it an integration of work and leisure or death and life:

> *hic vero subitum ac dictu mirabile monstrum*
> *aspiciunt, liquefacta boum per viscera toto*
> *stridere apes utero et ruptis effervere costis,*
> *immensasque trahi nubes, iamque arbore summa*
> *confluere et lentis uvam demittere ramis.*
>
> (4. 554–58)

> Here, to be sure, a miracle sudden and strange to
>   tell of
> They behold: from the oxen's bellies all over their
>   rotting flesh
> Creatures are humming, swarming through the wreck-
>   age of their ribs—
> Huge and trailing clouds of bees, that now in the
>   treetops
> Unite and hang like a bunch of grapes from the pliant
>   branches.

True to the spirit of its dialectic, however, the *Georgics* ends and does not end with the regeneration of the bees. The "sacred time" of that repeated ritual, like the *illud tempus* in which the poem was composed, now yields to a consciousness of public action in history: thus I sang, says Vergil, while Augustus earned immortality in distant combat and I lingered in the shade, enjoying a leisure which seems unworthy (*ignobilis oti*), singing of Tityrus lolling in the shade. At the same time, he has labored on this book that it might be contemplated by such a man of action, even as the purpose of imperial conquest (as the book's argument reiterates) is to earn an authentic golden age in history—to make the book come true. The book —like other leisurely experiences—is something we do without in order to have. It is, of course, the one book that has given that theme so commanding a form. True to its complexity, the last line raises the curtain even as it lowers it, echoing the first line of the *Eclogues* yet also insisting that the time for poetry is over, *cecini*. Reminded of that restored farm of Tityrus, we close the *Georgics* mindful of the leisure which it celebrates and summoned to the action which makes leisure possible.

Probably the most important critical rehabilitation of the *Georgics* in our time was that of T. S. Eliot when, in his essay on Vergil, he stressed the special importance of this poem for the medieval Christian world, which translated its dialectic into the Benedictine fusion of work and prayer.[30] We shall consider that medieval phenomenon soon enough. Here, as a final commentary on this still-neglected poem, it might be fitting to notice how the dialectical mystery at the conclusion and throughout the *Georgics* shapes Eliot's own poetic practice in the *Four Quartets*, especially in the Vergilian vision of the fisherman's labor in "The Dry Salvages." There, before the last poem's Dantesque contemplation in the monastic retreat, work "and every lawful traffic" is seen as itself a kind of prayer, action is one with contemplation, and even in frustration there is fulfillment:

> And right action is freedom
> From past and future also.
> For most of us, this is the aim
> Never here to be realized;
> We who are only undefeated
> Because we have gone on trying:
> We, content at the last
> If our temporal reversion nourish
> (Not too far from the yew-tree)
> The life of significant soil.[31]

So, it seems to me, the *Georgics* speaks to our age.

THE PRIVATE FOCUS

Horace's Satires *and Retired Leisure—The Daydream of
the Moneylender and the Liberations of the Contained
Life: The Father, the Friends, the Patron, the Farm*
(Epodes *2;* Satires *1. 1, 4, 6; 2. 6*)

The tradition that begins with Archilochus and Alcaeus and
runs through Montaigne to, say, Wallace Stevens instead of
Eliot has another view of such striving and of the civic or religious context that lends the soil such significance. One of the
supreme ironies of literary history is that, from the Renaissance
to the Enlightenment, Vergil's *O fortunatos nimium . . . agri-
colas,* praising the farmer's happiness as an emblem of civic
toil and leisure, should have been conflated with this description of rural bliss:

> *Beatus ille, qui procul negotiis,*
> *ut prisca gens mortalium,*
> *paterna rura bobus exercet suis,*
> *solutus omni faenore,*
> *neque excitatur classico miles truci,*
> *neque horret iratum mare,*
> *forumque vitat et superba civium*
> *potentiorum limina.*
> (Horace, *Epodes* 2. 1–8)

> Happy the man who, far away from business
> cares, like the pristine race of mortals, works
> his ancestral acres with his steers, from all
> money-lending free; who is not, as a soldier,
> roused by the wild clarion, nor dreads the angry
> sea; he avoids the Forum and proud thresholds
> of more powerful citizens.

To most readers who know anything about Horace this may
represent his typical theme: the busy city-dweller longs for the
leisurely innocence of the countryside, free from un-leisure
(*neg-otiis*). A denial of the flux of the busy world is soon fulfilled in the visionary affirmation of a golden age renewed. The

happy man spends his day in works that are more like amusements or hobbies: marrying vines to trees, surveying his grazing
herd, pruning his trees, storing his honey, shearing his sheep,
and, when autumn comes, plucking his pears and grapes (ll.
9–22). Even in winter he enjoys hunting boar, catching thrushes
by spreading nets on the polished pole, or laying snares for
small game (ll. 33–38). Enjoying this good life, why should he
care for the distractions of love (ll. 137–38)? Better to settle for
the happy man's *pudica mulier* of the old Sabine type or the
sunburned wife of a husky Apulian (ll. 39–42). There follows
an exhibition of the attractions of her pious economy: how
she piles high the fire on the sacred hearth, how she pens up
and milks the frisking flock, how she draws the wine and prepares a meal that doesn't cost a penny (ll. 43–48).[32] Enjoying
this simple table, our happy man casts a last scornful glance at
the great world's fancy—and expensive—cuisine (ll. 49–60). So
in the joys of the feast we leave him, *inter epulas*, watching his
sheep and oxen return, while his slaves keep to their place by
the gleaming household gods (ll. 61–66).

It seems too good to be true. And it is. Suddenly we discover
that our idyllic vision has been the daydream of one Alfius, a
moneylender—a contingency which, if it recalls the opening
solutus omni faenore, does so only to enforce a ludicrous reversal. Just when he was thinking of a farmer's life, he called
in all his money on the Ides—but he put it all out again by
the next Calends (ll. 68–70). The vision of leisure is dissipated
by the pressures of the calendar.

Thanks to a convenient excision of these last lines, this epode
came to enjoy its traditional status as a classic instance for the
Horatian myth of the Sabine farm.[33] It can, of course, be
pointed out as a historical fact that Horace had not received
his famous farm when this poem was composed; but a more
crucial question involves the literary and moral quality of the
poem itself: the poetry Horace wrote when he was his own
"happy man" will seem essentially different. It has doubtless
been evident from the tone of my review of its evocative features that this poem's view of rural bliss seems to have been

set off in a special way. When properly understood, the Second Epode is a delightful *jeu d'esprit*, but it is not as characteristic as its reputation suggests: it tests our comprehension of what is really central to the poet's vision. If we fail to distinguish between this epode and such authentic later statements as, say, *Satires* 2. 6, *Odes* 1. 7, or *Epistles* 1. 11, we shall never understand what is best in Horace, although, alas, we may share a widely held view of his work.

Perhaps because of the Second Epode's later influence, there has been, even among the poet's most astute readers, a critical reluctance to dismiss this bubble, which is inflated for sixty-six lines, as Wilkinson puts it, only to be pricked by the concluding word.[34] They therefore reduce the poem's conclusion to the status of a whimsical afterthought; they play down ironic awareness in order to restore the glamorous attractions of a less equivocal poem. To Fraenkel, most of the poem is "fundamentally true, if slightly idealizing." The "Heinesque" surprise at the close "is a characteristic dose of self-mockery."[35] The problem with these readings is their unwillingness to let Horace have it both ways throughout the poem. The question is worth considering, both to understand the intrinsic delights of a historically influential, if possibly misread, poem and to prepare us for the characteristic conclusion of the Horatian quest that began with a summons to depart for the Isles of the Blest. For it seems to me, at least, that the first sixty-six lines of the Second Epode have been designed to detach the careful reader from uncritically slipping into this kind of leisurely daydream. The "dose" at the end has trickled through the earlier lines. If the reader has the rug pulled out from under him in his own Alfius-like reverie, he has never enjoyed a very sure footing.[36]

Horace's tactic is to overstate the case so that the reversal has its earned necessity.[37] In the most rudimentary way, this is reflected in the quality of the syntax which the critics have noted, its very (un-Horatian) simplicity: one declarative proposition follows another with very little grammatical complexity or interweaving of words.[38] The tone is one of confident, indeed, too confident, even smug, assertion. Similarly—and here one proceeds tentatively—the meter seems to enforce this mood. There is first the regular beat of the iambic strophe, at once insistent and routine; against this pattern there is the peculiar effect of spondaic substitution, especially in the alternate (dimeter) line, as the iambs dilate into sonorities that swell the mold and virtually invite deflation.

Finally, as might have been evident in the tone of my summary, there is the special accent of the poem's manipulation of familiar motifs: it provides just too much of a good thing. From the opening *solutus omni faenore*, the daydream is informed—and exposed—by the economic considerations which we might expect from a character like Alfius. Rereading the poem as a moneylender's reverie, we perceive his satisfaction in the consumption of the goods of nature; indeed, we ironically enjoy the very imperturbability of his cutting, shearing, plucking, hunting, snaring, penning, draining, and pouring.

The same awareness should help us enter into the spirit of the final domestic scene. One suspects immediately an overdose of primitivism in the sunburnt wife (ll. 41–42). After all, why bring her in? Because, if the poet's moneylending Walter Mitty may shun sexual involvement, he can still cherish someone who makes a supper from *dapes inemptas*—food you don't have to pay for! The disingenuous simplicity of this feast is accentuated if we recall Vergil's praise of his happy farmer's living without, for example, foreign dyes or exotic spice, like cinnamon, to spoil his olive oil (*Georgics* 2. 465–66). For Horace's Alfius, rural simplicity involves otiose convenience and a veritably lip-smacking catalogue of the exotic food he does without (ll. 49–60). Vergil's lines contrast the corrupt city to a kind of life in which the good citizen finds his emblem of the authentic city. Alfius only has in mind two sets of comestibles: Lucrine oysters, African fowl, and Ionian pheasant as contrasted to the home-grown vegetables and the lamb slain at the feast of the boundaries or a kid rescued from the wolf. Rescued from the wolf—but delivered to the carving knife! This is why it is hard to keep from smiling when, in the midst of the feast that concludes his reverie, the would-be country gentleman joyfully contemplates the sheep hurrying homeward from pasture (ll. 61–62). Of course insights like these need not prevent us from enjoying the whimsy on its own terms—there is probably a bit of Alfius in all of us. Calypso's island, too, was delightful to read about, and most delightful when we knew why Odysseus must leave it. But there is more to Horace's characteristic vision than the yearning of the daydreaming city-dweller, and it is indeed ironical that he should continue to be appreciatively associated with a fantasy that in my view he took some pains to subvert.

What we have seen is another encounter between Theocritus' Lycidas and Simichidas, and again Simichidas has had the last word. Whether or not Alfius has been reading too deeply in Vergil's *Eclogues*, his speculations are pastoral in two ways: he regards the artificial naturalness of the rural creature comforts as "given," and the "pastimes" of the poem he inhabits curiously reflect (or "purify") the norms of the city. Just as the cultivated Alexandrian would turn poet-shepherd, so the Roman moneylender will become a gentleman farmer. In deflating the daydream of Alfius, Horace exposes both the unreality of the former and the materialism of the latter. But—witness the great dream of the Sixteenth Epode—there is, nevertheless, much in the pastoral ideal to appeal to him. For, as I have already suggested, the Horatian imagination aspires to the conditions of pastoral conceived not as fabulously given but as personally earned. The daydream of the "happy man" served Horace as *Amadis of Gaul* served Cervantes; what he began by mocking he ended by reconstituting, finding leisurely innocence not in an earthly paradise given to an improbable *beatus ille* but as a condition of mind achieved in tension with the real world, as the personal experience of a profoundly characterized *ego*. We have seen how, in the *Georgics*, Vergil could situate his pastoral ideal in the "context of history"; we can find the first expression of Horace's personal transformation of the *beatus ille* ideal in the unlikely vehicle of his *Satires*.

We need another name for Horace's *Satires*, one like the Latin *Sermones*, or Montaigne's *Essais*, which suggests affirma-

tive reflection and rumination as well as ridicule and castiga-
tion.[39] More than that, we need to appreciate the special
achievement of his *Satires* and *Epistles*, perhaps the most un-
justly neglected writings in the canon of classical literature.
There is "satire" here, but much more too. It is true, of course,
that even the most negative excoriation will speak up for certain values; Juvenal's *saeva indignatio*, for example, is the outraged response to an idealized *vir bonus*, whose rural, old-
fashioned, stoic way of life provides a norm with which to
indict urban, new-fangled decadence. Nevertheless, such affirmations are normally of an implicit kind; the satirist typically
voices a more destructive urgency. When we put down, say,
Juvenal's Tenth Satire, we are not so much moved by the wisdom of praying for a sound mind in a sound body as we are
contemptuously aware of the vicious folly of most human aspirations, such as those of Sejanus or Hannibal or Alexander.
It is quite otherwise in the *Sermones* of Horace that we are
going to consider. Here, it is the poet's definition of the good
life which leaves its impression, long after particular follies
are scorned and forgotten. The deepest analogy is not with
Juvenal but with Montaigne. What gives Horace's positive
ethical instruction its enduring appeal would seem to be precisely its assimilation of those symbolic motifs we have been
discussing, especially those we noted in the two "golden age"
Epodes. Here that dream of ease is absorbed into, and in turn
transmutes and inspires, a poetic world that seems, at first
glance, nothing but that merely representational mimesis fabled by the daughters of memory and ironic realism.

The line of argument which is the ethical justification for
the retired life in the *Sermones* is at least as old as the negative
or satiric fragments of Archilochus, transmuted, as these were,
into the affirmative and symbolic forms of festive lyric and
ideal landscape. Much the same transformation awaits us in
Horace's vision of content.

Why is it, he asks Maecenas at the start of his First Satire,
that no man lives content with his lot, but each man envies
the quest of another (*Satires* 1. 1. 1–3)? With this statement of

the satire's theme, the curtain rises on a crowded, obstreperous panorama; on every side we hear a restless cry. "Businessmen have it easy," gripes the old soldier. "The soldier's life for me," complains the merchant during a storm at sea. When a client's knocking wakens him, the lawyer praises the farmer's life; but the farmer, dragged into court from the country, yells that only city folks know how to be happy. Abruptly, a *deus ex machina* interrupts the turbulence: "All right, have the life you wish. Presto chango." Yet no one moves—no one really wants to change. "Well, what do they want anyway?" (ll. 4–23).

"Let us be serious for a moment," urges the poet, and then, with seeming artlessness, yet with masterful psychological insight, he hurries us into an extended attack on greed and avarice. Although this apparent divergence in the objects of the satire perplexes some readers, the two themes can easily be reconciled, and indeed the very necessity of their integration attests to the depth and subtlety of the poem's ethical view of restless unleisure. From a jocular view of human dissatisfaction, he has probed to what is for him the root of civilization's discontents. Why will no one live content? Because no one will accept the logic of the word's etymology and live contained. Instead, the reality that can be found only in accepting the contained self is sought in expansive projections, typically in the busy heaping-up of external goods (ll. 32–44, 51, 70–71). Opposed to these fantasies of expansion and accumulation is the poet's insistence on the self as it really is, subject to limitations, which, in the full sense of the Latin *finis*, are not only restrictive but purposive and liberating (ll. 49–50, 92, 106).

Now moderation *can* be one of the duller virtues, and there is probably sound folk insight registered in the customary connotations of the word "mediocrity." In Blake's words, "The cistern contains, the fountain overflows." The rare achievement of Horace is to celebrate the fountains of leisure which spring from content, to render the potentially humdrum norms of a *modus in rebus* not as a static, cistern-like platitude but as a dynamic response to life. Indeed, it is significant that the phrase *modus in rebus* should arise near the close of the poem

(l. 106), as if in acknowledgment that only one aspect of the question has occupied the author's attention. The poet has spent such energy in attacking avarice that he can hear someone objecting that he advocates the other extreme—"live like a spendthrift" (ll. 101–2). One knows, of course, the answer: "Why fly from one extreme to the other—there is measure in all things" (ll. 102–7); but at the same time one can hardly claim that the poem's emphasis reflects this balanced proportion. Erroneous as it is, the appearance of commending prodigality nevertheless points up a vital, liberating factor in the contracted focus as Horace characteristically sees it.

In the attack on the restless acquisitiveness of the uncontained self, it is important to see that the insistence on man's limitations springs from a willingness to consume and enjoy what comes within his scope. The heaping-up of material goods stands condemned not only for its expansive aspirations but also for its diminution of the self, its static denial of use. This is nicely illustrated in the opening discussion of the kind of "retirement" most men know—the secret piling-up of wealth for some distant future, *senes ut in otia tuta recedunt* (l. 31). Compare, says Horace, the ant, whose industry men admire, but who, when winter comes, makes use of the store she has gathered (ll. 32–37). It is not so with men during such seasons; in burning summer or freezing winter, man still will accumulate and accumulate (ll. 38–40). To achieve a timeless stasis for his heap of "retired" wealth, the discontented man thus subjects himself to time; to preserve what is human, the contented man retires himself, consuming his dwindling supply of material goods. In both lives we have versions of detachment and action. The difference lies in the choice between values, human and material: which is worth saving, which is worth using. As the material wealth of the uncontented man swells, his humanity is depleted; the contained man's limitation is the condition for his expansive liberation (ll. 73–79).

We notice also the tendency to define useful wealth within the contracted focus of food and drink. As a practical necessity, of course, these items have their place in the contented man's budget, but their function tends to be symbolic as well. The transfiguration of moderation begins when utility can be conceived as festivity.

This leisurely transformation is celebrated at the satire's conclusion in a meditation on the final limitation, death. There we have our climactic glimpse of the centrifugal flux of the uncontained life, like a futile chariot race (l. 113). Contrasted with it, and recalling the leisurely acceptance of death by Odysseus or Montaigne, we are shown the man, seldom seen, who is fulfilled in his limitations and who leaves the feast of life sufficed (ll. 118–19). *Conviva satur*: the latter word, which gives a name to the random hodgepodge of satire, is here restored to the sense of festive plenitude which is the goal of Horace's satiric insistence on limitations.

Engaging as these liberating elements are, the reader will be drawn to another quality, which first makes its appearance in the Third Satire of the first book: the outrageous idea (as Pascal complains of Montaigne)[40] of painting a portrait of yourself, of converting pedestrian biographical data into something representative and fabulous. For, at their best, the moral reflections of Horace persuade us not as disembodied statements but as convictions imbued with the particular coloring of a very personal life-story. This is especially evident in the Fourth Satire of the first book, a poem which begins with literary considerations and ends with a poignant reminiscence of Horace's father and an engaging apology for the poet's present behavior. The poem's structure, typically, is determined by the opposition of the uncontained and the contracted, this time conceived in literary terms as the difference between verbosity and brevity, popularity and limited readership, and (implicitly) quantity and quality. Looked at another way, it is the difference between a satiric vision which is harsh and censorious and loquacious and one which is jocular, tolerant, and reticent. Along these lines, the poem begins with a view of Horace's predecessor, the satirist Lucilius, an imitator of the crude jests of the Old Comedy and, in many ways, the epitome of all that our poet is out to replace. Lucilius was a witty fellow, in his rough way, says Horace. He could dictate two hundred lines while standing on one foot. There was much to remove in that muddy stream of his verbosity, but he was unwilling to revise (*Satires* 1. 4. 9–13).

Horace's first reaction, in the manner of Archilochus, is to shrug and to disqualify himself from any aspiration to such an output or to the comparable torrents of Crispinus or Fannius (ll. 14–22). Besides, he is not rich in imagination or facile in expression (ll. 17–18), and, anyway, satire is bound to offend the many who deserve it (ll. 22–25). No sooner do we hear the last item than we again behold the centrifugal flux of the uncontained life: adulterers, perverts, spendthrifts—all, like the merchant who rushes headlong for wealth from dawn to dusk, are "like dust caught up in a whirlwind" (l. 3).

By the time Horace asks us to hear a few words in self-defense (l. 38), he has defined himself both as a poet careful with his words, writing within a limited range, and as a satiric reformer opposed to a flood of excesses. But he is also working toward a positive justification for a kind of poetic statement and a way of life which looks beyond the exigencies of the simply satiric performance and seeks to define the mythless myth of his own life in an idiom suited to the transformation of the pedestrian. He claims he is not a poet at all but a mere versifier of lines more suited to conversation (*sermoni propiora*, l. 42), whereas a true poet has a godlike soul and a gift of noble eloquence (ll. 43–44). And so he slips into contrasting Lucilius with the more sublime Ennius (ll. 43–62). His own achievement will be precisely to blend the random conversational stream of Lucilius with the divine mind and noble expression he praises in poets like Ennius, and nowhere will this be more moving than in his description of his father's role in shaping his satiric attitude, a private equivalent, perhaps, of the epic past of an Ennius. If he is too free in his language, he says, please understand: it is a habit the best of fathers taught him (ll. 103–5). In his father's discourses, the moral message will be characteristically enlivened by a certain droll *savoir-faire*, as in the slyly solemn intonation of the warning against squandering a patrimony (ll. 110–11) or in the rich understatement recalling an adulterer caught in the act (*deprensi non bella est fama Treboni*, l. 114). All in all, while it inculcates a heritage, *traditum ab antiquis morem*, the father's sermon ends on a less serious, even whimsical note in describing the self-sufficiency Horace will soon come to enjoy in the flux of life: "then you will swim without the cork" (*nabis sine cortice*, l. 120).

It is just this buoyancy which enhances the poem's final sequence, an account of Horace's way of life, which is the climax of the poem: a scene of happy isolation which recreates the private legend of a *pater optimus* and which provides, in both manner and content, a counterstatement to the flux of discontent imaged earlier in both the muddy stream of verbosity and the whirlwind of vices deserving satire. He has a few failings, Horace admits, but here is how he regulates his life:

> *neque enim, cum lectulus aut me*
> *porticus excepit, desum mihi: "rectius hoc est:*
> *hoc faciens vivam melius: sic dulcis amicis*
> *occurram: hoc quidam non belle; numquid ego illi*
> *imprudens olim faciam simile?" haec ego mecum*
> *compressis agito labris; ubi quid datur oti*
> *illudo chartis. hoc est mediocribus illis*
> *ex vitiis unum; cui si concedere nolis,*
> *multa poetarum veniat manus, auxilio quae*
> *sit mihi (nam multo plures sumus), ac veluti te*
> *Iudaei cogemus in hanc concedere turbam.*
>
> (1. 4. 133–43)

> . . . for when my couch welcomes me or I stroll in the colonnade, I do not fail myself: "This is the better course: if I do that, I shall fare more happily: thus I shall delight the friends I meet: that was ugly conduct of so and so: is it possible that some day I may thoughtlessly do anything like that?" Thus, with lips shut tight, I debate with myself; and when I find a bit of leisure, I trifle with my papers. This is one of those lesser frailties I spoke of, and if you should make no allowance for it, then would a big band of poets come to my aid—for we are the big majority— and we, like the Jews, will compel you to make one of our throng.

With consummate expressiveness these "pedestrian" lines suggest the workings of that faculty which, quoting the passage in the seventeenth century, Sir Thomas Browne called his "solitary and retired imagination." We are first impressed by the inward drama (*mecum / compressis agito labris*, ll. 137–38) of defining the contracted focus: how the choppy effect of the extra caesurae (indicated by modern punctuation) registers the disjunctions of a dialogue with the self or how the concentration of the thought is felt in the brevity and point of the phrasing: *hoc . . . hoc . . . sic . . . hoc.* Yet from this agitation within compression there springs, typically, a release, a playful expansiveness inaugurated by the promise of leisure (*quid datur oti*, l. 138), epitomized in the reference to satiric composition as itself a kind of game (*illudo chartis*, l. 139), and preposterously aggrandized in our isolated poet's paradoxical claim that he has hosts of fellow writers on his side (ll. 139–43). And hosts of readers too, we might add, as we find ourselves playing at reading as he composed, *illudo chartis.* Thus finally, when contemplated from the perspective of his happy island, even the muddy river finds its place in the scheme of things; and so too (though this is not explicit), once the center of calm has been discovered within the self of the author and his reader, the whirlwind of other men's discontents will come to enjoy the toleration which both accord to the remote and the irrelevant.

This study is not the first reading of Horace to remark, as he himself does, on the absence of *saeva indignatio* in his most characteristic satires (ll. 101–3). Nor is this the first observation of the poet's special kind of self-portrayal: what we might call, in Jamesian parlance, "Horace as the intruding narrator." But these two characteristics of the Horatian *sermo* have not been seen as creatively related to each other in a special way, best exemplified by this poem. Let us, in reviewing for a moment that miniature type of the Horatian satire, the reminiscence of Horace's father criticizing the town, be mindful that the poem's significance may dwell as much in its portrait of the *pater optimus* as it does in its satire—though there are vices aplenty condemned in the father's opening remarks. What happens to the satiric itch can be explained by the fact that we

become less concerned with the evil of the vices than with how
Horace's father saw them. Our participation in his point of
view leads to our absorption in the brief portrayal of his way
of life. These are the conditions, I suggest, for the peculiar
benignancy of the father's "condemnations" and of Horatian
satire in general. The leisurely reader does not see the satiric
scene as such; he sees a narrator who lets him record how he
contemplates it. As we are admitted to the personal pleasures
of the narrator's retired life, we come to share with him a certain detachment, like that of the gods who live at ease.

One way of defining the difference between tragedy and comedy is the difference between the apprehension of life as experience and life as spectacle.[41] These features probably account
for the difference between the more tragic, even "more satiri-
cal," attacks of Juvenal and the typically detached attitude of
Horace. Take, for example, one of Juvenal's most incisive
lines: *nil habet infelix paupertas durius in se, quam quod ri-
diculos homines facit (Satires* 3. 152–53).[42] "Luckless poverty
has no harder woe than this—that it makes men ridiculous."
Reading it, we are engaged. We perceive a bizarre aspect of
human misery which we had not previously observed, and we
"realize" it. To a certain extent we share that degradation.
At the same time, we must reflect that we are all among those
who laugh at the ridiculous poor—but that was in our "normal"
state of detachment from life, which is, in this respect, detachment from Juvenal. In "satire as experience" we can be both
victim and victimizer; we judge and are judged.

On the other hand, in what might be called "satire as contemplated spectacle" we are not the author's adversary, or, at
best, his fellow combatant, but his intimate. And we share in
his Olympian detachment. The very perspective that in Juvenal's world results in a callous laugh at the victim's expense
becomes with Horace a way of laughing at the victimizer from a
still superior place of privilege, which is, of course, accessible to
the imagination of most victims. The insistence here, then, is
not on the confrontation with evil but on the shared consciousness of the abiding primacy of a valid alternative, an ethically

informed "content" which is not (as in Juvenal) a lost heritage of virtue but rather a very lively and personal possibility.[43] Horace's depiction of his private life, his invitation to the reader to share his leisurely point of view as he did his father's—these aspects are not the added attractions of Horatian satire but the very conditions of its essentially contemplative quality, its tolerance, and its comedy.

In a later satire (*Satires* 2. 1) Horace paid tribute to Lucilius for the very quality of self-preservation and self-recreation which distinguishes his own satire. Lucilius' life, Horace tells us, is as open to view as if painted on a votive tablet. He shared his secrets with his books as if they were his closest friends (ll. 28–34), and the secrets are most engagingly those of friendship. He exposed vice in high places and was a friend only to virtue and her friends; but when he joined Scipio and Laelius in a private party, they gave themselves to folly and cast off restraint (ll. 68–73). *Nugari cum illo et discinti ludere*—this unbuttoned frivolity, so expressive of candid affection, epitomizes what will become a leading motif in Horace's delineation of his retired way of life: the convivial circle of intimates. There, as he once was with his father, he is now with a few select contemporaries; and so he will be perpetually with his leisurely readers, as he is in the Fourth Satire of the first book, disdaining large crowds and textbook adoption, as long as the readers, fit though few, applaud the performance (ll. 74–77).

We have begun this account of Horace's circle of friends by characterizing them (as he himself does) as judges of literary value. If their invocation attests to a growing acceptance of—and by—the great world, it is instructive to notice in the Tenth Satire of the first book that one list is more than an exercise in name-dropping. Indeed, as a clue to the poet's "conversion" to the regime, the catalogue is more remarkable for its allegiance to the past, its inclusion of names from the days of Brutus' lost cause (*Sat.* 1. 10. 76–86). Similarly, even as he enjoys the benefits of the regime, the poet's representation of his contemporary friends and patron will be notable for the features he chooses to heighten or to omit; typically, the intensity of the private communion will tend to displace the larger civic loyalty.

We catch more than a glimpse of this convivial ideal as it first emerges in and transforms the Fifth Satire of the first book, an account of a journey to Brundisium in the entourage of Maecenas and Cocceius, who had been sent on an embassy to Mark Antony. That important mission is, of course, precisely what the poem is not about; nor, on the other hand, can its special quality be reduced to the imitation of a Lucilian proto-type.[44] To understand it, one must grant the author his sense of holiday excursion, a departure, as announced in his opening words, from the great world of the city (*Egressum magna me . . . Roma*, l. 1) to the limitations of rural simplicity (*Aricia . . . hospito modico*, ll. 1–2). The latter are soon translated into those values of release and free time (*hoc iter ignavi divisimus*, l. 5) which pervade the business of the journey's stops and starts in a way that may call to mind the goings-on of some-thing like *Three Men in a Boat*. The effect here, to recall our preceding chapter, is comparable to the mood of the excursion of Theocritus' city-dwellers to the harvest festival, or the free time of the Epicurean garden, or the pastoral sequence cited in *De Rerum Natura*. And, as in these instances, the rural set-ting invites not only release but affirmation. Leaving the me-tropolis behind and neglecting those state affairs which are the mission's goal, the poet is able to define and exalt a less mo-mentous but more authentic kind of community, as he does, for example, in the unbounded festivity heralding the arrival of Plotius, Varius, and Vergil (ll. 39–44). As Fraenkel reminds us, there is one parallel to the expressiveness of these lines: "He prizes these friendships as he prizes the memory of his father."[45] One may, I hope, rephrase this to say: "He prizes these friendships *because* he prizes the memory of his fa-ther," or even "These friendships are a way of recreating the relationship he once enjoyed with his father." For that is how, it seems to me, the point of view in the perambulations of the original pair becomes the perspective of the travelogue which the circle of friends—and readers—enjoys. So, too, one relishes "as spectacle" the mock-epical combat of Sarmentus and Cicirrus (ll. 51–70),[46] the fiery alarums of the innkeeper at Beneventum (ll. 71–76), even the narrator's own arch embarrassment at his attempted assignation (ll. 81–85). Thus, finally, we arrive at Gnatia and share a laugh at the local superstition that incense melts without fire on the temple threshold. We know better; we say with the author (who is quoting Lucretius) that the carefree gods never bother themselves about such petty human concerns.[47] Neither, indeed, do "we.'" The perspective of the gods is the point of view of Horatian satire, and it is no less godlike for its transformation of detachment into the friendly festivity of unembarrassed embracing and joy: *o qui complexus et gaudia quanta fuerunt* (l. 43).

The preeminent member of Horace's private community of friends was, of course, his patron, Maecenas; and it is fitting that, though his name has been invoked earlier, Maecenas should first emerge as a "character" in Horace's fable of the self in the Sixth Satire, which is the center, if not the summit, of the first book. The ostensible occasion of the poem is the poet's humble origin as a freedman's son, and hence one way of conceiving it is to say that it is Horace's defense against the charge of social climbing. But the theme of the poem can also, perhaps more profoundly, be described not simply as the dismissal of public notions of aristocratic distinction but as the reassertion of such a distinction in the personal sense: who one's father was becomes indeed the radical question. In its meaningful answer, in relating the values of the past to the prosperity of the present, the self-destructive satire becomes, as in Pope's "Imitations of Horace," an apologia pro vita sua.

The theme of true aristocracy is announced at the start of the poem, where Maecenas' open-minded and, so to speak, "democratic" behavior is shown to issue from the noble ancestry sonorously evoked in the opening lines (*Sat.* 1. 6. 1–4). As Horace points out, Maecenas' elevation of a freedman's son attests to a genuine nobility, which has its model in the venerable precedent of a heroic past, the days before the reign of Tullius, when, despite their low birth, countless men enjoyed

the dignity of high office (ll. 7–11). The true aristocrat disregards the vulgar appearances of nobility. From the detachment
of this shared perspective, Maecenas, Horace, and the reader
enjoy the satiric spectacle of those dumbfounded by the public
images of class (ll. 17–18). Even more ludicrous than the
shallow status-consciousness of the mob is the ambition of those
who aspire to these trappings. We see them soon enough in
another derisive survey of the conspicuous consumption of the
uncontained self (ll. 19–44). There, behind Reputation's glittering chariot, rush all those who presume to public promi-
nence and are exposed to the accusation of social climbing, the
charge of being a *novus homo*. "Where did he come from?
What did his father do?" people will ask. "Publicity begets
jealousy; no one envies a private man." This satire will end in
a celebration of the privacy of Horace's unambitious way of
life; but by that time (and this is the special achievement of
this poem's movement away from satiric negation) such a life
will be exalted not because it is free *from* envy but because it
is free *for* its own sake as a consummation of what is "noblest"
in Maecenas and in Horace's father.

Hence the poet resumes his autobiographical fable with an
account of his first meeting with Maecenas. Compared to the
idealizing allegory of Vergil's account of Tityrus' journey to
Rome, Horace's plain tale seems a pedestrian vehicle, as if we had
turned from a romance to a novel. In conversational language
—*sermoni propiora*—divested of pastoral's aureate glow, the
poet offers a probing social and psychological dramatization, a
scrupulous sensitivity to the nuances of manners, from the
slight details of the preliminary introduction of Vergil and
Varius (ll. 54–55) to the poignant entrance of Horace, who
comes like Telemachus to the great house of a Menelaus; and
if, this time, the father is dead, the quest will not go unfulfilled.
Hence we remember the tongue-tied embarrassment and final
blunt declaration, so suited to this realistic literary form: "I
was not a famous father's son," he says, "but what I was I told
you"—*sed quod eram, narro* (ll. 56–60). Horace of course uses
the present-tense *narro* (an untranslatable effect in English),

which is enforced by the continuing narrative present of the poem. He "tells" Maecenas who he is, as he tells his readers. Maecenas says little in response, as is his custom, but after nine months Horace is invited into his circle (ll. 60–62). Horace will not be able to say of Maecenas, as Vergil's Tityrus could of Augustus, that a god has given him leisure; but his experience of his own kind of leisure gives him, if not a god, at least a mythic transformation of autobiography. His acceptance by Maecenas depends not on a famous father but on a father who personally shaped his moral identity. This, we begin to feel, is history at least as authentic as the Vergilian myth of an Augustan recreation of the Age of Saturn.

Yet the poet's memory of his private golden age evokes more than a moral condition free from corruption and scandal. It evokes a state of being free for its own sake—as in the contemplative leisure of a liberal education, which was this father's supreme gift to this son. The lost garden was a grove of Academe. For though the father was struggling on a farm, he sent his son to the school of Flavius, where the sons of centurions used to go, and dared to have him taught the same studies that a knight's or senator's son would learn (ll. 71–78). Horace regards this "liberal" education as a gentleman's privilege, but the economic condition becomes a kind of moral metaphor. In Horace's enjoyment of the gracious leisure of a highborn student, a real nobility is engendered, so that neither father nor son need disdain baser occupations (ll. 85–87). For the same reason, the poet would never wish for another father, even if he might live his life over. As Niall Rudd puts it nicely, "It therefore turns out that Horace is more free than those who despise him, thanks to the guidance of a man who was once a slave."[48] Content with the innocence and leisure which are his father's legacy, he would not exchange them for a nobility which can be defined only by the emblems of high office. "The world may think me mad," Horace confides to Maecenas, "but you at least will understand" (ll. 96–98).

As it is set forth in the following lines, the poet's way of life is first defined as the sane alternative to the status-seeking which

has been his satiric target. Recalling the embarrassments which
beset the ambitious Tillius (*invida accrevit, privato quae minor
esset*, 1. 26), he now conclusively elaborates the negative advan-
tages of a life which is private and contained, free from envy
and expense (ll. 107–11). As the debonair recreation of a cherished paternal ideal, the final appeal of this condition springs,
typically, from its transfiguration of the contained life. Freedom from envy and expense becomes freedom for its own sake.
Within the limited scope of private content there is liberated
an expanded self-awareness:

> quacumque libido est,
> incedo solus; percontor quanti holus ac far;
> fallacem Circum vespertinumque pererro
> saepe Forum; adsisto divinis . . .
>   (*Sat*. 1. 6. 111–14)
> Wherever the fancy leads, I saunter forth
> alone. I ask the price of greens and flour; often
> toward evening I stroll round the cheating Cir-
> cus and the Forum. I listen to the fortune-
> tellers; . . .

Here, to alter Blake's proverb, the overflowing fountain wells
up from within the cistern that "contains," as the carefree
release joyously announced in the first line (*Quacumque libido
est*) animates that detached point of view (*incedo solus*) in
which it originates and on which it depends. The very openness of the poet's invitation to observe all experience, to ask
the price of groceries, "to draw us into quarters which at that
hour the respectable citizen would rather avoid,"[49] even to lis-
ten to fortune-tellers, the whole irresistible exhibition of a
consciousness which calls nothing human alien, which, like
Montaigne's, sees man as *un subject merveilleusement vain,
divers, et ondoyant*, is possible only because it is, significantly,
an openness not so much to experience itself but to the detached contemplation of experience (*incedo solus*). Green-
grocers and fortune-tellers are enjoyed by Horace not because
he is a man interested in greens or fortunes but because he is

a man seeing. Though the sights may even deserve satiric scorn, he visits them as he would read a book or observe a work of art. The city becomes his grove of Academe, the life of leisure becomes a continuing liberal education; but this is possible only because there has been the initial containment of experience, exemplified by his content with a simple supper (ll. 114–18).

Even Horace's sleep seems to epitomize this distance from worldly cares (ll. 119–21). And, in the account of the next day, even such a slight detail as the jocular admission of the late hour of his rising seems to have its intrinsic and leisurely significance.

> *ad quartam iaceo; post hanc vagor, aut ego lecto*
> *aut scripto quod me tacitum iuvet unguor olivo* . . .
> (ll. 122–23)
> I lie a-bed till ten; then I take a stroll, or after
> reading or writing something that will please
> me in quiet moments I anoint myself with oil—

Clock time has lost its meaning, and this most mundane hint of the ease a god granted to Vergil's Tityrus is the keynote of the freedom and variability which enlivens the duration of the morning's amusements. Our awareness expands again with the promise of release (*post hanc vagor*); and in the alternative conjunctions and the absolute and subjunctive verb constructions (*aut ego, lecto / aut scripto quod me tacitum iuvet*) which precede the final simple *unguor olivo*, the very syntax registers a variety of possibilities and times which blend together in one timeless consciousness of personal duration. One notices, too, the bookish nature of these amusements; more explicitly than those of the previous afternoon, these recreations recall those humanistic pursuits which the poet first enjoyed in the leisurely education of his youth. And we are reminded also, as in the *incedo solus* of the first sequence, that, like Milton's Il Penseroso, his contemplative expansion of the possibilities of the self is the fruition of a contraction from the busyness and glare of the uncontained life (ll. 125–26).

This dialectical progression from restraint to liberation is perfectly restated in our glimpse of the poet as he returns home:

> *pransus non avide, quantum interpellet inani*
> *ventre diem durare, domesticus otior.*
>
> (ll. 127–28)

After a slight luncheon, just enough to save me
from an all-day fast, I idle away time at home.

Given the Sixth Satire's critical response to the centrifugal forces of experience, its conclusion might indeed be "otiose" in the unhappy contemporary sense; and without its promise of self-liberating *scholē*, its insistence on restraint might be only a negative and fruitless self-denial. To put it another way, it is the uncontained life which is the self-indulgent; it is the centripetal focus which expands the central consciousness to include centers outside the circle of the self. *Pransus non avide . . . domesticus otior*: it is late afternoon in the poet's daily round, and this dialectical progress of contraction and release will end, as it began, in the continuing transfiguration of detachment: *quacumque libido est, incedo solus.* This, then, is the leisurely life of the man who liberates himself by containing himself. It recalls to mind the innocent leisure of *Epodes* 16 and 2, but it comes to us as neither prophecy nor daydream, nor, as in the opposite argument of the *Eclogues* and the *Georgics*, does it represent the fabulous consummation of civic order. It insists on contentment with a humble paternity, but a contentment irradiated by the patronage of an aristocrat who, even as he prompts the remembrance of that earlier condition, reminds us of its true nobility, not in civic but in personal terms. Such is the life of men freed from the burden of ambition, Horace says; and he comforts himself that he lives more happily than if his grandfather or father or uncle had held political office (ll. 128–31).

Though fortuitous, it may be instructive that this examination of the emergent fable of the *Sermones* has so far been concerned more with the reality of the mind's world than, as might be expected, with the pleasures of a Sabine farm. As a

matter of fact, it is not likely that Maecenas had given Horace
the farm by the time the first book was composed;[50] but this
accident of biography may serve to remind us that, though the
rural ambiance provides the retired poet with a perfect theater
for the transfiguration of the contained life, the particular
locale is not an essential condition or an inevitable theme of
that poetry.[51] There is, to borrow the language of England's
greatest nature poet, nothing "far more deeply interfused" in
the countryside of the retired imagination comparable to the
immanent civic or religious significance of the gardens of Alcinous or the rural Italy of the *Georgics*. Horace celebrates
the delights of his earthly paradise because they give symbolic
expression to the free time of a paradise within the mind.

As such an emblem of the life of leisure, the Sabine farm
first emerges in the Sixth Satire of the second book. Undoubt-
edly the finest of Horace's "satires" (though here, if ever, the
term is misleading), the poem is also a superb climax to that
quest for the blessed isle whose definition and gradual fulfillment we have been studying.

> *Hoc erat in votis: modus agri non ita magnus,*
> *hortus ubi et tecto vicinus iugis aquae fons*
> *et paulum silvae super his foret. auctius atque*
> *di melius fecere. bene est. nil amplius oro,*
> *Maia nate, nisi ut propria haec mihi munera faxis.*
>
> (*Sat.* 2. 6. 1–5)
>
> This is what I prayed for!—a piece of land
> not so very large, where there would be a gar-
> den, and near the house a spring of ever-flowing
> water, and up above these a bit of woodland.
> More and better than this have the gods done
> for me. I am content. Nothing more do I ask,
> O son of Maia, save that thou make these bless-
> ings last my life long.

Conversational yet lyrical, the lines are charged with a quiet
excitement—"quiet" because the scope here is limited and contained (*non ita magnus*); "excitement" because the continuing
urgency of these contrasted expectations is registered so tell-

ingly in the use of the imperfect (*hoc erat in votis*) and is fulfilled in a vision of free time which absorbs this past and overflows from present to future (*fecere . . . bene est . . . oro . . .
faxis*); "excitement" too as the initial limitation is transformed
by suggestive details of landscape—garden, fountain, and grove
—to enact a vision of plenitude (*nil amplius oro*) which expands from within the contracted focus. This joy, which springs
from the transfiguration of contentment, belies its origins; and,
in the lines before us, the final if not the first proof of this kind
of expansion is the fact that we have been reading a humanistic
prayer, a mythless celebration of the Horatian myth.

The first fifteen lines of the poem address Mercury in his
role as god of good fortune. As in those quoted, the remaining
ten insist on the limitations of ambition which, paradoxically,
entitle Horace to the farm (ll. 6–13) and thus renew the plea
to continue those delights which transform contentment (ll.
14–15). And yet, what a difference there is between the god
of Vergil's First Eclogue and this god, who, instead of being
the divine giver of human leisure, represents the "divine"
possibility which is given to man in the life of leisure. The
poet's conscious elevation of the tone (which virtually overturns
the expected limitations of conversational language) exalts not
a beneficent deity but the godlike situation of his own blessed
isle, free not only from the flux of place-seeking but from the
seasonal reminders of mortality. He has retired, he says, to his
castle in the hills. Is there anything more important to excite
his pedestrian muse? There is no scrambling for position here,
nor does the sirocco come, nor autumn's plagues.

Characteristically, however, the poem will not allow the ease
of the gods merely to be asserted. Instead, the authentic significance of retired leisure will be realized dramatically as it is
sought from within the flux and press of the busy world. To
that end, Horace devotes the next forty lines to his own quest
for this calm harbor, beginning his urban odyssey with a sublime invocation of the god of the morning—ironically lofty
lines, which soar above the middle flight of the pedestrian

muse (ll. 20–23) only to expose the banality of the turbulent world which they introduce (ll. 23–26). Impetuously summoned to Rome, reminded of wind and winter, the reader is hurried back to a world where no ambition is contained and where time is never interrupted by leisure. The prayerful wish, already fulfilled for the poet in the opening lines (*Hoc erat in votis*), is dramatized in all the urgency of its fulfillment. Like Odysseus on the stormy seas, Horace is caught up in the centrifugal whirl of the city's discontents. As the friend of Maecenas, he is especially buttonholed for favors (ll. 27–39), and (to use the patois of the Washington correspondent) for "news leaks" (ll. 51–58). Yet, as he reminds us, the very nature of his relationship with Maecenas—the reserve of the patron, the reticence of the poet—presupposes the value of detachment, of the sanctity of privacy. The topics of their conversation are slight, as Horace records them (ll. 40–50), but they testify to an authentic intimacy far more than would subjects of greater political moment. In his role as "informed source," Horace is asked, for example, where he would guess the veterans of Actium will be rewarded with grants of land (ll. 55–57), but there is only one question that concerns our disinterested veteran of Philippi. It is answered at the start of the poem, but its insistence is felt in every line of this urban *nostos* and nowhere more than in the (literally) nostalgic poignancy of the climax of this sequence: *Perditur haec inter misero lux non sine votis; / o rus, quando ego te aspiciam!* (Amid such trifling, alas! I waste my day, praying the while: / O rural home: when shall I behold you!) (ll. 59–60).

This poem began at the farm with the freshness of a dawn rite and the promise of a timeless renewal. To review the opening from the perspective of these lines not only would indicate the difference between sunrise and nightfall, countryside and city, free time and devouring time (though the manipulation of these contrasts is impressive); it would also demonstrate the earned necessity of retired leisure (*hoc erat in votis*) by the very intensity of its prayerful anticipation, all the more telling for its final ironic litotes (*perditur haec inter misero lux non sine votis*). One need not, however, return to the start of the poem to find the fulfillment of this passage's yearning:

> *Perditur haec inter misero lux non sine votis:*
> *o rus, quando ego te aspiciam? quandoque licebit*
> *nunc veterum libris, nunc somno et inertibus horis,*
> *ducere sollicitae iucunda oblivia vitae?*
> *o quando faba Pythagorae cognata simulque*
> *uncta satis pingui ponentur holuscula lardo?*
> *o noctes cenaeque deum!*
>
> (ll. 59–65)

> Amid such trifling, alas! I waste my day, praying the while: O rural home: when shall I behold you! When shall I be able, now with books of the ancients, now with sleep and idle hours, to quaff sweet forgetfulness of life's cares! O when shall beans, brethren of Pythagoras, be served me, and with them greens well larded with fat bacon! O nights and feasts divine!

These climactic lines exhibit most of the leading motifs traced in this and the preceding chapter, but perhaps they are best introduced within the specific rhetorical structure of the poem. I mean the way in which, through successive exclamatory questions, Horace here shifts the reader's sense of place from the city to the country. The countryside first appears in these lines as something distantly yearned for, more desirable for its very distance: *o rus, quando ego te aspiciam!* Then, as the delights of the retired life are defined more particularly, the reader is invited into the daydream, to realize the poem's vision in his own leisurely contemplation of its commemoration in verse. The note of distance and futurity begins to yield to an assurance of proximity and presence (ll. 60–62), and this note of confidence is curiously heightened by the bantering circumlocution about beans, which prepares us for the poem's great affirmation, *O noctes cenaeque deum!* We experience it not as a distant ideal but as a vividly apprehended reality, the reality of the very process of reading the poem, as well as enjoying its subject.

The next lines (65–75) are recounted in the present tense, but this present is the future of an immediate past: *hoc erat in votis*—one recalls—but with a renewed appreciation of how the present and the past intersect in this poem, here where the timeless and time engage. *O noctes cenaeque deum*—we have heard this affirmation before. Yet, even as we acknowledge an affinity with the classic context of leisure, we must recognize the crucial difference between the public and the private conceptions of these values, the difference, as suggested at the start of this chapter, between Vergil's god, who makes leisure possible, and the gods whom leisure makes possible. Here the holiday has created the holy day. Here, one might say, there are no such things as gods without a feast. The private celebration we enter into here is literally a symposium, an Epicurean drinking party, where, liberated from the conventions which govern public behavior, the participant finds his private satisfactions transfigured in a communion of self-fulfillment. But the occasion is also a symposium in the modern and the best classical sense. We start to talk, Horace says, not about homes and estates or about manners, like the dancing of Lepos, but about issues that concern us at the deepest level: Does wealth or virtue make men happy? Which leads to friendship? and What is the nature of the good? What is its highest form? The very circumstance of the symposium is, of course, the essential answer to these questions regarding the good life.

Horace's depiction of his festive academy is likewise enlivened by its own drama and play within his play. There is, for example, a neighbor, Cervius by name, always ready with an old wives' tale to suit the occasion, especially to reprove someone, ignorant of the city's discontents, who looks back admiringly on the attainment of wealth: "Once upon a time —so the story goes—there was a country mouse who, despite his humble lot, generously entertained a city mouse. . . ."

The fable which concludes the Sixth Satire of the second book has enjoyed such popularity out of its context that the integrity of the whole poem has probably suffered from the emphasis. The following reading will attempt to relate the fable to the structure of the entire poem, the theme of which, if it must be fixed in a title, seems to be announced in the opening lines, *Hoc erat in votis*. This is one way of discovering that the poem's beginning is peculiarly its end. Indeed, in approaching the fable, it is useful to recall that the whole satire has been notable for its fluid sense of place and time. It begins on the Sabine farm at daybreak, but soon, as if drawn by the initial *hoc erat*, the scene shifts from the country to the city and from the actual present to a narrative present describing apparently past events; thence we come back to the farm, this time to an evening feast, as if from a busy day in the city. We come back to a present which was the future of a vividly realized past. Viewed within this pattern of excursion and depletion, withdrawal and renewal, the fable of Cervius enacts the final movement. Returning us to the anxiety of uncontained existence, it does so only to expose the "real" world finally as merely the proper setting for a Tom and Jerry cartoon and to reassert the enduring reality of the contracted world of retired leisure, not only of Horace and his immediate circle but of all those "guests" at this symposium, including the readers, who have been present at that feast which is the reading of the poem itself.

The complexity of the parable also demands an awareness of its dramatic occasion: it is narrated at a specific symposium of "country mice." The opening description of *mus rusticus* finds him enjoying a state not a little like that which is also the privilege of Cervius' audience: Horace's guests—which is to say, his readers. Once upon a time a country mouse welcomed his old friend from the city into his poor hole. He fared roughly and was frugal of what he had, yet his thrifty soul could expand in acts of hospitality, begrudging not his hoard of vetch or oats, and even serving a dried raisin and nibbled bits of bacon to a guest so fastidious as hardly to touch a morsel. Meanwhile, the master of the house stretched out on fresh straw and ate spelt and darnel, leaving the tidbits to his friend. (ll. 79–89).

The poem's strategy will be to define the difference between rural contentment and urban ambition by exhibiting the symbolic qualities of their representative feasts. The contained life begins on a rather negative note of frugality (l. 82), a theme which is likewise suggested by the detailed minuteness of the particles left over after the rural repast. Yet, as the very mention of the victuals should serve to illustrate, the contracted focus is soon transformed by a festive generosity. The characteristic tone of the passage has precisely this lively sense of release from the constrictions of the thrifty soul, a release that paradoxically originates in the acceptance of those limitations. Horace's country mouse reconciles the most attractive features of both Aesop's frugal ant and festive grasshopper. The only sour note at the feast comes from the guest, whose self-indulgence fussily enforces self-denial, a behavior which seems even more petty in view of the contrast with the superb concluding image of the master of the house, presiding like some benevolent deity over a world assured of leisure and festivity (ll. 88–89) —presiding, indeed, like the very audience of this tale, whether at Horace's farm or at its recreation in this poem.

This assurance of the good life in the countryside renders the discontented speech of the city mouse a masterpiece of dramatic irony:

> *"carpe viam, mihi crede, comes; terrestria quando*
> *mortalis animas vivunt sortita, neque ulla est*
> *aut magno aut parvo leti fuga: quo, bone, circa,*
> *dum licet, in rebus iucundis vive beatus;*
> *vive memor, quam sis aevi brevis." haec ubi dicta*
> *agrestem pepulere, domo levis exsilit; inde*
> *ambo propositum peragunt iter, urbis aventes*
> *moenia nocturni subrepere.*
>
> (ll. 93–100)

> "Take my advice: set out with me. Inasmuch as all creatures that live on earth have mortal souls, and for neither great nor small is there escape from death, therefore, good sir, while you may, live happy amid joys; live mindful ever of how brief your time is!" These words struck home with the rustic, who lightly leaped forth from his house. Then both pursue the journey as planned, eager to creep under the city walls by night.

With their keen sense of the mutability of man's lot and their
longing for a moment of festive free time, the lines persuasively draw from a heritage of Epicurean sentiments, as Horace himself was often to do. (One might readily compare the
mouse's *carpe viam* with the poet's own famous *carpe diem*
ode, the Ninth of the first book). Ironically, the very reasons
the city mouse unwittingly advances should lead to a life of
retired leisure, not to the centrifugal hazards of urban flux
(ll. 96–97).

Unfortunately, however, the country cousin has taken his
own real beatitude for granted. Soon, with a flurry of plosives
(*pepulere . . . ambo propositum peragunt . . . subrepere*) contentment is forsaken for the great world:

>   *Iamque tenebat*
> *nox medium caeli spatium, cum ponit uterque*
> *in locuplete domo vestigia, rubro ubi cocco*
> *tincta super lectos canderet vestis eburnos,*
> *multaque de magna superessent fercula cena,*
> *quae procul exstructis inerant hesterna canistris.*
> *ergo ubi purpurea porrectum in veste locavit*
> *agrestem, veluti succinctus cursitat hospes*
> *continuatque dapes nec non verniliter ipsis*
> *fungitur officiis, praelambens omne quod adfert.*
> *ille cubans gaudet mutata sorte bonisque*
> *rebus agit laetum convivam . . .*
>
>   (ll. 100–111)

> And now night was holding the mid space of
> heaven, when the two set foot in a wealthy pal-
> ace, where covens dyed in scarlet glittered on
> ivory couches, and many courses remained over
> from a great dinner of the evening before, in
> baskets piled up hard by. So when the town
> mouse has the rustic stretched out on purple
> covers, he himself bustles about in waiter-style,
> serving course after course, and doing all the
> duties of the home-bred slave, first tasting every-
> thing he serves. The other, lying at ease, enjoys
> his changed lot, and amid the good cheer is
> playing the happy guest.

The mock-heroic tone of the narrative underscores what is probably the most conspicuous feature of this banquet—the disproportion between scene and actors. The vehicle, which began as an Aesopian way of pointing up the theme, tends to *become* the theme ("Let mice stand for men because those men who parade before such grand settings are radically like mice"). Thus, in comparison with the frugal particulars of the country feast, the cuisine available in the city is grandiose and only vaguely apprehended. One notices also how ludicrously incongruous amid the Lucullan accommodations is the slave-like bustling of the "host." There was an assurance of repose in the modest hospitality of the country mouse; here, as course after course is served up, the very strenuousness of the repletion suggests a fatal restlessness. Despite the seignorial lounging of his rustic guest, the city mouse cannot provide the gift of free time on the stormy seas of unchecked aspiration. And he suffers their perils when suddenly a terrible banging of doors tumbles them from their couches. Terror-stricken, they run the length of the hall as the lofty mansion echoes with the barking of Molossian hounds. In this nightmare, which is still hilarious, the poet's fantasy transcends the satiric and the instructive to yield to a radical image of the plight of uncontained, urban, self-indulgent, ambitious, discontented man. The reader whose first comparison is to the Tom and Jerry cartoon might think of Kafka or Céline.

Nevertheless, the final importance of the fable is not the inevitable anxiety of the city mouse but what emerges as its irrelevance in the light of the enduring validity of the retired life, which opposes to the nightmare of Molossian hounds the reassurance of that Saturn-like figure of the rustic master of the house, sharing his simple table with the country mouse. *Hoc erat in votis*—the opening thanksgiving for Horace's own deliverance applies to the country mouse's reaction at the turning point of his adventure into the great world. Goodbye to all that, he says. In my hole in the forest, secure from dangers, I can find comfort with a bit of vetch (ll. 115–17). Here we might recall the reversal by Alfius, the usurer, in the *Beatus ille* epode, with which we began this discussion; there, like-

wise, we witnessed the collapse of a fantasy before the pressures of the real world. The difference between the two poems,
however, is more like the difference between the beginning and
the end of *Don Quixote*. The ideal that began as a daydream
to be exposed is now revealed to be more "real" than that busy
world to which we customarily assign the label. It is the great
world which now is essentially an illusion; the center of reality,
as the country mouse discovers, is the retired cave.

This reordering of our sense of reality is not only affected
by the events of the narrative but is also promoted by what I
have called the radical aspect of the fable. Even before the story
ends, urban and ambitious man has been reduced to his proper
dimensions, as seen from the perspective of Horace's guests,
who behold the spectacle of the mice in the same Olympian
way as might the *pater ipse domus* of the country mouse from
the height of his rustic table. If we compare this perspective
with that of the reader, it is the busy world outside the leisurely experience of the book which is unreal. To regard the
poem's structure in a more formal way, this reconstitution of
reality is the special profit that accrues from its incorporating
one kind of fiction within another. The country mouse's "ca-
tastrophe" not only exposes the illusions of the great world but
brings down the curtain on the fable which he inhabits. The
effect, presumably, is to return the reader from the make-believe
world of talking mice to the "real" world. Yet the world of
whose validity the reader is so compellingly assured is that of
the preceding fiction: the world of Cervius and the convivial
audience of Horace's friends, the world consummated in the
reader's leisurely celebration of the poem. The busy urban
world which we are accustomed to call the real world (in a
sense, even the world "outside" the poem) suffers the same
displacement as the fable for which it was the setting:

> Like the baseless fabric of this vision
> The cloud-capp'd towers, the gorgeous palaces,
> The solemn temples, the great globe itself,
> Yea, all which it inherit shall dissolve

> And like this insubstantial pageant faded
> Leave not a wrack behind.
> (*The Tempest*, 4. 1. 151–56)

What "shall dissolve" in Shakespeare's lines is what has dissolved in Horace's poem: in the termination of the fable, the great world fades from view. For if the conclusion of Prospero's masque of rural holiday prompts an intuition of the great illusions of civilization, the ending of Horace's fable on the illusions of civilization restores us to the reality of rural holiday.

Viewed from this perspective, there is an extraordinary effect achieved by having the ending of the fable also terminate the poem (ll. 115–17). Horace achieves that effect, not by a romantic masque on a fabulous island, but in a homespun tale in a setting that could hardly be more down to earth. To end the poem in this way is abrupt but not abortive, indeed not really conclusive. There is an important sense in which the poem describing the good life at the farm may be said to continue beyond the fable's conclusion, that is, beyond its own last line on the printed page. This effect is possible because of the absence of further lines of the poem in which the fable originates, such as, "Thus Cervius spoke, and each guest joined me in praising his wit over a fresh draught of wine," etc. Instead, the fiction of the Sabine farm remains unterminated and unquestioned; it becomes the really "real" world to which we awaken when the nightmare of the fable, the bad dream of what we like to call the "real" world, is over. We awaken to the start of the poem, not only because thematically the country mouse's wishes are fulfilled (*hoc erat in votis*), but because we are finally convinced of the reality of that opening perspective by the collapse of the concluding fiction: *auctius atque | di melius fecere. bene est. nil amplius oro* (ll. 3–4). The singular achievement of this poem in its close and in its total structure is the dramatic fulfillment of the promise of that dawn prayer: to read it is to awaken to the dream of ease.

This "satire" has engaged our attention at some length because of its relatively unappreciated intricacy and because of its significance in this essay as the climax of those evolving and globing images and attitudes which have informed this reading of the *Sermones*. The poem virtually proclaims that the composition of the *Odes* is at hand, and its own stature is not diminished by the prospect.

Nunc vino pellite curas: *Horace's* Odes *and the*
Internalization of Time and Place
(Odes *1. 1, 4, 9, 7; 2. 4*)

Although they are clearly his finest achievement, this is not the place to attempt anything like a thorough reading of Horace's *Odes*. What we can begin to see more clearly, and more emphatically, I hope, is that the distinction of these incomparable poems is perfectly consonant with the theory and practice of the *Sermones* and *Epistulae*, which appeared before and after their publication. If they seem more patently lyrical in one way, we deny their unique accomplishment if we do not relish their un-lyrical quality: their distrust of the portentously fanciful, the overtly mythic. This is admittedly the "low-mimetic" aspect of Horace's lyrics; he is not Pindar or even Catullus. The fascinating affinity of the *Odes* is still with the *sermo pedestris* of the earlier and later works. We might review the characteristic argument of the Horatian poems already read as a movement from (satiric) negation of the flux of the uncontained life to an insistence on contraction and, finally, to the transfiguration of content, liberating and expanding the self in a new affirmation. If we allow for the absence of a critical or didactic urgency in the first phase, we shall find that, to an extraordinary degree, the rhetorical pattern of the *Odes* conforms to the habit of mind defined in the *Satires* and earlier texts. Especially striking, perhaps, is the number which explicitly begin on a note of withdrawal ("others may . . . but as for me . . .") or a more explicit denial ("not for me is . . . ; as for me I prefer . . .").[52]

One might also note how the author often begins by disclaiming some presumed ambition of competence.[53] There are

not many odes of Horace that begin in an unqualifiedly affirmative or immediate statement. One awaits the inevitable systole,
"but as for me," contracted and reassuring, subversive yet affirmative. Inevitably, like Montaigne, Horace comes to the
point *chez lui*. He comes to himself as he did in his introduction to Maecenas, *sed quod eram narro*. This initial denial or
distancing gives the affirmative conclusions of the *Odes* their
rhetorical force, their sense of dramatic fulfillment, even necessity.

The First Ode of the first book is a fairly representative
instance of the poet's lyric imagination working in this way
which is so reminiscent of the pattern of the "retirement"
satires. Two-thirds of it is taken up with the activities of other
men, activities which at the start are deftly detached from the
contemplative perspective of Horace and Maecenas, the poet
and the reader, in a shared moment of free time:

> *Maecenas atavis edite regibus,*
> *o et praesidium et dulce decus meum,*
> *sunt quos curriculo pulverem Olympicum*
> *collegisse invat, metaque fervidis*
> *evitata rotis palmaque nobilis*
> *terrarum dominos evehit ad deos;*
> *hunc, si mobilium turba Quiritium*
> *certat tergeminis tollere honoribus; . . .*
> (*Odes* 1. 1. 1–8)

Maecenas, sprung from royal stock, my bulwark
and my glory dearly cherished, some there are
whose one delight is to gather Olympic dust
upon the racing car, and whom the turning-post
cleared with glowing wheel and the glorious
palm exalt as masters of the earth to the very
gods. One man is glad if the mob of fickle Romans strive to raise him to triple honors; . . .

The flux of the active or public life was a paramount theme
in all of Horace's poetry, but nowhere in all his writings is
there a complex of images so suggestive of the centrifugal
energy of the uncontained life. The opening description of the

charioteer, stirring up clouds of dust and rounding the turning
post with hot wheels aglow, is not only a compelling dramatization of a strenuous whirl (of the sort which, we may remember,
Pythagoras chose as a symbol of the active life), but its mo-
mentum virtually spins into the lines introducing the political
career accelerated by the *mobilium turba Quiritium*. Even more
suggestively, these images of centrifugal turbulence meet in the
same desired elevation: *terrarum dominos evehit ad deos . . .
certat tergeminis tollere honoribus*. But the exciting reversal
of this poem is precisely its realization that elevation to the
level of the gods springs not from the accumulation of Olympic
dust—a phrase itself expressive of apparent accomplishment
and essential triviality—but from the collection and concentration of the self. In the end, it is the retired poet who will
enjoy an elevation that towers over the glory sought by the
charioteer and the politician (ll. 29–36). The horizontally expanded man can never rise as he desires; contraction is the first
condition of elevation. The poet's detached observation of the
other occupations cited is an adroit blending of the complementary and the contrasting.[54] The rich man, happy with his
stored heaps of grain, yields to the peasant hoeing his ancestral
fields. The latter would not go to sea for any price, and that
brings to mind the merchant longing in a storm at sea to return
to the quiet fields of his home town; once ashore, of course, he
sets sail again, unable to endure a peasant's poverty (ll. 9–18).
On the other hand, there are some men who can retire and
enjoy it, snatching a few hours from the busy day for a bowl of
wine, relaxing beneath a shady tree by some gentle brook (ll.
19–22). In sharp contrast is the active life of the man who loves
the soldier's camp, with its bugles and trumpets and "the wars
that mothers hate" (ll. 23–25). Compare him with the hunter,
out all night beneath a cold sky, neglecting his wife for the
game (ll. 25–28). Noticing how each succeeding example is
connected with and subversive of the previous case, one is
doubtless struck first by the circularity and pointlessness of
all these lives, and that is not an impression I wish to remove.
Upon closer inspection, however, there seems to be a certain

pattern in the pairing of opposite values; on the one hand, the granary heaps, the storms at sea (and business profits), the fanfare of war; on the other hand, the peasant's fields, the shady tree and brook of the retired scene, the nightly solitude of the hunter.

Like the charioteer and the politician, Horace will finally enjoy in retirement the fulfillment of these desires for wealth, quiet, and music. A more interesting question is raised by the second grouping, the relatively contracted or isolated figures. There are some not above sipping old Massic wine, snatching some time from the business day to stretch out in the shade while a gentle brook bubbles nearby (ll. 19–22). One could learn a good deal about the Horatian vision of retired leisure in general, and about this poem in particular, by comparing these lines with the concluding description of the poet's own seclusion and its transfiguration. Their difference attests to the continuing significance in the *Odes* of the mind's world already noted in the *Satires*. The joys exhibited here are attractive in their way, but they are sensual delights, such, for example, as Catullus immortalized at Sirmio or, more equivocally, such as inspired the reverie of our friend Alfius. Nothing could be more misleading than to equate this indulgence in the pleasure principle of a terrestrial paradise with the inward condition which exfoliates in the cool grove of the poem's conclusion and which is so characteristic of the ethical and imaginative significance which inheres in retired leisure throughout Horace's best poetry. Before Horace introduces his climactic "but as for me . . ." celebration, he has his survey of the busy world conclude in two occupations, the soldier's and the hunter's. Each is the culmination of alternative patterns of imagery, but what finally must strike the reader is the acute resemblance of both the involved and the solitary figure in one crucial respect: their indifference to the claims of mothers and wives (ll. 24–26). These details contribute to a remarkable effect in the transition to the poet's grove. In leaving the great world, the reader feels that he is leaving, not the scene of responsibility and attachment, but a lonely and cheerless place; and, conversely,

when he enters the cool grove, the effect is not one of further
detachment but of incipient festivity. Surrounded by dancing
nymphs and satyrs, attended by Euterpe and Polyhymnia, the
retired poet is infectiously convivial, assuredly creative, even
sociable. The one reminder of the poet's withdrawal (*secernunt
populo*) is completely absorbed into the celebration's insistent
expansiveness:

> *me doctarum hederae praemia frontium*
> *dis miscent superis, me gelidum nemus*
> *nympharumque leves cum Satyris chori*
> *secernunt populo, si neque tibias*
> *Euterpe cohibet nec Polyhymnia*
> *Lesboum refugit tendere barbiton.*
> *quodsi me lyricis vatibus inseres,*
> *sublimi feriam sidera vertice.*
>
> (ll. 29–36)

> Me the ivy, the reward of poets' brows, links
> with the gods above; me the cool grove and the
> lightly tripping bands of the nymphs and satyrs
> withdraw from the vulgar throng, if only Eu-
> terpe withhold not the flute, nor Polyhymnia
> refuse to tune the Lesbian lyre. But if you
> rank me among lyric bards, I shall touch the
> stars with my exalted head.

This poem began with the vividly centrifugal image of a
charioteer rounding a turn. It ends with the poet, and his
readers, at the center of a dance at the heart of a grove which
secludes him from the world. It ends with the withdrawn, contemplative man enjoying a triumph which towers over all those
apotheoses sought by the activities of the uncontained.

Not all the *Odes*, of course, sustain these affirmations, not
even the ones specifically devoted to the theme of retired leisure. It is no accident that the Western world's greatest poet
of free time was also particularly haunted by the impermanence
of all things human and by the inevitability of death. Again
and again, in many of Horace's finest *Odes*, as Steele Commager puts it, a "*dum licet* boxes the occasion."[55] A classic in-

stance is the first celebration of spring, with its abrupt and haunting reminder at the end that *pallida mors* knocks at the doors of princes and paupers. *O beate Sesti*, the poet concludes, *vitae summa brevis spem nos vetat incohare longam* (*Odes* 1. 4. 14–15). "O happy Sestius [though the poignancy of the vocative springs from a concessive connotation—'even though you are happy'], life's brief span prevents entertaining any far-reaching hope."

Yet, acute as is the poet's awareness of "the blight man was born for," the perennial appeal of these poems would seem to lie rather in the internal permanence which they wrest from external change, a state of being which originates in a vivid apprehension of becoming and flux, a spiritual approximation of that winterless climate which we noted first in the Isles of the Blest and which we have seen to inspire so much of Horace's early writing. As was suggested in the reading of the First Ode and in the evolved transformations of the *Satires* of retired leisure, one must distinguish between external and internal recreation. In turning from the *Satires* to the *Odes*, one finds that free time tends to be regarded not so much as the proper reward for the good or contained man but as the central discovery of the imaginative man. To put it another way, the centrifugal imagery representative of the ambitions of the discontented man on the level of ethics is now frequently charged with a more radical significance as the symbol of time's destructive flux. Like his great inheritor, Montaigne, Horace anticipates Bergson's distinction between clock time and human duration. Man cannot change the passage of time or ultimately the fact of death, but he can alter their significance, for any significance they have is of his making. Just as he punctures the pastoral reverie of Alfius, Horace, in his "Ode to Spring" and elsewhere, (typically) subjects the terrestrial paradise to the pressures of mortal experience. The persistent recognition of Death's *et in Arcadia ego* is the condition of a still greater affirmation, that even with death there may be Arcady, in the only sense that can liberate man from time, that of a paradise within the mind.

In a poem which drew its title from the line of the *pallida mors* sequence, quoted above, Ernest Dowson wept that "They are not long, the days of wine and roses." Horace's sense of life's fleeting delights was equally acute and could be as achingly phrased, but it is crucial to understand how little wine and roses ultimately mean to him.[56] Their significance, like that of the Sabine farm itself, is derived from an interior state; they might be called humanistic sacraments. The festive center of the *Odes*, as in the First Ode of the first book, lies—beyond the bowls of Massic and the lovely landscape where spring yields to winter—in the cool grove of the mind's world and the deathless reality which is the poet's creation. It was another English poet who truly apprehended the leisurely dimension of Horatian festivity when he celebrated, not wine and roses, but "The Feast of Reason and the Flow of Soul."

This characteristic tendency of the retired imagination could be illustrated throughout the *Odes*, and it is baffling to select one; but we might consider, for example, the inevitable winter companion piece to the "Ode to Spring," a poem whose later structural peculiarities still vex the critics but whose opening clearly conforms to a familiar pattern:

> *Vides ut alta stet nive candidum*
> *Soracte, nec iam sustineant onus*
> *silvae laborantes, geluque*
> *flumina constiterint acuto.*
>
> *dissolve frigus ligna super foco*
> *large reponens atque benignius*
> *deprome quadrimum Sabina,*
> *o Thaliarche, merum diota.*
> (*Odes* 1. 9. 1–8)

Look how Soracte stands glistening in its mantle of snow, and how the straining woods no longer uphold their burden, and the streams are frozen with the biting cold. Dispel the chill by piling high the wood upon the hearth, and generously bring forth in a Sabine jar the wine four winters old, O Thaliarchus!

The imaginative process informing the lines is a classic instance of withdrawal and transfiguration. We have already discussed its prototype in Alcaeus, but here we might notice how the metaphor of the storm and the island is particularized by the suggestive details of height or magnitude to represent exterior cold and interior warmth (*alta . . . nive; ligna super foco / large reponens*) or, more literally, how the next stanza uses the tempest on the deep and the stable old trees ashore to express the flux of time and the expanding significance of the present moment (ll. 9–12). This is why the poet can celebrate an interior liberation from past and future, expressed in love-making and dancing, the springtime rites of renewal (ll. 13–18).

So intense is our involvement in the mind's regeneration that we easily accept the poem's metaphor as literal fact. Spring *is* at hand, we begin to feel, as an insistently reiterated *nunc* turns today into tomorrow and our vision expands from this secluded hearthside to the open city squares on a balmy spring evening:

> *nunc et campus et areae*
> *lenesque sub noctem susurri*
> *composita repetantur hora,*
>
> *nunc et latentis proditor intimo*
> *gratus puellae risus ab angulo*
> *pignusque dereptum lacertis*
> *aut digito male pertinaci.*
>
> (ll. 18–24)

> Now let the Campus be sought and the
> squares, with low whispers at the trysting-hour
> as night draws on, and the merry tell-tale laugh
> of a maiden hiding in the farthest corner, and
> the forfeit snatched from her arm or finger that
> but feigns resistance.

This particular shift has incurred the displeasure of no less a reader than Fraenkel. But the troublesome feature, "a season wholly different from the severe winter at the beginning," far from being an accidental inconvenience in this one poem, is in fact characteristic of Horace's imagination, his composing of precisely these "heterogeneous elements" of winter and spring in a typical process of contraction and liberation into another dimension.[57] In the most sensitive, but still somewhat "apologetic," interpretation that has appeared, Steele Commager writes: "The seasonal inconsistency between the poem's beginning and end is less disconcerting once we recognize that Horace's terms are not exclusively external. *Nunc . . . nunc* indicates the nonliteral direction of his thought, unless we suppose him guilty of a total aberration and forgetful of what he is writing about."[58] The poem uses the language of spring and youth to enliven our sense of an interior spring, a blessed isle within the self. More than a compensation for the "spring-yields-to-winter" reflections of the Fourth Ode of the first book, the Ninth does not ask "Can spring be far behind?" but proclaims that it is already here, in that world within us which is winterless. Fraenkel's objection to the seasonal "incongruity" of the lines beginning *nunc et campus et areae* can serve to remind us that here, as often when the poet uses *nunc*, a repeated insistence on the present signals the transition from clock time to the festive free time of human duration.

There is another aspect of the conclusion which might seem even more incongruous than the temporal shift to spring, and that is the boldly continued use of spatial imagery. For not only does the initial contraction, from the elevation of the snow-covered mountains to the intimacy of the blazing fireside, issue in a festive intuition of spring, but this temporal expansion is described spatially. We leave the enclave of retirement for the *campus et areae* of the city on a balmy evening, and yet—such is the remarkable suggestiveness of the poem— we still preserve a sense of withdrawal, for the opening-out of this return to the city has its latent intimacy in the low whispers, the coming-on of night, the *intumo . . . angulo* of the last stanza's tryst, which "draws us in as surely as does the second."[59] Indeed, as it has led us farther out, it draws us even farther in, to a stiller point than the hearthside but, at the same time, to a nucleus which quickens to life even more than that convivial scene. More suggestive than the familiar image of the feast, the sexual symbolism of the nocturnal tryst is virtually inexhaustible to meditation. The poet celebrates the transfiguration of withdrawal at that moment when the self is least alone. From the lofty mountain, gleaming with snow, through the blaze indoors of the high-piled fireplace, one is led to a dark corner of intimacy and interiority which, paradoxically, implicates the poem's most expansive and urban setting. Like the sweet laugh which betrays the maid *intumo . . . ab angulo* (ll. 21–22), the last stanza opens out even as it contracts. Like the lover's resistance to the theft of the love pledge, the stanza, the poem, the retired imagination itself, deny that they may affirm, say no when they most mean yes.

This Ninth Ode of the first book was selected for discussion because both its affirmative contrast with the argument of the Spring ode and its own structural peculiarities illustrate the expansion of personal duration and interior distance which is central to the working of Horace's imagination in the *Odes* and which has been seen to emerge in certain *Satires'* transfiguration of content. The Seventh Ode of the first book, in praise of Tibur, provides an even more provocative transformation of our sense of external landscape, and time, in the country of the mind. Without provoking the critics' displeasure as much as the Soracte ode, just discussed, its shift in direction has nevertheless accounted for a venerable tradition (reflected in several codices) that this ode is in fact two poems.[60]

That the place celebrated in the Seventh Ode happens to be not the Sabine farm but a retreat at Tibur (Tivoli) is perhaps an instructive accident; for as the second "heterogeneous" half of the poem will demonstrate, one can be removed from Tibur itself and still enjoy everything it means. What it first means is characteristically introduced by a dismissal:

> *Laudabunt alii claram Rhodon aut Mytilenen*
> *aut Epheson bimarisve Corinthi*
> *moenia vel Baccho Thebas vel Apolline Delphos*
> *insignis aut Thessala Tempe:*

sunt quibus unum opus est intactae Palladis urbem
   carmine perpetuo celebrare et
undique decerptam fronti praeponere olivam:
   plurimus in Iunonis honorem
aptum dicet equis Argos ditisque Mycenas:
   me nec tam patiens Lacedaemon
nec tam Larisae percussit campus opimae,
   quam domus Albuneae resonantis
et praeceps Anio ac Tiburni lucus et uda
mobilibus pomaria rivis.

(Odes 1. 7. 1–14)

Others shall praise famed Rhodes, or Mitylene,
or Ephesus, or the walls of Corinth, that over-
looks two seas, or Thebes renowned for Bacchus,
Delphi for Apollo, or Thessalian Tempe. Some
there are whose only task it is to hymn in unbroken song the town of virgin Pallas and to
place upon their brows a wreath of olive gathered from every quarter. Many a one in Juno's
honour shall sing of horse-breeding Argos and
of rich Mycenae.

   As for me, not hardy Lacedaemon, or the
plain of bounteous Larisa has so struck my
fancy as Albunea's echoing grotto and the tumbling Anio, Tiburnius' grove and the orchards
watered by the coursing rills.

Nothing is more important in a consideration of Horace
than to see that the importance of the rural scene was not the
special charm of a particularly picturesque location but its
effect on the poet's inner reality—its faculty, as he said in an
epistle to the keeper of his farm, of returning him to himself,
mihi me reddentis (*Epistles* 1. 14. 1).[61] This is why, in another
ode, when he tells a friend ready to fight barbarians or defy
the tossing waves, that while he hopes his own odyssey will
happily conclude at Tibur, he can still accept the fact that it
might not (*Odes* 2. 6. 1–8). Well, if not, let it be Tarentum—
and there follows one of the loveliest evocations of the *locus
amoenus*, the lovable landscape, in all of Horace's poetry (2. 6.

10–24). "Can we imagine Catullus equally amenable," asks
Commager wittily, "if he had been told he might not return
to Sirmio?" One cannot, indeed, think of Catullus' finding a
paradise other than Sirmio, any more than one can conceive of
the *Georgics'* vision of civic leisure anywhere else than in the
Saturnia tellus of rural Italy in the course of Roman history.
But Horace could readily substitute Tarentum for Tibur or
even a Sabine farm for Tibur; and the reason is not only a
certain equable inclusiveness but, much more significantly, a
vision of leisure as the consummation of interior and not exterior order. Catullus and, more profoundly, Vergil celebrate
the genius of the place. But Horace's imagination, his Muse,
is the genius of the place. The Horatian celebration of the
locus amoenus becomes, typically, a poem about the powers of
poetry, in any scene that will return us to ourselves:

> *vester, Camenae, vester in arduos*
> *tollor Sabinos, seu mihi frigidum*
> *Praeneste seu Tibur supinum*
> *seu liquidae placuere Baiae.*
> (*Odes* 3. 4. 21–24)

> As yours, yes, yours, O Muses, do I climb to
> my lofty Sabine hills, or go to cool Praeneste, or
> sloping Tibur, or to cloudless Baiae, has it but
> caught my fancy.

This stanza is the final triumphant great moment in the
patriotic Fourth Ode of the third book, which is modeled on
Pindar's sublime First Pythian. It is the difference from the
original, however, which needs underscoring, for the difference is precisely the internality of the process which I have
been trying to describe, and nowhere is it more apocalyptic
than in the lines before us. The ode which Pindar composed
—one is prompted to say sang—is public and ceremonial, drawing from a rich tradition of religious and civic festival. Horace
is the celebrant of an interior ceremony. Describing his poetic
performance, Pindar characteristically compares it to that of a
javelin-thrower at the games, striving to hurl it beyond any

other's reach.[62] To describe his own performance, Horace begins with a haunting description of the poet's seclusion that
beautifully anticipates the lines already quoted:

> *Descende caelo et dic age tibia*
> *regina longum Calliope melos,*
> *seu voce nunc mavis acuta,*
> *seu fidibus citharave Phoebi.*
>
> *auditis, an me ludit amabilis*
> *insania? audire et videor pios*
> *errare per lucos, amoenae*
> *quos et aquae subeunt et aurae.*
>
> (ll. 1–8)

Descend from heaven, O Queen Calliope, and
play upon the flute a long-continued melody, or
sing with thy clear voice, dost thou prefer, or to
the strings of Phoebus' lyre! Do you hear me?
Or does some fond illusion mock me? I think
I hear her and am straying through hallowed
groves, where pleasant waters steal and breezes
stir.

Between this opening and the climactic passage quoted
above, the poet indulges in a famous reminiscence of his childhood: how one day, on trackless Mount Vultur, he strayed beyond the limits of Apulia (his old nurse), and, tired with play,
went to sleep in the woods and was covered with leaves by the
doves, "a wonder to all who dwelt in Acherontia's high nest
and Bantia's glades and the rich fields of low-lying Forentum"
(ll. 9–17). These "autobiographical" lines have offended many
distinguished critics by their apparent irrelevance to the theme
of the poem.[63] Yet it hardly seems an exaggeration to suggest
that to understand the function of this personal allusion is to
understand Horace.

One may begin to see its relevance if one recalls the way
Horace drew from similar resources in the *Satires* to fashion
an image of his private life that was both representative and
fabulous.[64] Let us admit that there may be the germ of some
actual event in the story as told. At least the homely place

names, as Fraenkel remarks, seem designed to give that impression. At the same time, however, there hovers over the episode, like its own storied doves, a symbolic dimension which invests the childhood scene with the sense of a prelude: of the growth of a poet's mind. Consider the fabulous climax of this reminiscence, the account of how one day, when he had strayed from home, he slept safe from bears and serpents because he was covered by laurel and myrtle, themselves the emblems of poetic transformation (ll. 17–20). Indeed, at this point, that would seem to be the primary significance of the covering; for here an extraordinary complication of inner and outer, present and past reality somehow still preserves a simple radiance. Whatever protected the boy while he slept becomes a type of withdrawal into the world of imagination in which the adult, too, overcomes the bear and the viper without fleeing to the Isles of the Blest (*Epodes* 16. 51–52). The child's seclusion thus sustains the opening reference to the poet in his sacred grove and is profoundly connected with the address to the Muses, quoted to introduce this poem. In our reading of the *Satires*, we have already noticed a certain tendency of the poet to see in retirement a way of preserving or reconstructing the kind of life he had once enjoyed in association with his father. As one reads this passage in the Fourth Ode, it would seem impossible not to feel the same movement of rediscovery and reassertion. To ascend to the Sabine hills is to return to Mount Vultur; it is a "homecoming," a *nostos,* to a landscape of the mind, vibrant, in the opening anaphora, with a sense of a poet's genesis:

> *vester, Camenae, vester in arduos*
> *tollor Sabinos, seu mihi frigidum*
> *Praeneste seu Tibur supinum*
> *seu liquidae placuere Baiae.*
> (ll. 21–24)

> As yours again, as yours once more, O Muses, do I climb to my lofty Sabine hills, or go to cool Praeneste, or sloping Tibur, or to cloudless Baiae.

This, then, is the *locus amoenus* of Horace's *Odes*: it can be Tibur or Tarentum, the Sabine hills now, or an Apulian mountain years ago. It is all of these places together, but it is nowhere that the poet is not, at least imaginatively. Like Wallace Stevens' girl whose singing orders the ocean's flux at Key West, Horace is the single artificer of the world in which he sings, and we, as we behold him striding here alone, must learn that there never was a Sabine farm or a Tibur except the one he sang and, singing, made.

Of course, as the next stanzas insist, and as we might expect by now, Horace's vision here is anything but solipsistic. With the blessed isle discovered at the center of the mind's world, the world's *tempestas* can be freshly confronted and ordered on one's own terms. He recalls how he was saved from the rout at Philippi and from a tree falling on him and from an accident in the Sicilian waves that took Palinurus (ll. 25–28). In fact, nurtured by this reminiscence, he will consider more wandering and warfare (ll. 29–36), and in the remaining lines (the Fourth of the third book is the longest of the *Odes*) will have a public statement to make. The widening perspective prepares us for the celebration of Jove's victory over the Titans, and it is tempting to describe this process in terms of going back "out of" retirement to resume the responsibilities of the real or public or busy or centrifugal world. So conceived, this is doubtless an excellent description of the function of retirement or pastoral withdrawal in certain longer (public) forms; Odysseus, for example, must leave Phaeacia to reach Ithaca. In Horace and the tradition of retired leisure, however, one is, so to speak, already home. Augustus himself, it is worth noting, is introduced in a retired role, in contrast with the overreaching enemy figured in the rebellious Titans. There is considerable imaginative logic in the transition from the self-description of the secluded priest of the Muses to the imperial contemplative, here even the philosopher-king (ll. 37–42). National order, to reverse the civic formula, becomes the consummation of private leisure. Ithaca can be restored on Phaeacia.

And Tibur can be restored when one is exiled from Italy. Let us return to the poem which initiated this discussion of

the meaning of the rural scene to Horace. We left the Seventh
Ode of the first book at the conclusion of its first "half," when,
after a survey of goodly states and kingdoms, the poet had
"come home" to Tibur's lovely groves and tumbling waters.
(Now, however, we can better appreciate what homecoming
meant to Horace.) What has been regarded as the beginning
of a "new poem" within the Seventh Ode is an address to a
certain Plancus urging a similar process of withdrawal and
recreation: as the south wind often dispels storm clouds and
leaves a clear sky, Plancus, dismissing life's glooms and labors,
should seek serenity over a cup of wine wherever he may happen to be, whether in camp beneath gleaming banners or in
the deep shade of his native Tibur (*Odes* 1. 7. 19–21). If these
lines read only "lighten your cares now that you have joined
me here in Tibur," this would be a simpler poem and one
that would doubtless conform to the widely received notion
of Horace's "message." But the locale is not that easily fixed,
and it is the "whereverness" of the last lines' alternatives that
must engage the careful reader's attention.[65]

The legend that concludes the ode is one of exile and aliena-
tion transformed by festivity and the power of the imagination.
Teucer, cast out of Salamis, was promised a "new Salamis" by
Apollo. Significantly, however, the poem ends not with that
Aeneid-like restoration but with a feast that is an end in itself
in the midst of the journey:

> *Teucer Salamina patremque*
>   *cum fugeret, tamen uda Lyaeo*
> *tempora populea fertur vinxisse corona,*
>   *sic tristis adfatus amicos:*
>
> *"quo nos cumque feret melior fortuna parente,*
>   *ibimus, o socii comitesque.*
> *nil desperandum Teucro duce et auspice: Teucri*
>   *certus enim promisit Apollo*
>
> *ambiguam tellure nova Salamina futuram.*
>   *o fortes peioraque passi*
> *mecum saepe viri, nunc vino pellite curas;*
>   *cras ingens iterabimus aequor."*
>
>   (*Odes* 1. 7. 21–32)

Teucer, as he fled from Salamis and his father, is yet said to have bound garlands of poplar about his temples flushed with wine, addressing thus his sorrowing friends: "Whithersoever Fortune, kinder than my sire, shall bear us, thither let us go, O friends and comrades! Never despair under Teucer's lead and auspices! For the unerring Apollo pledged to Teucer that there should be a second Salamis in a new land. O brave heroes, who with me have often suffered worse misfortunes, banish care now with wine! To-morrow we will take again our course over the mighty sea."

In Teucer's feast "the new Salamis" is already in the process of being discovered. The festive moment is not a flower of time plucked in defiance of the future—it incorporates the future, just as the emphatic postcaesural *nunc vino pellite curas* gathers up into itself the concluding *cras ingens iterabimus aequor.* The future is virtually contained in the present, a "now" whose becoming is limitless in duration. The renewal has already begun.

One begins to see, then, the structural significance of the opening travelogue. If in that first movement Horace returned "home" to his native Tibur, in the second half he demonstrates how the exile can likewise fulfill his nostalgia in a Tibur within the mind—which, I hope, has been demonstrated to be the true significance of Tibur for Horace, too. The import of the Teucer myth lies not so much in the "oblique assurance," as Commager suggests, that, like the new Salamis promised to Teucer, a new Rome awaits the exiled Plancus,[66] but in its more humanistic affirmation that, like Teucer, Plancus can realize the future in the present. To come home, Horace seems to be saying, again and again, and never more emphatically than in this ode, is not to come to a specific piece of land but to come home as Montaigne does in the fullest sense of being *chez lui*: it is to return to oneself.

This reading of the Seventh Ode of the first book can be deepened if one compares these lines to Aeneas' famous speech in somewhat parallel circumstances in the first book of the *Aeneid*. "Comrades," he says, "there will be a meaningful end to our quest. Someday we shall look back with pleasure on these events. Whatever happens, we must push on to Latium, where Troy will rise again" (1. 198–207). Though Vergil's hero and his men are eating and drinking, indeed doing so after a storm, one can hardly call the occasion "festive," as Teucer's celebration clearly—and invitingly—is. This difference in attitude, it seems to me, can be traced specifically to a different sense of place and time. Aeneas' gaze is fixed on his destination and his destiny: the where and when of the present are assimilated to that of a *forsan et haec olim . . .* , an *ubi*, an *illic*. Seen in that perspective, the present is already in the process of being converted into a past memory (*meminisse iuvabit*); it has, indeed, already become something to look back upon. The difference from Teucer's speech is manifest: as Aeneas sees the present in terms of the future and a new Rome, Teucer sees the future and a new Salamis in terms of the present and wherever he happens to be. More open than Vergil's hero to the delights of gardens, feasts, and songs, Odysseus could praise "the fairest thing there is" and yet, true to the complex imperatives of civic leisure, grow restive the next day at the same scene. For Horace's Teucer, however, there is no such summons in the setting sun. He need not do without leisure to have leisure. The journey's urgency is suspended like the tides of time themselves. He is at home on Phaeacia, enjoying "the fairest thing there is" on his own Ithacan terms. One thinks of Shakespeare's exiles, such as the old Duke in the Forest of Arden or Prospero on his enchanted island. With them, too, it is possible to speak of a "return" to the reality of the busy world; yet again, it seems more accurate to speak of an assimilation of reality into the focus of retirement, an expansion within contraction. The old Duke's reaction, "meanwhile," to the news of his restored dignity would seem to correspond perfectly to Teucer's "recollection" of his future happiness in the festive present:

> First, in this forest let us do those ends
> That here were well begun and well begot;
> And after, every of this happy number
> That have endured shrewd days and nights with us
> Shall share the good of our returned fortune
> According to the measure of their states.
> Meanwhile, forget this new-fall'n dignity
> And fall into our rustic revelry.
> (*As You Like It*, 5. 4. 176–82)

Otia liberrima: *Horace's* Epistles *and Ultimate Retirement* (Epistles *1. 11, 9, 1, 7, 16; 2. 2*)

This reading of the *Odes* from the perspective of the *Satires* has been a very selective one, concerned with the retired imagination not only in its pattern of withdrawal from the flux of the great world to the rural scene but, more importantly, in its retreat from a simply external time and place to one "within," whose duration and extension constitute the reality of the mind's world. As I hope to demonstrate, such a view of the *Odes* may also serve to introduce the characteristic quality of Horace's most neglected poems—his *Epistles*. To appreciate the incomparable artistry of the *Odes* and ignore these later poems is to deny ourselves some of the fullest, toughest expressions of his deepest themes. Like the later poetry of Stevens, the later poetry of Horace has been overshadowed by the aesthetic delight of the very lyrics which might serve to introduce it.

We might, for example, begin by comparing the relatively neglected Eleventh Epistle of the first book with the ode in praise of Tibur, which has just been read. The epistle is addressed to one Bullatius, a traveler, and, much like the Seventh Ode's *Laudabunt alii* sequence, this poem begins with a survey of those glamorous public sites which might attract the tourist:

> *Quid tibi visa Chios, Bullati, notaque Lesbos,*
> *qui concinna Samos, quid Croesi regia Sardis,*
> *Zmyrna quid et Colophon, maiora minorane fama?*
> *cunctane prae Campo et Tiberino flumine sordent?*
> *an venit in votum Attalicis ex urbibus una,*
> *an Lebedum laudas odio maris atque viarum?*
>
> <div align="right">(<i>Epistles</i> 1. 11. 1–6)</div>
>
> What did you think of Chios, my Bullatius,
> and of famous Lesbos? What of charming
> Samos? What of Sardis, royal home of Croesus?
> What of Smyrna and Colophon? Whether they
> are above or below their fame, do they all seem
> poor beside the Campus and Tiber's stream?
> Or is your heart set upon one of the cities of
> Attalus? Or do you extol Lebedus, because you
> are sick of seas and roads?

Then, in a shift quite like Horace's declaration of his own preference for Tibur, the next lines are an admission of this very distaste for the ocean and the highways. Presumably a quotation from a letter or the reminiscence of a remark in conversation, Bullatius' own words are an oddly touching confession of the traveler's nostalgia, probably because of their way of reiterating the place's name while disclaiming its popular appeal and then converting this negative description of the place's desolation to an intimation of the attraction of its solitude, that of the calm isle from which the distant tempest can be serenely contemplated.[67] "You know about Lebedus, a town more desolate than Gabii or Fidenae, yet I'd love to live there, the world forgetting, by the world forgot, and gaze in contemplation at Neptune's rage" (ll. 7–10).

Here is a lovely evocation of the longing to retire, but the nostalgia of Bullatius is for a particular place on the map: only in the secluded coastal town can he enjoy the vision of the tranquil isle.[68] Moreover, there lingers over the evocation of Lebedus a profound world-weariness, a lonely melancholy, which probably accounts for the lines' poignancy but should also distinguish them from Horace's typical aspiration. The notable conclusion of this poem, however—and this is the essential test-

ament of the *Epistles*—is that no external circumstances of time
or place can guarantee the kind of escapist retirement for
which Bullatius longs at Lebedus.[69] In our reading of the *Odes*
we have focused on a certain inward tendency of the poet's
imagination in order to stress the symbolic quality of his landscape and feasts; it is, of course, also true that their external
details are also presented most vividly, and this doubtless serves
to enhance their inner significance. In the *Epistles*, however,
the poet's inward focus is so acute as to preclude any attachment to external place or time.[70] Teucer, in the Seventh Ode,
is anticipating a specific "new Salamis" that will be his at some
future time. Compare the lines in the Eleventh Epistle which
follow Bullatius' praise of Lebedus:

> *Sed neque qui Capua Romam petit, imbre lutoque*
> *aspersus volet in caupona vivere; nec qui*
> *frigus collegit, furnos et balnea laudat*
> *ut fortunatam plene praestantia vitam.*
> *nec si te validus iactaverit Auster in alto,*
> *idcirco navem trans Aegaeum mare vendas.*
>
> (ll. 11–16)

> Yet he who travels from Capua to Rome,
> though bespattered with rain and mud, will not
> want to live on in an inn, nor does he who has
> caught a chill cry up stoves and baths as fully
> furnishing a happy life. And so you, though a
> stiff south wind has tossed you on the deep, will
> not for that reason sell your ship on the far side
> of the Aegean Sea.

An interlude at an inn, a pause at the baths, a calm after a
rough voyage—these moments of recreation may dispel the cold
and the storm, but they do not last. A first impression might be
that this line of thought would deny a transfiguration such as
animates Teucer's feast—that it would lead to a reassertion, let
us say, of the *cras ingens iterabimus aequor*, the return to involvement. As we shall see, however, this awareness of the impermanence of the moment of free time tends to generate a
more acute contraction and a more radical transformation. For

the poet does not seem about to repudiate the ideal of the place isolated from seasonal extremes or centrifugal involvement (as we see in the next passage, which is a typical indictment of the great world and, especially, of such exotic centers as Rhodes and Mitylene). Such places do as much for a man as a heavy cloak in summertime or a wrestler's tunic in snowy weather, as a stove in August or the Tiber's waters in January. Places like that should be praised at a distance, by a man happy he had never left Rome (ll. 17–21).

The reasons for Bullatius' yearning for secluded Lebedus seem irresistibly persuasive, and yet at this very point the poem will release its most expansive affirmation, a celebration of perpetual becoming, at any time, in any place. It reads almost like an endorsement of traveling:

> *tu quamcumque deus tibi fortunaverit horam*
> *grata sume manu neu dulcia differ in annum,*
> *ut quocumque loco fueris vixisse libenter*
> *te dicas; . . .*

                                                     (ll. 22–25)

And you—whatever hour God has given for your well-being, take it with grateful hand, and do not put off joys from year to year. This way, in whatever place you have been, you may say that you have lived happily.

But—and this seems to me to be the key to the poem and to the *Epistles*—this unparalleled openness is possible only if a radical contraction will free the self from its dependence on any special time or place—not only the past but the future, not only an exotic city but also a festive inn and, as we shall see, even that longed-for quiet coastal town. To retire is to retire from retirement itself:

> *nam si ratio et prudentia curas,*
> *non locus effusi late maris arbiter aufert,*
> *caelum non animum mutant qui trans mare currunt.*
> *strenua nos exercet inertia: navibus atque*
> *quadrigis petimus bene vivere.*

                                                     (ll. 25–29)

> For if it is reason and wisdom that take away
> cares, and not a site commanding a wide ex-
> panse of sea, they change their clime, not their
> mind, who rush across the sea. It is a busy idle-
> ness that is our bane; with yachts and cars we
> seek to enjoy life.

To retire is to be most contained and yet be truly free, enjoying even at Ulubrae, a town in the Pomptine swamps, noted
for clamorous frogs, the peace which earlier in the poem has
been vainly sought in the solitude of Lebedus:

> *quod petis hic est,*
> *est Ulubris, animus si te non deficit aequus.*
> (ll. 29–30)

> What you are seeking is here; it is at Ulubrae,
> if there you do not lack a mind well balanced.

It is typical of the widely received image of Horace that in
eighteenth-century Scotland Lord Auchinleck had these lines
inscribed over the entry to his home and that his son, James
Boswell, complained throughout his wanderings from home
that what he lacked was just this *animus aequus*, meaning, presumably, an almost inhuman kind of placidity.[71] Yet, as the
poem itself demonstrates, Horace, while certainly no young
Boswell or melancholy Bullatius, is scarcely advocating the
severely limited sensibility one associates with *animus aequus*
when it is extrapolated as a motto. Horace's insistence is on
the variousness and potentiality of life for the man who has
found himself (*quamcumque . . . horam . . . quocumque loco,*
ll. 22–24). The repudiation of travel captured in the brilliant
paradox of *strenua inertia* is a rejection of the travail that
issues from ennui. In dismissing the strenuous, the poet would
also save his friend from the inert.

The reminder that crossing the seas is no assurance of interior renewal (*caelum, non animum, mutant, qui trans mare
currunt,* l. 27) is a quotable aphorism and has an evident rele-

vance to Bullatius' present wanderings; but we do scant justice to the subtlety of the poet's insight if we ignore the implications of the condition which leads us to this conclusion (ll. 25–26). Linked not only imagistically but verbally to the apodosis (*maris arbiter . . . trans mare currunt*), this protatic admission would seem to repudiate the other alternative of not traveling at all, of simply beholding the sea's expanse in a way that recalls the view from that secluded Lebedus which world-weary Bullatius longs for (ll. 6, 10). In their full complexity, then, the lines deny intrinsic value not only to the sea voyage but to the place of calm seclusion. Bullatius must learn to seek at Lebedus not what Catullus finds at Sirmio but what Horace finds at Tibur or his Sabine farm. He must learn to seek not a place but a self, to become, like Wallace Stevens' Crispin, "an introspective voyager." Indeed, so much more acute is Horace's inward focus now that he postmarks his letter, not from his own famous lovely resorts, but from Ulubrae—no *locus amoenus*, but rather, in the contemporary translation of Smith Palmer Bovie, a "Frogville, or Swamptown, or Rattle-kazoo." It is the superb incongruity of this locale which gives the endorsement of abstractions like *ratio* and *prudentia* and *animus aequus* a special pungency. For, though logically the meaning of the last line is "What you seek can be even at Ulubrae if you do not lack equanimity," the words Horace has chosen lack this hypothetical cast. Instead they are insistently declarative and chiastically emphatic, *quod petis hic est, / est . . . .* Thus the climax of "Frogville" (*est Ulubris*) somehow seems to survive anticlimax; it is curiously satisfactory, almost as if the line read, say, *est Tiburi*. Here, one feels, is precisely the place for Bullatius. Of course, one is soon reminded of the condition of this appreciation of the place (*animus si te non deficit aequus*), but, nevertheless, the consummate delightfulness of the poem springs from its freedom genuinely to accept the unlikely scene.

This liberating acceptance of "Swamptown" as a leisurely recreation for the mind which has found itself perfectly illustrates the ultimate transfiguration of the retired focus in Horace's later poems. However much he might claim the *animus aequus*, it is hard to imagine Lord Auchinleck being content there, but it is a place that Montaigne might have savored.

The repudiation of both Bullatius' wandering and his solipsistic yearning for Lebedus' solitude was notable because of its acute inwardness and because of the even more uninhibited expansiveness that was liberated. In both these respects the Eleventh Epistle offers much in little to illustrate the characteristic temper of the first book of the *Epistles*. But, unhappily, it is only the former, negatively more "retired," tendency that is usually recognized. Horace, to summarize this argument, is older and wiser. Disappointed, perhaps, in the reception of his *Odes*, he has turned to a more prosaic medium. He is less of an Epicurean now and more of a Stoic.[72]

Now there are certain grounds for this impression, for Horace himself gives these as his reasons for choosing a different idiom. As he tells Maecenas in the First Epistle of the first book, he is like an old gladiator, allowed to retire from the arena, who hangs up his weapons and hides in the country from the mob (*Epist.* 1. 1. 4–6); and so he too retires from lyric verse and its typical festive and amatory themes to the more serious form suited to the ethical reflections which are his new concern (ll. 10–12).

Yet the employment of this form is, of course, nothing less than the rediscovery of the conversational idiom of the *Satires*, the idiom more suited, like those of Montaigne's essays, to self-portraiture. It had already been brought to perfection in that least "satiric" but most memorable Sixth Satire of the second book (*Hoc erat in votis*). And, as in that early instance, the style of the *Epistles* (many of which could be read as odes) is not without its muted lyricism. Here, then, is what Pope, praising Cowley's imitations of Montaigne, called "the language of the heart." Here too, perhaps, is what the modern Epicurean poet means in "The Comedian as the Letter C," by the essential prose "To which all poems were incident, unless / That prose should wear a poem's guise at last."

But, granting Horace's successful manipulation of his medium, one may insist that, nevertheless, the typical themes of the *Epistles* betray the imaginative impoverishment which might be associated with a Stoic address to life. Instead of the transfiguration of retirement symbolized in the festive *O noctes cenaeque deum* or *nunc vino pellite curas*, we have, to cite a conspicuous example, a poem that begins with the famous negative injunction: *Nil admirari prope res est una, Numici, | solaque quae possit facere et servare beatum* (" 'Marvel at nothing'—that is perhaps the one and only thing, Numicius, /that can make a man happy and keep him so") (*Epist.* 1. 6 1–2)—a poem that ends with a sarcastic dismissal of *amore iocisque.* Or, what of that reading of the *Odyssey* which commends Odysseus as the very type of Stoic *ataraxia*, imperturbable in the storm-tossed waves and immune to the blandishments of Sirens' songs and Circe's cups (*Epist.* 1. 5. 22–23), and then proceeds to scorn the easy life of the courtiers of Alcinous in terms which would seem to deny any appreciation of that interlude? The key to an understanding of such passages lies in recognizing not simply this most acute containment of the self but, much more importantly, its unexpected consequences in a transfiguration of retirement that is remarkable for its inclusiveness. Freed from all attachments in the enjoyment of *otia liberrima*, Horace engagingly presents himself as more open to all experience than he has ever been before. And, just as in the Eleventh Epistle, there is ample compensation for the absence of any celebration of particular festivity or landscape. Nowhere else than in the *Epistles* is Horace more like Montaigne, transforming extreme solitude into a condition of unlimited accessibility, accepting the centrifugal whirl, paradoxically, from within the centripetal focus. For, returning to the opening of the First Epistle, one discovers that, after the initial insistence on detachment and prosaic imitation (ll. 10–14), there emerges an unqualified acceptance of life as *divers et ondoyant*, extraordinarily rendered here by the tempestuous imagery which we have known for so long as a symbol of the perils of the active life:

> *quo me cumque rapit tempestas, deferor hospes.*
> *nunc agilis fio et mersor civilibus undis,*
> *virtutis verae custos rigidusque satelles; . . .*
>   (*Epist.* 1. 1. 15–17)
> . . . wherever the storm drives me, I turn in for
> comfort. Now I become all action, and plunge
> into the tide of civil life, stern champion and
> follower of true Virtue; . . .

We have met this image of the passing guest before, but in
those earlier characterizations the rhetorical emphasis was on
the stability of the festive moment, its contained completeness
in personal duration. But now there is something new, and the
veritably Faustian language of Jacques Perret's appreciation
of the lines perfectly captures the transforming spirit which is
the great affirmation of the *Epistles*: "These are not the gropings that seek a sure passage and access to a port. There is no
port: these gropings are wisdom itself."[73] One inevitably thinks
of Montaigne's acceptance of the flux of his own retired life,
for example in his memorable dismissal of "Repentance": *Je
ne peints pas l'estre. Je peints le passage* (*Essais* 2. 2. 899). Or,
to quote Wallace Stevens again, as seems so inevitable in a
consideration of Horace and Montaigne: "Let the place of the
solitaires / Be a place of perpetual undulation." And yet what
arrests our attention in such celebrations of life *ondoyant et
divers* is how remarkably *un*centrifugal is the process. Rather it
is, as Georges Poulet said of Montaigne, "simply the reverse
side of the constant need to find himself again."[74] For as Poulet
puts it in another place, "by dint of portraying *passage*, Montaigne obtains communication with being."[75] This same paradoxical relationship between continuity and novelty, contraction and expansion, should be discerned in the lines before us.
For if Horace is a "guest," in the sense which Perret endorses,
this is only because he is also a guest like Telemachus, whose
detachment from Menelaus' gifts we now have as a type of
Horace's independent acceptance of Maecenas' hospitality. It
is true, as Perret means it, that the lines declare "there is no
port"; but another way of phrasing the same insight would be

that there *is* a happy haven anywhere such a traveler stops: indeed, *est Ulubris*. Horace's image of the guest displays the man who is at home anywhere because he is at home nowhere or, more accurately, because he is at home within himself. This is why, for example, in the same essay in which he voices this acceptance of *passage*, Montaigne insists on his own lack of centrifugal agitation. *Si je ne suis chez moy, j'en suis pres tousjours bien pres* ("If I am not at home, I am always very near it").[76]

Similarly, to touch on Horace's use of the Homeric situation, already discussed, there is in the treatment of his occasional plunges into the waves of the active life and civic responsibility (*Epist.* 1. 1. 16) still a sense of that buoyant detachment which we have seen him praise elsewhere in Odysseus (*Epist.* 1. 2. 22). If the speaker of the poem is *agilis*, he is stable too; indeed, he is more the latter because of the former. Once again, his grasp of being is surer for its renewal in becoming. The limitless aspirations which Perret endorses in the First Epistle of the first book are possible only because of Horace's very limited expectations for anything other than self-knowledge. This Faustian openness to all experience is the fruit of a Candidelike cultivation of one's own garden.

Such a progression is the radical dynamic for the ultimate transfiguration of the contracted focus: the release of the utterly centrifugal within the absolutely centripetal. In Horace's *Epistles* and Montaigne's *Essais*, the speaker who has returned to himself readily affords such contradictions; indeed, he tends to exult in them. In the celebration of self-discovery he is large, he contains multitudes. Which is to say that, even at Ulubrae, he can find himself. This "eccentric" quality of Horace's intensively concentric self-portrayal gives the *Epistles* their characteristically comic tone, a gaiety one notices first in the inherent amusement of incongruous conclusions but which, in a more profoundly comic way, enacts an idealized vitality blended with chance and mortality.

True to the promise of the lines just discussed, the conclusion of the First Epistle is an engaging instance of this comic

spirit. The main part of the epistle relates how the opening
example of a gladiator's retirement is like the wise man's retirement from the stormy voyages that drive men to the Indies
in pursuit of wealth (*Epist.* 1. 1. 41–46). The poet offers two
reflections: one, the familiar maxim that the good man is king
(*rex eris . . . si recte facies*, ll. 59–60); the other—so unlike the
first—the Roscian law, which reserved the first fourteen rows
of seats in the theater for knights. The poet obviously sub-
scribes to the first norm; but what gives his appropriation of
the *rex sibi* topic such appeal is his remarkable skill in avoiding
the static or Stoic condition he had once mocked, for the au-
thority he cites here is simply children at play. The phrases
we are discussing were a refrain sung by Roman children, and
the word play on *rex* and *recte* referred to the rewards of the
winner: "You have sense, morals, eloquence, and honor, yet
you lack six or seven thousand to make the four hundred. Still
boys at play cry, 'You'll be king, if you do the right thing.'
Let that be our motto, as it was for the manly Camilli and
Curii: 'Rex eris . . . si recte facies' " (ll. 57–64). Thus, what
happens in the last lines of the poem gives dramatic life to the
intimations of transfiguration previously elicited from the image
of the guest or of the child at play. The poet who can insist on
his detachment from the mob now—unexpectedly—presents
himself as unkempt, askew, *ondoyant*, and not a little mad:
"Suppose some slipshod barber has cropped my hair—you'll
laugh, Maecenas, as at my tattered shirt or tunic awry. Well,
my judgment doesn't know what it wants, and my whole way
of life shifts like the tides, pulling down, building up, changing
square to round. Yet you who fret over an ill-pared nail accept
this madness with no suggestions of consulting a doctor" (ll.
94–105). Consequently we relish the tone of the conclusion's
assertion that the virtuous sage is second only to Jove; he is a
king—and all good things as the catalogue of virtues accumu-
lates; he is most of all *sanus*—a sound mind in a sound body—
until, unexpectedly, he comes down with a cold (ll. 106–8). It
is, of course, the measure of Horace's achievement in this poem,
and in the *Epistles* as a whole, that his claim to the title of *rex*

sibi and to proximity to the gods is all the stronger for its outlandish admission of these imperfections. The very eccentricity of the characterization still persuades us of its concentric focus, just as, in the earlier example, the inclusion of Ulubrae attests to the liveliness of the *animus aequus*. At once visionary and pedestrian, zany and typical, enrapt and sly, the dramatized self of the *Epistles* is nowhere more triumphant than in his acceptance of one of the least majestic of defeats—*nisi cum pituita molesta est.*

One poem to consider in the light of these speculations on the unexpected workings of Horace's retired imagination is the Seventh Epistle of the first book. In the most provocative passage of this poem Horace cites Telemachus' refusal of Menelaus' proffered gift as a precedent for his own independence of Maecenas—even, as some have suggested, to the extent of giving up his Sabine farm. Earlier in the poem Horace distinguished between two kinds of benefactors, then between two kinds of beneficiaries.[77] In the first place, there is the example of the Calabrian host pressing on his guest the pears he would otherwise feed to the swine—a "generosity" which elicits only ingratitude (*Epist.* 1. 7. 14–21). On the other hand, there is the generosity of a patron who is a *vir bonus et sapiens*, like Maecenas, and so knows that the value of money deserves the best efforts of a protégé to glorify his name (ll. 22–24). As for the various kinds of beneficiaries, there is first the pushy fellow who traps himself like the fox who crawled through a narrow chink into a bin of grain and stuffed himself so full that he could not get out (ll. 29–33). Then there is the example of a guest like Telemachus, or Horace. In each pair of contrasts it is, of course, the second style which Horace embraces; and, taken as a whole, the sequence really attests to the depth, within (or despite) moderation, of friendship between the tactful patron and the independent protégé.[78]

Yet, when all this is accepted, we may wonder whether the cordial relationship between Horace and Maecenas should not itself be seen under the aspect of the *otia liberrima* which Horace claims to enjoy in the country and which is the central

issue of the Seventh Epistle. It is this quality of his life in the
country which, as he explains at the opening of the poem, has
kept him away from the city, not just for the five-day vacation
he had announced to Maecenas but for the whole of August.
And this, too, is why he would live there for the rest of the
year, far from the city's foul weather, disease, and busyness,
returning to Maecenas in the spring with the zephyrs and the
first swallows, as if he too had migrated to some happier place
of fair weather (ll. 1–13). *Parvum parva decent*, he concludes,
small things for small folks, so he'll stay at Tibur or Tarentum, not go to Rome (ll. 44–45). Yet the latter half of the
poem is devoted to a fable which, although it has been called
"the most accomplished of all the paradigmatic stories in Horace's *sermones* and altogether one of the happiest products of
his pen,"[79] is nevertheless a most anomalous justification of
Horace's preference for the country and a fascinating reversal
of the simple contrast of city mouse and country mouse which
might have been expected. As Fraenkel's analysis demonstrates,
the carefully planned structure of this fable, the precision and
vivacity of its organization, and its pervasive *humanitas* deserve
more attention than the more familiar poems.[80] It tells of one
Philippus, a famous pleader, vigorous and courageous, and, we
suspect, not a little like Maecenas (ll. 45–46). One afternoon
he comes upon a certain Volteius Mena loitering in the shade
of a barber's booth and manicuring his nails. Mena is an auctioneer whose private life reminds one of Horace or, as Fraenkel suggests, even of Horace's father. He is an auctioneer of
small means but a blameless life. He works hard and spends
readily, enjoying friends, his home, and the public sports (ll.
56–59). Philippus takes a fancy to the auctioneer and graciously
invites him to supper, but Mena hesitates to accept. The next
morning Philippus meets him at his job of hawking odds and
ends. Embarrassed, the poor man tries to make his work an
excuse for his absence, but he is pressed with another invitation. Mena gives in; but, once he arrives, he chats confidently
about anything and everything, until he is sent off to bed.

Significantly, the hubris of Volteius Mena will suffer its reversal not in the city but in the country. Out one day with his
patron, he never ceases to praise the Sabine soil and climate;
soon enough, with the backing of Philippus, he obtains a little
farm (ll. 82–85). It is as if the daydream of the usurer Alfius
had been fulfilled—and that is precisely its flaw. Mena has run
to the country to satisfy the same kind of illusions which had
inspired the Second Epode's mockery. Soon his sheep are stolen,
his goats are diseased, his crops disappoint him, his ox is worked
to death. Obsessed, Mena rides off to Philippus in the middle
of the night. "You seem so overworked," says the patron; and
Mena pleads to be restored to his previous city life (ll. 86–95).

Although it may be said to have the same abstract moral
(*parvum parva decent*), what distinguishes this story from the
tale of the city mouse and the country mouse is its reversal of
settings. While the *mus rusticus* returns to the country to find
peace of mind, Mena returns to his old life in the city. If this
parable had had Horace's surrogate leaving the country for the
city and then returning to the country, the parallel with the
poet's own announced preference would have been apt in an
obvious way—the way most readers think of Horace. But Horace's condition in this poem is such that it can be represented
by both surrogates: the country mouse and the urban auctioneer. Indeed, his condition would seem to be the result of their
dialectical interplay. In an important sense he is obviously a
country mouse; his usual preference has provided the dramatic
occasion for the epistle in the first place, and his defense of his
preference colors the first half of his poem. To use the example
from Homer, the country is Horace's Ithaca, it gives him back
to himself: *parvum parva decent . . . non regia Roma.* At the
same time, however, to continue the parallel with Telemachus,
this Sabine Ithaca is not really his own home but is the Phaeacian gift of Menelaus-Maecenas.[81] It is equally true that, like
Volteius Mena, Horace's proper place was in Rome, until the
kindness of his patron gave him his farm—but it is important
to see that the very self-discovery which the farm makes pos-

sible liberates him from dependence on it. Such to me, at least, is what Horace means here by *otia liberrima*. Like Volteius Mena, he can now return to his old haunts, but only because, unlike Mena, he has found himself in the countryside.

Thus, the very course of returning to the city—the repudiation of which prompted the epistle—becomes the regenerative action of the fable. As it leads back to the city from the country, the fable justifies Horace's determination to stay in the country. Horace's retirement is at once the same and the opposite in its setting and the quality of its action. Taken in its complex entirety, the Seventh Epistle is thus a masterful articulation of that "retirement from retirement" which is not so much a "return" to urban action as a radical insistence on retirement itself. This is not a thrust toward a particular goal but a continuous process whose goals, once achieved, become the very conditions from which to retire. The Sabine farm liberates its owner to the extent that he becomes free to dismiss it. That is why it is worth enjoying and not dismissing.

Finally, however, and most ironically, one puts the poem down, not dizzy with the dialectical progressions with which the critic tries to explicate the configuration of meanings which the poet has deftly dramatized in the fable and the epistle, but, rather, calmly reassured of what looks like an easygoing relativism on the poem's own terms: Let each measure himself by his own rule (ll. 96–98). Exasperatingly, the lines knit the surface together, leaving us superficially with the kind of platitude that has distracted so many from Horace's imaginative genius. But for the careful reader, I hope it has been demonstrated, the lines vibrate with a sense of an earned resolution. Reading them, one must not forget how Mena left what he had sought to seek what he had left, or that Horace can leave what he has found because he has found what he had sought.

So far, this reading of the *Epistles* has been concerned mainly with their retired sense of place and personal relationships. Following the approach used with the *Odes*, let us bring this survey to a close by turning to two poems which unite these themes with another (though it is a theme which has always been implied): the passage of time and human mortality. This theme has already been anticipated in the reading of the First Epistle of the first book, and the parallel with certain affirmations of Montaigne and Stevens was suggested. The Sixteenth Epistle of the first book, addressed to a certain Quinctius, is a veritable summation of the Horatian condition, *la pièce maîtresse du recueil*, as Courbaud calls it. The poem opens with one of the loveliest descriptions of his farm that the poet ever wrote (*Epist.* 1. 16. 5–16). *Continui montes*: one's first impression is of an unbroken horizon, a sense of harmony and continuity which is curiously confirmed even as it is qualified by the cleavage of the valley, whose daily balance of sunshine and shade seems an emblem of the place's year-round temperate climate. The description of the shrubs and trees begins, of course, with an emphasis on the ripeness and abundance of the fruits and nuts where the cattle roam. Typically, however, Horace's own enjoyment of the scene involves a certain withdrawal from these georgic satisfactions to the repose of the shade and to the waters whose cool and healing quality perfectly symbolizes the humanistic attraction of the secluded place.

Typically, too, the poet's meditation proceeds from this sense of place to the condition which finds its image there, the happiness of the good and wise man. These are the qualities in which Quinctius, whose tendency is to judge by more popular standards, needs instruction. Consequently, the body of the poem is taken up with the importance of a morality grounded on inner integrity and not merely external appearances, on the positive love of the good rather than merely the negative shunning of evil (ll. 17–72). What interests us here, however, is the last few lines, a sequence which, with the opening description of the farm, frames the exhortation to Quinctius in a context which brings these instructive reflections to imaginative life. For Horace's final characterization of the *vir bonus et sapiens* involves an appeal to myth and, rather unexpectedly, to the figure of Dionysus. He presents his version of the situation in Euripides' *Bacchae*, lines 492–98,[82] when Pentheus, the ra-

tional, antitraditional king of Thebes, confronts his captive,
a Lydian stranger who is Dionysus in disguise:

> *vir bonus et sapiens audebit dicere "Pentheu,*
> *rector Thebarum, quid me perferre patique*
> *indignum coges?" "Adimam bona." "Nempe pecus, rem,*
> *lectos, argentum: tollas licet." "In manicis et*
> *compedibus saevo te sub custode tenebo."*
> *"Ipse deus, simul atque volam, me solvet." opinor*
> *hoc sentit, "moriar."*

(Epist. 1. 16. 73–79)

> The truly good and wise man will have the
> courage to say, "Pentheus, lord of Thebes, what
> shame can you inflict on me?" "I will take away
> your goods." "My cattle, couches, plate, take
> them all!" "I will keep you in fetters under a
> cruel jailer." "God himself, the moment I
> choose, will set me free." This, I take it, is his
> meaning: "I will die."

The lines to some degree parallel those of the *Bacchae*, except
for the *moriar*, which, as the poet's inferences indicate, is obviously central to his own meaning. The meaning is usually
interpreted as "I will commit suicide." Such a reading has its
Stoic lesson, to be sure,[83] but it disregards what is probably
the most distinctive feature of the poem, the surprising selection of Dionysus as the type of the *vir bonus et sapiens*. The
god of Euripides' play would seem to be anything but an
obvious candidate for the relatively static (one could call it
Apollonian) role of Horace's ideal of moderation. For Dionysus is, in the words of William Arrowsmith, "the incarnate
life-force itself, the uncontrollable chaotic eruption of nature
in individuals and cities; the thrust of the sap in the tree and
the blood in the veins, the 'force that through the green fuse
drives the flower.' "[84]

In using this exuberant figure to illustrate the self-contained
ideal of the *vir bonus et sapiens*, the poem enacts a consummate transfiguration of retirement. Dionysus' acceptance of
poverty and imprisonment and death becomes the condition

for his liberation from these ills. Nor does it seem to me that *moriar* must mean only "I will die by my own hand"; instead it can have the more inclusive sense "the god will let me die when I please." Like the ending of the *Odyssey*, both the context of the poem and the play itself seem oriented less toward death than life; or, more precisely, the poem's acceptance of death is a testament to the meaning of life. To recall the example of the Eleventh Epistle of the first book, death in the last lines here becomes a kind of ultimate Ulubrae; what one seeks can be there, even there, *animus si te non deficit aequus.* Incarnate in Dionysus, that centripetal equanimity expands beyond one's normal associations of it with the life of contented leisure to become transformed into a celebration of becoming whose apprehension of being is simply that ripeness is all.

In a more muted and more personal way this liberation from time by the acceptance of time suffuses the climax of the epistle to Florus, the Second Epistle of the second book, a poem whose remembrance of things past has unfortunately been appreciated mainly for its biographical evidence.[85] It was, of course, not the last poem which Horace wrote, but it does seem to be the last to exhibit so finely the workings of his retired imagination. Despite the incompetence for the public myth-making mode which he protested in the epistle to Augustus (*Epist.* 2. 1. 250–59), Horace did go on to devote himself to civic and heroic themes in the composition of the *Carmen Saeculare* and the fourth book of *Odes*; but the life memorialized in the epistle to Florus lacks this public dimension and this heroic commitment. The only battle it recalls is the defeat of a lost cause, and its view of that allegiance is most disenchanted. Still, one suspects that this private statement may claim a significance as universal as the larger and later utterances.

The poem begins with a self-deprecating justification of Horace's reticence, both as a letter-writer and a poet. In the first case, you can't complain about a slave's vices when the seller admitted them in the first place. In the second case, he is like a soldier whose fortune was stolen and who fights for

booty the next day. Once he is rich, though, he has a reply
worthy of Archilochus: "Let him dash into the breach who has
lost his wallet." The comparison deepens in a reminiscence
whose parallel of loss and "recapture" is underscored by its
piquant contrast with the martial success of the soldier in the
anecdote, as Horace tells of his original "wealth" in the heritage of his schooling at Rome and in the grove of Academe
(*Epist.* 2. 2. 41–45) and of the destruction of that first garden
of leisure by the raging tides of civil war, by which he was
disinherited (ll. 46–52). Like the soldier of his story, Horace
earns back, by means of these poetic sallies, the leisurely life
which had been "stolen" from him, and his explanation for his
retirement from the field echoes the soldier's reasons (ll. 52–
54).

I have already suggested the importance of this sense of loss
and reconstitution in the emergent personal myth of the *Satires.*
While the poem before us lacks the particular characters and
scenes which the earlier poems celebrate, it would seem to
enact the same pattern in a more profound way, as the images
of theft and storm recur and combine to implicate meanings
more universal than their first sense of personal loss. Thus, for
example, after having boasted of the restoration of his fortunes
through his poetry, Horace's very next lines poignantly describe a more essential depredation:

> *Singula de nobis anni praedantur euntes;*
> *eripuere iocos, Venerem, convivia, ludum;*
> *tendunt extorquere poemata; quid faciam vis?*
> (*Epist.* 2. 2. 55–57)

> The years, as they pass, plunder us of all joys,
> one by one. They have stripped me of mirth,
> love, feasting, play; they are striving to wrest
> from me my poems. What would you have me
> do?

Beginning with this sense of ineluctable depletion, the rest
of the poem applies it to literary and moral questions. Horace
slips into a meditation on the incoherence of literary taste (ll.

58–64) and then, inevitably, moves on to the centrifugal flux of urban existence that makes the writing of poetry impossible: the contractor with mules and porters, while his cranes raise stones and beams; the funeral colliding with traffic; a mad dog running off here, a mud-spattered sow running there (ll. 72–75, 84–86, 97–98). If these images recall the tides of civil war that snatched the young Horace from Athens' grove of Academe, they dramatically justify the poets' flight from the city to the peaceful grove: *scriptorum chorus omnis amat nemus et fugit urbem, / rite cliens Bacchi somno gaudentis et umbra* ("The whole chorus of poets loves the grove and flees the town, / loyal to Bacchus, who finds joy in sleep and shade," ll. 77–78). In this epistle Horace does not quite count himself among the *scriptorum chorus* (although he shares their retreat); nevertheless, his praise of the poet whose integrity can survive the debasement of urban taste is interesting as a literary equivalent of the moral identity which he will assume at the end of the poem.

Judging by the last quotation, one might expect the ideal poet to be identical with that retired figure described in the grove at the conclusion of the First Ode of the first book. If he is, however, it is not his withdrawal that Horace now chooses to emphasize but his total participation in the flux of time. If in the First Ode the secluded artist stands at the center of a dance, in this poem he participates in the dance of time through his immersion in and ordering of the flux of language (ll. 111–19). This is why, as he is finally presented to us, the ideal poet is not the inhabitant of a grotto but is compared to a river, the embodiment of time which has been accepted and ordered by the inner radiance of artistic vision (*vemens et liquidus puroque simillimus amni*, l. 120). This streaming exuberance secretly tempered, this union of antic becoming and inner being, animates the next lines' personal use of georgic imagery (ll. 120–23).

Hence, the conclusion of the poem turns from the style of poetry to the style of life, not to search out words that will fit the music of the Roman lyre, but to master the rhythms and numbers of a genuine existence (1. 144). *Composer nos meurs est nostre office*, as Montaigne will say, *non pas composer des livres* (*Essais* 3. 12. 1247). Horace's view of the human condition is charged with the same sense of depletion and affirmation that informed his reflections on verbal art. It will be recalled that, as early as the First Satire of the first book, he had distinguished between the miserly "retiring" of material goods from time and the retiring of human beings to use the wealth the first type might heap up. Deepening this insight, he begins his concluding remarks on man's quest for happiness by distinguishing between possession and use. Paradoxically, "use" is shown to be the only authentic kind of "possession" available to men (ll. 159–66). Conversely, those who seek permanence by purchasing possessions have purchased only use. Man may long for a terrestrial paradise, but nothing on earth is timeless. The man who buys a farm buys only greens for his dinner and firewood to keep the kettle boiling (ll. 167–69). With a satisfaction in boundaries comparable to that of Alfius, he may call the place his own even up to where the poplars have been planted by the property line. But it is his only to use, not to possess.

The image of time's predatory waves reminds us that there is only one island which cannot be so eroded: a state of being, within, sustained by perpetual becoming—indeed, expanding as its material resources dwindle (ll. 190–92). Of course the poet will deny that he advocates prodigality, but, as in the First Satire of the first book, the rhetorical thrust of his argument tends to upset the nice balance of the *modus in rebus*. For, having defined the extremes to be avoided, he offers as a model the example of the festive schoolboy, which, with its implications of youth, vitality, freedom, and even liberality, transfigures the mean: *ac potius, puer ut festis Quinquatribus olim, / exiguo gratoque fruaris tempore raptim* ("you snatch enjoyment of the brief and pleasant hour, like a schoolboy in the spring holidays," ll. 197–98).

The free time of the schoolboy's holiday also recalls the poem's earlier reminiscence of Horace's youthful enjoyment of contemplative leisure, but its suggestions now are more liberating than static: to regain that calm island, one must win one's way by yielding to the tide, as in the dynamic image which concludes the sequence, the image of riding out the tempest. Whether his vessel is large or small, the poet says, I shall remain the same passenger, not blown before a favorable north wind or struggling with southern gales; in strength, wit, person, virtue, station, fortune, behind the foremost, ever before the last (ll. 200–204). In this last and greatest epistle, Horace celebrates a conclusion that must summon any careful reader of poetry to reconsider the neglected vision of his later manner. Just as the previous passage moves from the exclusion of balanced extremes to the liberation of the schoolboy's holiday, this passage, after conceding that the extreme of poverty is to be avoided too (l. 199), communicates an acceptance of life as process which transfigures what could have been a perfunctory exercise in avoiding extremes. The passage, to be sure, is presented in the language of alternatives: a ship, large or small; the weather, favorable or stormy; the wind, north or south. Clearly, however, anyone looking for the design of a medium-sized ship or a prescription of temperate weather has come to the wrong poem (though he probably shares a popular image of Horace). What we need to see is that these alternatives (and there is more at stake here than the size of boats or the state of the weather) are not simply extremes to be rigidly shunned but parts of a dialectical process in which the self accepts external change as the very condition of an internal consistency which is as heroic in its way as the other quests we have considered. *Ego, utrum / nave ferar magna an parva, ferar unus et idem* (ll. 199–200). That line typifies the passage, for the *ego* which casually allows the first disjunction rises through the iterated verb to a heroic affirmation of that constancy of identity (*unus et idem*) which is triumphantly manifest in its very acceptance of diversity and becoming (*utrum . . . magna an parva*).

Here, in contrast to the quest of Odysseus or even the festivity of, say, Horace's Teucer, the peace or festivity of the

destination or the interlude is located in the very process of
the journey itself, one in which the poet has emphasized precisely the note of process, in the variability of sizes and seasons.
We noted earlier how a condition of free time was symbolized
by the absence of extreme seasonal variation. In these lines,
however, free time is joyously celebrated in the interplay of
opposed conditions whose very impermanence assures libera-
tion: *non agimur tumidis velis Aquilone secundo; | non tamen
adversis aetatem ducimus Austris* ("Not with swelling sails are
we borne before a favoring north wind, yet we drag not out our
life struggling with southern gales," ll. 201–2). It is important
to see and capture the note of process here, for the total effect
of the passage is not the mere dismissal of extremely good or
bad sailing weather. Indeed, the Latin seems implicitly to contain rather than to deny these poles of experience. What *is*
denied is the claim of either alternative to an absolute status.
We are simply never "always" (to add the crucial word to the
literal translation) in one circumstance or another, nor do we
feel we should even be in fair weather forever. Unlike earlier
exemptions from seasonal variation, the sense of liberated time
here participates in the "freedom" of the seasonal process itself.

   Similarly, as the symbols of ship and weather yield to the
more mundane variables of any man's journey, the apparent
randomness (if not anticlimax) of the list of the virtues prepares
us for the curiously indeterminate character of "our" final place
in the journey, which is now seen as something of a race: *extremi primorum extremis usque priores.* The place and the
ethical norm are, of course, the middle one; yet, if ever there
was an instance where dialectical rhetoric transfigured the moderate theme and the conversational idiom, it is this one. The
personal and the private here include the civic and the expansive. To savor their pungency, one need only reflect on how
much more straightforwardly (and uncreatively) the lines might
have pointed the moral in another, more logical (if unmetrical)
arrangement of the terms: *primorum extremi priores usque
extremis.* In his more creative version Horace has done nothing

less than to make his ethical means into his poetical extremes. He has transposed the terms of his chiastic central norm to enclose rhetorically the very terms which themselves should "logically" enclose that center. This expansion of the ethical mean is even more dynamically registered in the reader's consciousness because the language used is sequential rather than quantitative, as we might expect it to be. In using the language of "first" and "last," however, Horace not only can resume the imagery of the journey but can dramatically transfigure the middle positions by literally making the "last" part of the opening segment first and the "first" part of the closing segment "last." Significantly, the reader is here not offered any simple description of the mean as such; rather, in an unsettling shift of perspectives, the reader is personally compelled to an enlargement of vision in which ethical truth is freed from the measurements of moralistic truism and he can rediscover the imaginative ultimacy of the personal center. The line stays with us, less for its implicit sense of abiding moderation than for the zest of its shifting perspectives and for the centrifugal openness of a centripetal norm, defined not tidily but by contraries and by the exuberant rhetoric which poetically includes the extremes it logically excludes.

The human depth of what may have seemed at first glance to be only an unusual aphorism is even more absorbing when we recall that this meditation is on the spending of the self in time's process. To think in terms of being first *or* last is to think of a temporal sequence, but to think of both together, and to envision both terms as somehow one, is profoundly to transform sequence into duration. By his unexpected placing of the "middle" points of his sequence at the ends of the line, Horace has invited the reader to perceive the future and the past simultaneously or as "spatially" enclosed by the first moment of the future and the last moment of the past—moments which are one in a continuing present. The reader's consideration of the future and the past literally begins and ends with the present. Here, in aphoristic summary of the central intuition which has matured throughout Horace's writings, the imaginative expansion of the ethical mean has its consummate symbol in the leisurely plenum of a continuing personal present.

The preceding reflections may not be the kind of attention one is taught in the schools to give to the *Epistles*, but they are the only ones appropriate here, before this last discussion of Horace concludes and before the poem itself comes to its close with a meditation on the end of life. As detachment from material possessions leads to "use," use leads to the acceptance of time as life itself is spent. Here, in what are perhaps the most unforgettable lines in all the *Epistles*, the final "retirement" of death becomes the condition for the poet's most haunting affirmation of festive free time:

> *Non es avarus: abi. quid? cetera iam simul isto*
> *cum vitio fugere? caret tibi pectus inani*
> *ambitione? caret mortis formidine et ira?*
> *somnia, terrores magicos, miracula, sagas,*
> *nocturnos lemures portentaque Thessala rides?*
> *natalis grate numeras? ignoscis amicis?*
> *lenior et melior fis accedente senecta?*
> *quid te exempta iuvat spinis de pluribus una?*
> *vivere si recte nescis, decede peritis.*
> *lusisti satis, edisti satis atque bibisti:*
> *tempus abire tibi est, ne potum largius aequo*
> *rideat et pulset lasciva decentius aetas.*
>
> (ll. 205–16)

You are no miser. Good! What then? Have all the other vices taken to flight with that? Is your heart free from vain ambition? Is it free from alarm and anger at death? Dreams, terrors of magic, marvels, witches, ghosts of night, Thessalian portents—do you laugh at these? Do you count your birthdays thankfully? Do you forgive your friends? Do you grow gentler and better, as old age draws near? What good does it do you to pluck out a single one of many thorns? If you do not know how to live right, make way for those who do. You have played enough, have eaten and drunk enough. It is time to quit the feast, lest when you have drunk too freely, youth mock and jostle you, playing the wanton with better grace.

The passage deftly transforms detachment from wealth into a liberation of the spirit from ambition and anxiety which itself is soon transformed from the laughing contemplation of the centrifugal imaginings of others to the positive acceptance of time and human frailty in the comedy of one's own life: *natalis grate numeras? ignoscis amicis?* These two motifs swell and blend beautifully as the imagery of organic ripeness merges with the language of festive satiety, even inebriety. Acceptance of the aging self and forgiveness of friends are quietly rendered in the suggestion of a softness which is at once ripening and disabling and which may also seem to mollify those thorns which cannot be extracted. If, unexpectedly, we discover that the "you" who has been addressed is dramatically imagined at the point of death, there is no shock here but a strange assurance in the discovery. For it is the very process of increasing imperfection, of final "softening," that also accounts for our humane perfection.

The last four lines take the Lucretian metaphor of life as a feast, noted already at the end of the First Satire of the first book, and superbly fulfill the festive promise of the image. The man at the point of death, one notices, has not only eaten and drunk enough but *played* enough too—like the schoolboys on their spring holidays perhaps, some twenty lines earlier. As the *tempus abire* recalls the jocular opening *abi* of line 205, the tone of the finale is one of convivial—as well as poignant—cajolery: "Come on now, you've had enough." Indeed—and this is the great comic achievement of these deceptively simple lines—there lingers a strong suggestion that the dying man has almost had more than enough to drink. This is not the case of one who has warmed both hands before the fire of life, which sinks, and he is ready to depart. Horace's dying man has reached the climax of his feast; he dies as he is about to have a larger draught of life than he can hold. This ripeness at the moment of passage is the consummate liberation that follows the acceptance of time. "Death," as Wallace Stevens has memorably said, "is the mother of beauty," meaning, as Marie Borroff puts it, not the cliché that transient things are precious, "but the profounder idea that all the beauty we as human beings can know is born of the process of change which is one with the process of death, the beauty of the fruit that has come to the end of its life upon the bough."[86] *J'en ay veu l'herbe et les fleurs et le fruit,* Montaigne will write, *et en vois la secheresse. Heureusement, puisque c'est naturellement (Essais* 3. 2. 913). "I have seen the grass, the flower, and the fruit; now I see the dryness—happily, since it is naturally." And this is the testament of Horace's *Epistles,* an acceptance of death and time which, seeking no larger context of significant soil or city of man or god, still finds a personal vision of free time even at the point of death.

For the reader who must depart, if not from the feast of life, at least from the leisurely experience of this poem, there is a special complexity to its kind of closure which is all the more appropriate as our last example from Horace. Many of Horace's poems are specifically addressed to readers who either share his leisurely perspective or who are being instructed in the true meaning of that perspective. In the poem before us, Julius Florus is first characterized as being impatient for Horace's correspondence and his poetry. Now, having enjoyed the richest example of the mode, his own situation especially seems to reflect Horace's theme on the acceptance of time as the basis of true leisure. When the poem ends with an address to a "you" who must depart from life someday, that fictive auditor includes not only Florus, or Horace talking with himself, but every reader for whom it is time to depart from this poem as, someday, from this life.

Horace, forever excerpted for the phrase *carpe diem,* should be remembered as the celebrant of the greater harvest which is perpetually shared with the reader who is also dismissed at the end of this poem. *Lusisti satis, edisti satis atque bibisti.* If we have played enough, eaten and drunk enough, we have done so not only at the feast of life but at the celebration of this poem; we have done so even in this line, to the plangent gaiety of the final music of those repeated syllables. In the next line, as the time to depart from life becomes, in the dramatic direct address, quite literally the time to leave the poem, the reader finds himself experiencing the end of the one as if it were the end of the other. It is not, of course, the time to depart from life—that is merely the drama of the poem's fiction. It is "really" only the time to leave the poem's moment of contemplative leisure; but also, we enjoy discovering, it is the time to return to that very festive life-force which has jostled the reader out of the poem and the dying man out of life. Yet, significantly, it is the time to depart which is itself first felt as over. Everyone who reads this poem will die, but that future certainty can now be seen as a past, even from the leisurely perspective of the present in process. The acceptance of death becomes for the reader the renewal of life.

It is profoundly appropriate that this poet, whom we first heard summoning his readers to voyage to the Isles of the Blest, should be finally honored for the much greater departure affirmed in these lines: out of the timeless into time, out of poetry into life, and, most importantly, out of life into death. With its meditation on death, the contemplative leisure of reading is over: the feast of life has begun. There will be no Phaeacian harpers to transform that feast into "the fairest thing there is." There need be only the book we are closing to remind us that life need be nothing but itself to be free time. In the words of one who opened that book more, perhaps, than any other, and whose own *Essais* show its deepest impress, *Nous sommes de grands fols: Il a passé sa vie en oisiveté, disons nous; je n'ay rien faict d'audjourd'huy. Quoy, avez vous pas vescu? C'est non seulement la foundamentale mais la plus illustre de vos occupations* (*Essais* 3. 13. 1247). ("We are great fools. 'He has spent his life in idleness,' we say; 'I have done nothing today.' What, have you not lived? That is not only the fundamental but the most illustrious of your occupations.") If this reading of Horace has had one purpose, it has been to suggest that no writer was ever more fundamentally or illustriously dedicated to that "occupation" than this greatest poet of free time.

4

Deus nobis haec otia fecit:
FROM CHRISTIAN CIVIC
LEISURE TO THE RETIRED
LEISURE OF MONTAIGNE

How happy is the blameless Vestal's lot!
The world forgetting, by the world forgot.
Eternal sun-shine of the spotless mind!
Each pray'r accepted, and each wish resign'd;
. . . .
Grace shines around her with serenest beams
And whisp'ring Angels prompt her golden dreams.
For her th' unfading rose of *Eden* blooms,
And wings of Seraphs shed divine perfumes . . .
              Alexander Pope, "Eloisa to Abelard"

                 a moving transparence on the nuns,
A light on the candle tearing against the wick
To join a hovering excellence, to escape
From fire and be part only of that of which

Fire is the symbol: the celestial possible.
Speak to your pillow as if it was yourself.
Be orator but with an accurate tongue
And without eloquence, O, half-asleep,
Of the pity that is the memorial of this room,

So that we feel, in this illumined large,
The veritable small, so that each of us
Beholds himself in you, and hears his voice
In yours, master and commiserable man,
Intent on your particles of nether-do . . .
        Wallace Stevens, "To an Old Philosopher
                          in Rome"

Two Retirements

In 1556, two years before his death, Charles V surrendered his powers as head of the Holy Roman Empire to his son and retired to live out the remainder of his days at the monastery of Yuste. Twenty-four years later, in a remarkable collection of jottings candidly entitled *Essais* (before that word meant anything like a literary form), Michel Eyquem de Montaigne praised the emperor's willingness to admit his declining strength and declared that his retirement was the "finest action" of his career (*Essais*, bk. 2, no. 7, p. 429). Appropriately enough, the tribute was rounded off with a reference to Horace's justification of his retirement in the First Epistle of the first book: two lines about turning loose an old horse, lest amid jeers he stumble, broken-winded (*Epist.* 1. 1. 8–9).

Long before he might have qualified for that description, the author of the essay had accomplished his own retirement: "In the year of Christ 1571, at the age of thirty-eight, on the last day of February, his birthday, Michel de Montaigne, long weary of the servitude of the court and of public employments, while still entire, retired to the bosom of the learned virgins, where in calm and freedom from all cares he will spend what little remains of his life, now more than half run out. If the fates permit, he will complete this abode, this sweet ancestral retreat; and he has consecrated it to his freedom, tranquility, and leisure." Inscribed in Latin on the wall of a study near his library, the proclamation was fulfilled during the next twenty-one years of Montaigne's life, even on those occasions when the circumstances of civil wars demanded his adroit public service, especially as an aide to Henry of Navarre.[1]

How inconsequential, at first glance, this withdrawal may seem in contrast with that of an emperor giving up the throne of Augustus and Charlemagne; how truly momentous it was, precisely in terms of this contrast, is the subject of this chapter. Whatever may have passed through his mind, the emperor, it

seems fair to say, could hardly have seen his decision as an unusual one. Even the former Augustinian monk whose reforms
had disturbed his reign would have seen that decision as part
of a tradition—albeit one he sought to correct; indeed, Luther's
objections nailed to a church door in Wittenberg are curiously
conservative compared to the inscription on Montaigne's wall.
The world from which Montaigne is retiring is the world not
only of secular activity but of the religious concerns to which,
however they might dispute them, Charles and Luther were
dedicated.

Montaigne was a practicing, apparently devout, Roman Catholic.[2] His public writing career begins in 1569 with a translation of a work of "natural" theology, Raymond Sebond's *Book
of Creatures*, which, as the title suggests, proposes the evidence
for the hierarchical cosmos of medieval Christianity.[3] Some ten
years later Montaigne wrote his own most eloquent defense of
faith in an "Apology for Raymond Sebond," the longest of the
Essais and perhaps the most influential. And yet the very influence of the "Apology" attests to its Pyrrhic victory in vindicating Sebond's facile rationalism. As Donald Frame has persuasively argued, Montaigne did not consciously intend to "betray"
Sebond, but it is hard to deny that the rhetorical excitement
and influential appeal of the "Apology" proceed as much from
its skeptical attack on the arrogance of human reason—so fal-
lible an instrument—in presuming to know anything so certainly and momentously as natural theology promises—as from
its more general attack on the vanity of man—so miserable a
creature—aspiring to glory of any kind.[4] The "Apology" will
end by quoting Seneca on the "vile and abject thing" that man
is "if he does not raise himself above humanity." *Voyla un bon
mot et un utile desir*, says Montaigne with an irony that already insinuates the concluding deflation, *mais pareillement
absurde.* For to make the handful bigger than the hand, the
reach larger than the grasp, is impossible and unnatural. Man
will rise only if God lends him a hand, *extraordinairement*:
"he will rise by abandoning and renouncing his own means,
and letting himself be raised and uplifted by purely celestial
means. It is for our Christian faith, not for his Stoical virtue,

to aspire to that divine and miraculous metamorphosis" (*Essais* 2. 12; Frame trans., p. 457; Thibaudet ed., pp. 682–83).

Now, moving and doubtless "sincere" as that conclusion is, a reader of Montaigne might also call to mind another and even more typical use of its key terms in another final passage —the lines which conclude Montaigne's contemplation of "Experience," his last essay and the one which we first evoked, in a reading of Archilochus, to express an insistence on personal limitation:

> (b) It is an absolute perfection and virtually divine to know how to enjoy our being rightfully. We seek other conditions because we do not understand the use of our own, and go outside of ourselves because we do not know what it is like inside. (c) Yet there is no use our mounting on stilts, for on stilts we must still walk on our own legs. And on the loftiest throne in the world we are still sitting only on our own rump. (b) The most beautiful lives, to my mind, are those that conform to the common (c) human (b) pattern, (c) with order, but (b) without miracle and without eccentricity [3. 13; F., p. 857; T., p. 1257].[5]

What these two climactic passages share is the rich configuration of the imagery of elevation and debasement imaginatively if not logically blended with the imagery of expansion and contraction. This configuration introduces the complex master image that will inform our interpretation of the phenomenological world of the *Essais*, a world that we shall find to be not unlike that previously introduced by a centrifugal storm and a central island of free time. Still, despite the similarity of their language, there is a fascinating dissimilarity in the rhetorical disposition and ethical affect of the like terms in the two passages. Looking more closely at the verbal texture, one notices first how effectively the end of each sentence is also its rhetorical climax; at the same time, however, one discovers how diametrically the thrust of the one passage is opposed to the other.

Thus, in the selection from the "Apology," the usual order of protasis and apodosis is left reversed for dramatic effect in the quotation from Seneca. The first sentence rises from *la vile chose . . . et abjecte* to the expectant *s'il ne s'esleve au dessus de l'humanité*. In the context of the "Apology"'s argument, of course, such a climactic protasis is merely wishful thinking. Hence, the next two sentences reverse the order and emphasis: now the iterated terms of elevation and expansion are debased and deflated by the end of the sentence:

> *un bon mot*
>   *et*
> *un util desir,*
>
>   *mais*
>   *pareillement absurde.*
> *la poignée plus grande que le poing,*
> *la brassée plus grande que le bras,*
> *enjamber plus que de l'estandue de nos jambes,*
>   *est*
>   *impossible*
>   *et*
>   *absurde.*

The second half of the passage from the "Apology" reverses the direction of the first half, as its anaphoras move from the possibility of man's elevation by God's grace to its heightened fulfillment. The final protasis (*il s'eslevera*) of the sentence from Seneca is now an iterated apodosis, rising first to its own even more expectant protasis (*si Dieu lui preste extraordinairement la main*) and then rising higher and higher through a series of participles which shift the tone from the conditional to the present and actual realization of the triumphant conclusion:

>   *purement celestes*
>   *par les moyens*
>   *et soubslever*
>   *hausser*
> *abandonnant*   *et se laissant*
>   *et*
> *renonçant*
> *à ses propre moyens*

Finally, after a parenthetical dismissal of the Senecan aspiration, the last sentence rises assuredly to the sublime possibility which concludes the "Apology"—*cette divine et miraculeuse metamorphose*. That divine and miraculous metamorphosis was the consummate aspiration of the world from which Montaigne retired, and the quest for it had inspired many men like Charles V to retire from the world.

In the contrasting passage from "Of Experience," however, we begin to perceive the distinctive nature of the "metamorphosis" at the center of Montaigne's retirement: it moves from the divine, so to speak, into the human, and not even the "elevated" human of the Senecan aspiration. It is a movement that is registered, too, when the terms and images of the "Apology" are now transposed to reverse the rhetorical direction noted above. The language of elevation and expansion is now neither set up to be debased and deflated because it is merely human (first half of the "Apology" passage), nor is it the climax of a progression from the human to the divine (second half). Instead, in each sentence, the elevated and expansive term "rises" to its fulfillment in affirming rhetorically the kind of term that, in the context of the "Apology" passage, would have seemed like an anticlimactic debasement or deflation:

C'est une absolue perfection
            et
      comme divine,   *de scavoyr jouyr*
                                          loiallement de son estre.
Nous cherchons d'autres conditions—
                              pour n'entendre l'usage
                                          des nostres,
et sortons hors de nous,
                        pour ne sçavoir
                                    quel il y fait.
Si avons nous beau monter sur des eschasses
                  car   sur des eschasses
                        encores faut-il marcher de nos jambes.
Et au plus eslevé throne du monde
            si ne sommes assis
                  que sus nostre cul.

Les plus belles vies   sont . . .
> *au modelle commun et humain*
> *avec ordre,*
>> *mais sans miracle*
>> *et sans extravagance.*

Not only within each sentence, but across the whole series, one perceives the same movement "rising" through bathos to a climactic decrescendo. To see how the first doublet, *une absolue perfection et comme divine*, is fulfilled in the last, *sans miracle et sans extravagance*, is to start to understand Montaigne's realization of that life of "the happy gods" with which this book began. To apprehend an absolute and almost divine perfection in a life without miracle and extravagance is, some might say, its own kind of miracle and extravagance. If the terms are granted their Latin weight, the sense deepens: a life without *miracula*, the life of *nihil admirari*, becomes worthy of that wonder in which Plato found the motive of contemplation; a life without *extra-vagare*, without wandering beyond limits, enjoys in retirement its own discovery of the happy island sought in a quest for free time.

Such, at least, is the interpretation of Montaigne which we shall discuss at greater length at the end of this chapter, and such, generally, is the difference between the consummation of his retirement and the kind of "divine and miraculous metamorphosis" which an emperor might have sought in retirement. "Transcendental humors frighten me," Montaigne says in the previous paragraph of "Experience," "like lofty and inaccessible places" (p. 856) (*Ces humeurs transcendentes m'effrayent, comme les lieux hautains et inaccessibles*, p. 1256). The retirement of Charles V was to a lofty and inaccessible place; Montaigne "descends" (the metaphor will recur) in retirement to a tower in which he becomes accessible.

So conceived, how then are the *Essais* related to the religious convictions ascribed to their author? How can one resolve the rhetorical and ethical divergence between the two passages just analyzed? Carried to its logical extreme the tendency of the second passage would seem to belie its author's orthodoxy, if not his Christianity. This is in fact the view of a perennial and variously inspired critical tradition distinguished by such interpreters as Pascal, Sainte-Beuve, and Gide. But, in the light of the best scholarship, it is not the view of the present study.[6] Neither, however, is an opposed tendency, which not only reacts to this with a reassertion of Montaigne's faith but goes to the other extreme of, for example, comparing Montaigne's retirement to that of a monk and the *Essais* to the *Imitation of Christ*.[7] The latter is doubtless the less attractive extreme to most readers, but its effort to show that Montaigne was not alone provides in fact an important introduction to the nature of his *Essais*. For the difference between the retirement of the emperor and that of Montaigne is not so much a matter of belief and disbelief; the difference is rather between the life of leisure conceived in a public context and that conceived in a private focus, as celebrated by a Vergil or by a Horace. In the conclusion of chapter 3 I have tried to describe a certain Montaigne-like quality in the affirmations of Horace's *Epistles*. Here we can consider why the customary association of these two writers seems apparently so inevitable and indeed is so profoundly meaningful. For example, the best way to describe the Christian commitment of Montaigne might be to recall the Roman patriotism of Horace. Each believes in the larger context, to be sure, but it does not profoundly shape his imaginative world. A passage of religious aspiration like the conclusion of the "Apology" might be compared to the great civic odes of Horace, but Montaigne's more characteristic celebration is the less exalted one which concludes "Of Experience," on the last page of the *Essais*, with a prayer to Apollo by Horace, celebrating the contained life.

We shall return to that conclusion; but to appreciate its significance more fully, let us, as in the previous chapter, consider the other way of conceiving leisure in a public context, this time that of traditional Christianity, which inspired the yearning for that "divine and miraculous metamorphosis" at the conclusion of the "Apology." The dimensions of this new context, as the imagery of that passage reminds us, were of course

more vertical than horizontal, sacred not secular, but it was
still distinctively "civic" in a way unfamiliar to the modern
mind. Though we might today think of Charles's abdication
chiefly as a movement away from a civic context, it is crucial
to see that it was this same civic aspect, heightened and transformed, which justified the contemplative leisure he sought.
If he resigned his throne, he did so to participate more fully
in another kingdom. The vision of civic leisure underwent a
profound metamorphosis with the advent of Christianity, the
effect of which was to assimilate the Greek *polis* or Vergil's
Rome into the free time of another city, one in which an
emperor might find even greater glory.

Indeed, one way to introduce that change would be to consider for a moment the transformation of "glory" itself as it
shifts from a classical to a Christian context. For, as Arendt
argues, the life of public "action"—which I have been calling
"civic leisure"—has as its goal the creation in history of "the
condition of remembrance." The division between the quest
for such "immortality" and the perception of "eternity" defines for her the nature of the split between "the men of action
and the men of thought" which she sees first in Socrates and
Plato and which culminates in the decline of the Roman *urbs
aeterna* and the rise of Christianity.[8] The word "glory," which
may have originally come, as *gnoria*, from the root *gno* (as in
ignoro) or, as *cloria*, akin to *clarus*, from the Greek *kleō* or
kluō, first meant "fame or "being well known," the equivalent of the Greek *doxa*.[9] In Roman, especially Vergilian, usage,
however, it acquired a civic and ethical character which lent,
as A. J. Vermeulen suggests, a grandeur to the patriotic virtue
of *pietas*. Thus, in the visionary center of the *Aeneid*, the revelation of Anchises in the underworld, Aeneas contemplates his
equivalent of Odysseus' "fairest thing there is," the final reason
for his labors, the future glory of the Dardan line (*Aeneid* 6.
756–57).[10] With the advent of Christianity, of course, such secular glory was to be rejected as an earthly vanity or, more accurately, was to be transferred to the new kingdom. Thus, in an
eloquent chapter of the *City of God* (2. 29), Augustine employs
Vergilian language to summon civic Romans to a new quest:

"Choose now your course, not to seek glory in yourself, but to find it infallibly in the true God." The ancient Roman glory, he continues, has found its truest expression in the martyrs. "They battled on all sides against hostile powers and conquering by their fearless death have purchased this country for us with their blood! To this country we pleadingly invite you."[11]

But the *gloria* which such new heroes were to enjoy was itself already undergoing another kind of transformation, more radical even than the assimilation of the Vergilian value. For *gloria* had also been used in translations of the Bible to render the Greek *doxa*, which in the Septuagint had already been used (in what Vermeulen calls "nothing less than a semantic revolution") to render the Hebrew *kabod* or the *kebod Yahveh*, instead of the more likely *epiphaneia*, which refers not to fame or opinion but to the dazzling majesty of God's theophany as he reveals himself apocalyptically to man in, for example, the Psalms, Isaiah, and Ezekiel.[12] In this sense we are close to the Christian liturgy's "We give thee thanks for thy great glory" and also to the connotations of "glory" in visionary evangelism: "Mine eyes have seen the glory of the coming of the Lord." By the fourth century, glory was increasingly understood in this new or at least unclassical sense, especially when it fused with the image of God as light and splendor.[13] The vision of that glorious manifestation (not merely reputation) is now seen as the climax of the Apocalypse, and, especially after the metamorphosis of Stoicism under Saint Ambrose, as the essence of the happiness of those in the heavenly kingdom whose "beatific vision" is simply the leisurely contemplation of divine glory in the exciting new sense.[14]

It is not surprising that this should have arisen in the fourth century, when persecution was ending and a certain note of triumph animated Christian culture; and Vermeulen's iconographic evidence richly reflects the new *gloria* of the saints and their radiant savior.[15] What may be surprising, however, is that this century should also have seen the rise of the first monastic withdrawal from that same "glory." What we must now begin to understand is the special "pastoral" character of this glory, first proclaimed by angels to shepherds—this glory in which the lilies of the field surpass the raiment of Solomon. At the same time, we must see that, in a kind of transformation of the Vergilian eclogue, this vision of Christian leisure was also the consummation of a new civic myth, even when it summoned a Christian emperor to resign the throne of Augustus.

THE PUBLIC CONTEXT

Christian Leisure: The Pastoral Image

Such considerations might begin some five hundred years after the birth of Christ with the emergence of Saint Benedict from his hermit's cave at Subiaco and the organization of a religious community on that most renowned of *lieux hautains et inaccessibles*, Monte Cassino. In his influential essay on Vergil and the Christian world, T. S. Eliot proposes a connection between the *Georgics* and the medieval resolution of action and contemplation, work and prayer, that, as we shall see, Benedict most fully exemplified.[16] Whether or not the poem itself was historically so influential, Eliot's suggestion invites further consideration because of the relevance of the georgic, and also pastoral, models as ways of analogously discussing the Christian vision of free time. For if, following the practice usual for tragedy or comedy, it is possible anywhere to speak of a pastoral or georgic "sense of life," it is so in describing the promise of the new faith. To explore the implications of the analogy somewhat more fully, the next pages will consider the expectations of the georgic and pastoral modes within the Christian imagination and their different appropriations by the contemplative spirit of the Eastern and Western divisions of the church.

For in general the Christian tradition has long held in solution two divergent tendencies, which might be called (among many other designations) pastoral or contemplative and georgic or active. Here too, as in Vergil's *Georgics*, the means of activity serves an end of pastoral, innocent leisure, but that active means is itself a later development. The pastoral motif begins

with the story of an original condition of innocence and contemplative leisure in a garden. Its emphasis, even after the loss
of this state, is on the hope of enjoying that beatitude once
again as "given." To this end it stresses a detachment from the
City of Man which is especially pastoral in a Vergilian way in
its celebration of the civic leisure of the City of God. That
"God made the country and man made the town" is a notion
extending as far back as the construction of the first city by
Cain, the murderer of the shepherd Abel, who also could be
taken to prefigure the "good shepherd" of the New Testament.
If that title recalls the language of the Twenty-third Psalm, it
likewise calls that psalm to mind in the distinctively pastoral
imagery of the New Testament, where this pastoral motif is
central to the theme of detachment from the great world and
of assured liberation within a higher community. In this connection it is worth recalling that the birth of Jesus among the
shepherds was to be long associated with the classic proclamation of the civic golden age in Vergil's Fourth—or "messianic"
—Eclogue.[17] Similarly, the range and quality of the story of his
life could readily lend themselves to a pastoral interpretation:
thirty years of obscurity among humble folk, and then the selection of fishermen as his followers, suggesting, as Izaak Wal-
ton was later prompted to observe, that "the hearts of such men
by nature were fitted for contemplation and quietness." Thus
the pastoral message of the New Testament becomes not so
much a declaration of alienation as an invitation to the happiness of free time conceived as "given," the idealization of a new
kind of civic leisure.[18]

In this context, let us consider the Sermon on the Mount.
It was less than a century after Vergil had begun his *Eclogues*,
in celebration of the happiness of Tityrus,

> *O Meliboee, deus nobis haec otia fecit*
> *namque erit ille mihi semper deus,*
> *(Eclogues* 1. 6–7)

that Jesus was to promise happiness, not to the recipient of an
emperor's favors, but to men like the dispossessed Meliboeus:

"Blessed are the poor in spirit: for theirs is the kingdom of heaven" (Matt. 5:3). Nowadays one is perhaps most struck by the reversal of the normal standards of success implied in these precepts, but it is worth underlining their traditional designation as "beatitudes": "Rejoice and be exceeding glad, for great is your reward in heaven: for so persecuted they the prophets who were before you" (Matt. 5:12).[19]

> Behold the fowls of the air: for they sow not,
>   neither do they reap, nor gather into barns;
>   yet your heavenly Father feedeth them. Are
>   ye not much better than they?
> Which of you by taking thought can add one
>   cubit unto his stature?
> And why take ye thought for raiment? Con-
>   sider the lilies of the field, how they grow;
>   they toil not, neither do they spin.
> And yet I say unto you, That not even Solomon
>   in all his glory was arrayed like one of these.
>   . . .
> But seek ye first the kingdom of God, and his
>   righteousness; and all these things shall be
>   added unto you.
>
> (Matt. 6:26–33)

Here, if anywhere, one might recall Vergil's words from the First Eclogue: *deus nobis haec otia fecit*.

As a subject of this "kingdom," the primitive Christian was, in Tertullian's words, "an alien in this world and a citizen of the city of Jerusalem which is above" (*Sed tu peregrinus mundi huius, civis supernae Jerusalem*).[20] Within the civic context of the classical world such a manifesto of a new kind of public leisure was a revolutionary announcement. Its challenge to the Roman scheme may already be apparent from our earlier reading of Vergil's *Eclogues* and *Georgics*. For, to use Christian terminology, there was an "eschatological" dimension to the claims of the secular *urbs aeterna*, and it was this quasi-religious conception of the Roman sense of history that the new religion resisted essentially.

But which it inevitably absorbed. With the conversion of Constantine and the ensuing Christianization of the imperial polity, opportunities arose for the resolution of these divergent commitments. The accommodation, however, had little appeal to the sensibility which Tertullian's declaration represents. Perhaps the genesis of monasticism in the East is best explained as a reaction not to barbarian invasions but to the secular success of Christianity: "The prospect of success was rather bright. Those who fled into the wilderness did not share these expectations. They had no trust in the 'christened Empire.' They rather distrusted the whole scheme altogether. They were leaving the earthly Kingdom, as much as it might have been actually 'christened,' in order to build the true Kingdom of Christ in the new land of promise, 'outside the gates,' in the Desert."[21] The monastic life thus arose as a reassertion of the primitive Christian pastoral vision. As Georges Florovsky demonstrates, it was conceived, not as a way for a few exceptional souls, but rather as "a consequent application of common and general Christian vows."[22] "Monks," as Dostoevsky's Father Zossima says, "are not a special sort of men but only what all men ought to be."

To describe the historical development in the language of Vergilian pastoral is not simply to indulge in a fanciful transformation of life into art but rather to emphasize the radical transformation of imaginative into existential reality which the monastic vision sought to achieve. Just as Vergil endowed the delights of Theocritean play with the sanction of history, so, taking literally the pastoral promise of Jesus, the monastic "pastoral" could supersede the Vergilian eclogues of civic leisure by making them "come true" more personally and immediately. We shall not be reading what is usually regarded as "literature" in the next few pages, but in letters, biographies, and histories we shall be reading what must surely be recognized as pastoral. This would at least seem to be what Newman meant when he called the monastic state "the most poetical" of religious disciplines: "It was a return to that primitive age of the world, of which poets have so often sung, the simple life of Arcadia or the reign of Saturn, when fraud and violence

were unknown. It was a bringing back of those real, not fabulous, scenes of innocence and miracle, when Adam delved, or
Abel kept sheep, or Noah planted the vine, and Angels visited
them."[23]

In advancing what I hope will prove to be a useful way of
considering the monastic imagination (and eventually of appre-
ciating the "Horatian" achievement of Montaigne), I want to
stress the two interrelated Vergilian aspects which it shares
with our Roman model: first its sense of a "civic" order—even
when it is most solitary; and second—even when it is most
ascetic—its vision of the consummation of that order in a condition of free time in an imaginative world equivalent to the
garden of Alcinous or the landscape of Vergil. If speaking of
"civic" allegiance in the origins of monasticism seems like a
contradiction in terms, it is so only in the secular terms of the
city which the movement repudiated.[24] What it sought to realize was nothing less than that other city of our quotation
from Tertullian. In this different but still civic context a man
might accomplish the goal of his earthly pilgrimage and find
the fulfillment of his destiny as *civis supernae Jerusalem*. Even
in its origins with Anthony in the Egyptian desert, austere and
inaccessible as he seems today, one is nevertheless surprised to
find this exciting sense of a new *polis* in which the flower of
life is at hand. *Erēmos epolisthē* says the *Vita Antonii* with
ineffable concision: "the desert was made a city" by Anthony's
call to the solitary life and by "monks coming out from their
own and enrolling themselves in the heavenly citizenship."[25]
Eight centuries later it is that same "city in the desert" which
a young canon will discover as he rests on his way to Jerusalem
at the abbey of Clairvaux and suddenly decides to spend his
life in contemplation there. In a letter which beautifully illustrates the monastic appropriation of the civic context, Bernard,
the abbot who received him, explains this unusual fulfillment
of the young man's pilgrimage:

> I write to tell you that your Philip has found a short
> cut to Jerusalem and has arrived there very quickly.
> He crossed the vast ocean stretching wide on every

hand with a favourable wind in a very short time, and he has now cast anchor on the shores for which he was making. Even now he stands in the courts of Jerusalem, and him whom he had heard tidings of in Ephrata he has found in the woodland plains, and gladly reverences in the place where he has halted in his journey. He has entered the holy city and has chosen his heritage with them of whom it has been deservedly said: "You are no longer exiles or aliens; the saints are your fellow citizens, you belong to God's household." His going and coming is in their company and he has become one of them, glorifying God and saying with them: "We find our true home in heaven." He is no longer an inquisitive onlooker, but a devout inhabitant and an enrolled citizen of Jerusalem; but not of that earthly Jerusalem to which Mount Sinai in Arabia is joined, and which is in bondage with her children, but of that free Jerusalem which is above and the mother of us all. . . . And this, if you want to know, is Clairvaux.[26]

Just as the apocalyptic New Jerusalem has at its center a river and tree of life, so too the "city" of the monastic imagination, like the court of Alcinous or the empire of Augustus, has its consummation in a condition of free time whose perfect emblem is paradise, both the lost garden of original innocence and the promised heavenly Isles of the Blest. When Justin Martyr suggested that Homer's garden of Alcinous was inspired by the biblical Eden, he had a more apologetic purpose in mind than the present study has, but he could have given no more compelling example of that Christian transformation of Odysseus' Phaeacian experience, the fulfillment of the monastic *nostos*, which we are concerned with here as an imaginative reality.[27] The life of the monk was envisioned as the fullest enactment of the pastoral promise of Christianity, "a return to paradise, a partial restoration of the joy and peace of Adam's contemplative life in Eden!"[28] So writes the modern monk, Thomas Merton, reflecting on the end of the monastic life as propounded by Abbot Isaias, one of the desert fathers.

It may seem incongruous to speak of a dream of innocent leisure in what was often a rigorously ascetic situation, but it must be remembered that it was precisely such mortification and detachment that returned the votary to his lost garden. In the words of Jacques La Carrière,

> The life in the desert was not, because of the familiar presence of angels, only the anticipation of a future paradise; it was also a reminiscence, a revival of a lost paradise. . . . [The purifications] permitted the ascetic for brief moments to live as "before the Fall," to live the life of Adam in paradise. They did even more than this, making it possible for him to be a new Adam. "Through the virtue of the Holy Ghost and spiritual regeneration," said Macarius the Elder in one of his Spiritual Homilies, "man rises to the dignity of the first Adam, for such a man is deified."[29]

As the contemplative is restored to his unfallen nature, so the world around him is seen as if irradiated by the same innocence. The lion lies down with the lamb in the mythopoeia of the desert. Like Adam, we are told, Anthony lives on his oasis in harmony with the beasts.[30] The garden of Cyriac, according to legend, is defended by a lion.[31] In the same visionary way the external landscape is seen redeemed and transformed; its "beauty" is itself a joyous object of contemplation. Thus, when a philosopher asks Anthony how he can endure the desert without books, he points to the mountainous wilderness around him and replies, "My book, philosopher, is the nature of created things, and it is present when I will for me to read the words of God."[32] Even Jerome, with all his austerity, can write from Rome of his yearning for a countryside which is transformed into a pastoral emblem of the heavenly city for which he likewise yearns. "There drowsiness will not blunt our prayers, nor gluttony our studies. In summer the shade of the trees will give us privacy; in autumn the delicate air and falling leaves invite us to stop and rest; in springtime the fields will be bright with flowers, and our psalms will find all the sweeter accompaniment in the song of birds. Even in the frost and snow of winter, we shall not have to buy fuel."[33] Though this is a description of seasonal variation, its symbolic details of shade, refreshment, song, and warmth intimate a freedom from the excesses of change, affirming a Vergilian sense of the shared values of leisure and fecundity that abide unchangingly. To recall the opening of the Fourth Eclogue, *Si canimus silvas, silvae sint consule dignae*: if the woodland which Jerome evokes does not attempt to be worthy of Vergil's consul and his new-born son, it nevertheless celebrates in a Vergilian way the values of a community that began with another birth.

We might conclude this account of the Eastern origins of the contemplative pastoral with an even more extraordinary evocation of the Homeric quest for the calm and fruitful island which began our survey of the classical image of leisure. Basil writes to Gregory of Nazianzus describing the ideal location he has found for a monastery. He envisions a *locus amoenus* rather like Jerome's countryside and lingers lovingly over "the redolence of the earth, and the river breezes, the carpet of flowers, the song of the birds." Significantly, he praises the spot for its island-like quality, cut off as it is by two deep gorges, a waterfall, and a mountain. "Not Homer's Paradise," he writes, "the island of Calypso, can have been more beautiful. Indeed this retreat of mine is itself an island, so cut off it is from all the world."[34] Hermes, we remember, found the joys of Calypso's island delightful even for a god used to Olympus; Odysseus, of course, had to leave them in order to find their human equivalent in rocky Ithaca. In Basil's vision of his "island," however, the leisurely delights of the place have already assimilated those of the Mount Olympus which is his Ithaca. On this enchanted contemplative island he has already come home to his city.

It is indeed the latter point which Gregory Nazianzen fails to recognize in his own evaluation of the site. It is really only a desert, he says; Basil is behaving like a shipwrecked mariner. The place is a mousehole, the woods are thickets, the mountains keep out the sun, the river is dangerous, not beautiful, the pass is hazardous.[35] But what Basil describes is the visionary transformation of just such an external fallen nature into that promised land whose landscape is the emblem of the Jerusalem he seeks. The young monk who found that city at the abbey of Clairvaux found it in "a valley of light" which was once, we are told, called a valley of wormwood.[36] Explaining the transformation, here—to resume our Western example—is Bernard writing to Ailred, abbot of Rievaulx, on the contemplative transformation of his northern desert into the promised land: "What you say about your mountains and rugged rocks does not disconcert me at all, nor am I horrified at the thought of your great valleys, for now 'the mountains drop down sweetness, the hills flow with milk and honey, and the valleys are filled with corn,' now 'honey is sucked out of rocks and oil out of the hardest stone,' and rocks and mountains are the pasture of the Lord's sheep."[37]

Ailred was once a kitchen steward and, lacking the schooling of the bookish contemplative, must be assured that, like Anthony's "book" in the Egyptian desert, his only object of contemplation need be the inner reality of the landscape transformed into an emblem of the ultimate academy. "And so I think that with that maul of yours you will be able to strike something out of those rocks that you have not got by your own wits from the bookshelves of the schoolmen, and that you will have experienced sometimes under the shade of a tree during the heat of midday what you would never have learned in the school."[38] What Ailred will experience is not unlike what Vergil's Tityrus experienced in the contemplative shade of the First Eclogue: *deus haec otia fecit.* As Bernard put it more personally in another place, "Believe me who have experience, you will find much more labouring amongst the woods than you ever will amongst books. Woods and stones will teach you what you can never hear from any master. Do you imagine you cannot suck honey from the rocks and oil from the hardest stone; that the mountains do not drop sweetness and the hills flow with milk and honey; that the valleys are not filled with corn?"[39]

But if Bernard's reference to actual labor in the woods strikes a note not stressed in Anthony's desert contemplation of the same "book," the difference illustrates the two divergent means of reaching the pastoral goal of monastic culture, which, following Vergil, we could call pastoral and georgic. For it is quite possible that the sense in which the term pastoral has been used may have begun to seem Pickwickian in the context of Western Christianity. Ironically, in locutions such as "pastoral office" or "pastoral responsibility" the shepherd metaphor suggests not liberation but occupation. In Vergilian terms, it is less pastoral and more georgic. Indeed, one useful way of conceiving the evolution of the monastic imagination, or, more accurately, of describing the difference between Eastern and Western monastic culture, is to see it in terms of the difference between the pastoral and georgic modes of realizing Christian leisure. To recall the previous discussion of Vergil's use of the two modes, the difference lies not so much in the contrast between the Saturnian or Edenic dream and its opposite but in the extent to which the georgic vision assimilates the usually unpastoral means of work and action in history to dramatize the final achievement of its golden age.

In the contemplative life as it evolved in Eastern Christianity there has been, along with the spirit of Father Zossima, the tendency which Dostoevsky dramatized in the character of Father Ferrapont. The very word "monk" is derived from the familiar Greek word for "one." The monastic life as first practiced by Anthony and his followers in the deserts of Egypt made very little practical allowance for communal or "cenobitic" activity.[40] Though spiritually a "city in the desert," it was primarily given over to the kind of solitary contemplation and detachment one might today associate with other Eastern religions that are not Christian. The cult of pillar asceticism among the Stylites is probably the most well-known expression of this tendency. Less familiar, but even more provocative perhaps, is the refusal of even the communal sacrament of the Eucharist by those who claimed already to have seen Christ

and entered his kingdom.[41] In calling this tradition "pastoral"
I wish primarily to describe the quality of this detachment, the
almost literal imitation of the birds of the air, who neither
sow nor reap nor gather into barns.[42] In the *Collations* of Cassian, as Butler observes, "Anything that withdraws the hermit
from the precincts of his cell and courtyard, and compels him
to go out for any work in the open air, 'dissipates his concentration of mind and all the keenness of the vision of his aim.
. . . Agricultural work is incompatible with the contemplative
life, because the multitude of thoughts generated by such work
makes unbearable the prolonged silence and quiet of the hermit's cell.' "[43] These precepts are extreme examples, and it must
be noted that in such great Eastern founders as Pachomius and
Basil there is considerable emphasis on a sense of community
and the importance of work—"practical" tendencies which
were to be accentuated by Benedict in the West. The temper
which they illustrate, however, is amply evident in the last
item in this brief survey of the contemplative life in the
East, the influential *Concerning Mystical Theology* of Pseudo-
Dionysius. With its doctrine of the "negative way" to union
with God, this treatise (the first to call "mystical" what was
previously simply termed "contemplative") provides the consummate statement of the Eastern spirituality of detachment.[44]

Christian Leisure: The Georgic Image

Eventually this version of the contemplative experience came
to prevail in the Western church too; but at the time the
Pseudo-Dionysian *Mystical Theology* was first spreading its
influence in the East, the contemplative life in the West was
being defined in just the opposite way, which might be called
georgic. To be sure, the primacy or superiority of the contemplative state was never overtly denied, but so pronounced was
the affirmation of labor that it is doubtful whether nowadays
one would call such an admixture of practical activity contemplative or "mystical" at all. Kenneth Kirk notes how Benedict silently eliminated the traditional justification of the con-

templative life as a state of "seeing" God.[45] Inasmuch as that practical transformation has been replaced by more "mystical" notions, it is not without reason that Cuthbert Butler's presentation of Western mysticism during these "Benedictine centuries" (550–1150) should bear the subtitle *Neglected Chapters in the History of Religion.*

The key to these neglected chapters is the endorsement of the "active" life, not reluctantly, as a necessary evil, but positively, as the very condition for the mystical experience of contemplative leisure. As it may already have occurred to a reader during our tracing of pastoral motifs in the Bible, there are also grounds for a "georgic" interpretation, beginning as early as man's fall from Edenic leisure and the doom to eat his bread in the sweat of his brow. For, as Milton's Adam declared, "Idleness had been worse," a resolution like the "paradoxical redemption" which Wilkinson perceives in the comparable fall in the *Georgics*: by doing without leisure, man might earn a more authentic beatitude than the one he had enjoyed as "given."[46] In the Old Testament this georgic motif is profoundly exhibited in the sense of history experienced by a chosen people. One thinks, for example, of Moses, whose solitary pastoral encounter with God in the burning bush came to stand as a type of the contemplative goal of the Christian life but whose own active life was characterized rather by commitment and even political involvement for the sake of accomplishing the ends of his God in history.[47] Similarly, in the New Testament, the idealized quality of pastoral detachment is not an exclusive motif. As Gregory the Great pointed out, "Christ set forth, in himself, patterns of both lives, that is, the active and the contemplative, united together. . . . For when he worked miracles in the city and yet continued all night in prayer on the mountain, he gave the faithful an example not to neglect the care of their neighbors through love of contemplation, nor to abandon contemplation by being immediately concerned with the care of their neighbors."[48]

There were other biblical precedents which, while never exalting labor *above* contemplative detachment, could neverthe-

less be cited as authorities for its worth; these were to be found
in the familiar paired figures of Peter and John, Martha and
Mary, Leah and Rachel. The difference in the first pair is obvious enough from their characterization in the New Testament narrative and their later careers. The meaning of the
second pair appears at the close of the tenth chapter of Luke.
While Martha bustles around the house, Mary simply sits at
the feet of Jesus. "Martha, Martha," he says, "thou art careful
and troubled about many things: But one thing is needful and
Mary hath chosen that good part, which shall not be taken away
from her" (Luke 10:41–42). The symbolism of the last pair is
probably the most suggestive. Jacob, who because of his dream of
the ladder of ascending and descending angels (Gen. 28:12–15)
became an obvious type of the contemplative man, labored for
seven years to win the hand of Rachel from her father Laban,
but he was deceived into first marrying Leah, the older daugh-
ter. Leah, who could not see well, eventually brought forth
many children. Rachel, whose eyesight was keener, produced
only two sons, but they were Joseph and Benjamin, the dearest
of the twelve (Gen. 29–35). The two sisters became types of the
life of action and contemplation. To recall an earlier formulation, just as one must do without leisure to have leisure, so one
must marry Leah to possess Rachel.

The "shepherd" of Hippo provides an interesting early instance of this georgic resolution of the tension between the
pastoral liberation of Christianity and the "pastoral" occupation necessary to attain that end.[49] In discussing the Martha
and Mary episode, Augustine is careful to do justice to Martha's
activity. Christ did not say that Martha had chosen a bad role,
he insists, but simply that Mary's was better. In fact, the rhetorical force of his argument in the following passage (underlined
by the internal rhyme of the last sentence) converts this simple
contrast into a relationship of condition and consequences:

> Thus in that home which received the Lord there
> dwelled two lives in these two women, both inno-
> cent, both praiseworthy. One was devoted to labor,
> the other was devoted to ease. Neither was the one
> evil-doing, nor the other slothful—evil-doing as the

> life of labor must avoid becoming, slothful as the
> life of leisure must avoid becoming. . . . In Martha
> there was the image of things present; in Mary the
> image of things to come. What Martha was doing—
> there we are now; what Mary was doing—for that
> we hope. Let us do the one well that we may have
> the other in full. [*Hoc agamus bene, ut illud habea-
> mus plene.*][50]

Similarly, in the nineteenth book of *The City of God*, Augustine declared his preference for a mixed life, devoted exclusively to neither contemplation nor action. "Wherefore the
love of truth makes one seek a holy leisure, the bond of love
makes one undertake a righteous occupation" (*Quamobrem
otium sanctum quaerit caritas veritatis: negotium iustum sus-
cipit necessitas caritatis*).[51] In these "practical" formulations
Augustine displays those distinctively "Western" qualities
which Erich Auerbach has singled out as so characteristic of
his achievement, "the fundamentally European determination
not to abolish reality by speculation, not to take flight into
transcendence, but to come to grips with the real world and
master it."[52]

Nor should one forget, as the very occasion of *The City of
God*'s composition reminds us, that historical events in the
West were far different from those that generated Eastern monasticism. Five centuries after Vergil had charged his *Georgics*
with his urgent sense of the need to restore civil order to a
shattered state, the same words—and the same message—might
have been addressed to the collapse of that order. In the fifth
century one could indeed see the need for Augustine's *negotium iustum*: "There was a Europe to be reconverted, Chris-
tianised, civilised anew; law and order to be restored; the fabric
of society to be rebuilt; the dignity of labour to be reasserted;
agriculture, commerce, education, the arts of peace to be revived; civil and political life to be renewed: in short, a Europe
to be remade."[53]

The Benedictine effort in that task has been sensitively described by Newman in a passage which also celebrates its
"georgic" dynamic:

St. Benedict found the world, physical and social, in
ruins, and his mission was to restore it in the way,
not of science, but of nature. . . . Silent men were
observed about the country, or discovered in the forest, digging, clearing, and building; and other silent
men, not seen, were sitting in the cold cloister, tiring
their eyes, and keeping their attention on the stretch,
while they painfully deciphered and copied and re-
copied the manuscripts which they had saved. . . .
By degrees the woody swamp became a hermitage, a
religious house, a farm, an abbey, a village, a semi-
nary, a school of learning, and a city.[54]

In an invocation of Vergil which anticipates and conceivably
influenced Eliot's account of the *Georgics* and the Christian
world, Newman had himself been meditating on

what congenial subjects for his verse would the
sweetest of all poets have found in scenes and histories such as the foregoing, he who in his Georgics
has shown such love of a country life and country
occupations, and of the themes and trains of thought
which rise out of the country! Would that Christianity had a Vergil to describe the old monks at their
rural labours . . . ; how could he have illustrated that
wonderful union of prayer, penance, toil, and literary
work, the true "otium cum dignitate," a fruitful
leisure and a meek-hearted dignity, which is exemplified in the Benedictine. . . . Herein then, according
to Vergil, lies the poetry of St. Benedict, in the "secura quies et nescia fallere vita."[55]

Prior to founding his "georgic" order, Benedict himself
had gone through a period of solitary contemplation after the
("pastoral") Egyptian manner, so that his personal development
provides a kind of summary of the different approaches to
Christian leisure described so far.[56] As an instance of the workings of his georgic imagination, one might consider the forty-
eighth chapter of his *Rule. Otiositas inimica est animae,* he
begins: "Idleness is the enemy of the soul. The brethren, therefore, must be occupied at stated hours in manual labor, and

again at other hours in sacred reading."[57] The most interesting discussion of the chapter is its regulation, and even suppression, of the singing of the canonical hours according to the exigencies of agricultural activity: "From Easter until September the fourteenth . . . let Nones be said early, at the middle of the eighth hour; and let them again do what work has to be done until Vespers. But if the circumstances of the place or their poverty require them to gather the harvest themselves, let them not be discontented; for then are they truly monks when they live by the labour of their hands, like our fathers and the apostles."[58] Though the birds of the air sow not, nor reap, nor gather into barns, Benedict seems to be saying, those who consider them must do so, that in doing so the toil may become itself the way of realizing the pastoral promise of free time.

The historical consequence of the doctrine of "work as prayer" was the reconciliation not only of cult and cultivation but of cult and culture, such as the scholarly conservation of literature through "the dark ages" or the active missionary work of an Augustine in England, a Boniface in Germany.[59] Perhaps the most dramatic representative of this georgic sensibility is the monk elected to the papacy at the close of the sixth century. The letter he wrote protesting his reluctance to assume that office is a moving recapitulation of the attractions of the contemplative "dream of ease" for Christians. He had been, he says, in a high place looking calmly down on the agitations of the world when suddenly he was caught up in a whirlwind, battered by waves, sunk amid tempests. He had cherished his Rachel, "not fruitful but of keen sight and beautiful," but now, by some unknown decision, Leah has been coupled with him in the night, she who is fruitful but dull of sight. He had longed to sit at the feet of the Lord with Mary, but he has been compelled to serve with Martha.[60]

Because of the depth of his devotion to the life of Rachel and Mary, the author of that letter was regarded as a master of mystical theology in the Middle Ages. Yet this very monk lives in Western history as "Gregory the Great" for the extraor-

dinary activism of his pontificate, especially for the first real
assertion of the temporal power of the papacy. His georgic resolution of these conflicting tendencies is described by Gregory's
most famous treatise, the *Liber Regulae Pastoralis*, or *Pastoral
Care*. There Gregory uses the occasion of Christ's meeting the
apostles as they were fishing, when he commissioned Peter to
feed his flock (John 21), precisely to underline the necessary active and public occupation of those who would enjoy the pastoral liberation of the good shepherd: "[There are those] who,
endowed, as we have said, with great gifts, in their eagerness for
the pursuit of contemplation only, decline to be of service to
their neighbor by preaching; they love to withdraw in quietude
and desire to be alone for meditation. Now, if they are judged
strictly on their conduct, they are certainly guilty in proportion to the public service which they were about to afford."[61]

The introductory chapter of this book referred to Dante's
condemnation in the *Inferno* of the otherworldly Celestine V
for his "great refusal," that is, his leaving the pressures of the
papacy in order to resume the contemplative life. We begin to
see now why the very same "poet of the secular world" could
assign the contemplatives the place of honor in the *Paradiso*,
placing them above the rulers and warriors in the sphere of
Saturn (whose emblem is Jacob's Ladder). Finally, in the sublime ending of the poem, as A. B. Giamatti has suggested, the
vision of the city and the garden, the amphitheater and the
rose, blend and transform each other.[62] These divergent dimensions intersect crucially at the conclusion of the *Purgatorio*,
during the illustration of the active life in "the earthly paradise." There, in what is certainly the finest medieval articulation of the interplay of georgic and pastoral motifs, the Christian imperatives of engagement and detachment are held in
an imaginative solution which may provide this brief survey
with its climactic example.

In the twenty-seventh canto of the *Purgatorio*, Dante has
passed through the wall of fire which signifies his final puri-
fication (ll. 1–57). The sun is setting, and, with the sense of
fleeting time which is so characteristic of this canticle, a voice

urges the pilgrim to hasten his steps (ll. 61–63). When night falls, Dante finally sleeps, like a goat watched over by shepherds (ll. 75–81). In his sleep Dante dreams of Leah, who, typically, distinguishes her activity from her sister's state of contemplation. What arrests the reader's attention, however, can only be called the leisurely quality of this representation of the active life:

> *Sappia qualunque il mio nome dimanda*
> *ch' i' mi son Lia, e vo movendo intorno*
> *le belle mani a farmi una ghirlanda.*
> *Per piacermi allo specchio qui m'adorno;*
> *ma mia suora Rachel mai non si smaga*
> *dal suo miraglio, e siede tutto giorno.*
> *Ell' e de' suoi belli occhi veder vaga*
> *com' io dell'adornarmi con le mani;*
> *lei lo vedere, e me l'ovrare appaga.*
>   (*Purgatorio* 27. 100–108)

Know, whoever asks my name, that I am Leah, and I go plying my fair hands here and there, to make me a garland; to please me at the glass I here adorn myself, but my sister Rachel never leaves her mirror and sits all day. She is fain to see her own fair eyes as I to adorn me with my hands. She with seeing, and I with doing am satisfied.[63]

The condition anticipated in the dream is fulfilled the next day, when the poet enters the earthly paradise, the "sacred wood" at the summit of the mountain. The place represents the perfection of the natural order, life as it was possible before the Fall. This does not mean, of course, that the state of innocence is an end in itself; it is rather, as Dorothy Sayers properly insists, "a starting point and not a stopping place for the journey to union with God."[64] As Dante himself put it in the *Monarchy*, Providence has ordained two goals for man: "the first is happiness in this life, which consists in the exercise of his own powers and is typified by the earthly paradise; the second is the happiness of eternal life, which consists in the enjoy-

ment of the divine countenance (which man cannot attain to
of his own power, but only by the aid of divine grace) and is
typified by the heavenly paradise."[65] In the terms of this book,
these two paradises represent two consummations of civic leisure, the one of the city of man, the other of the city of God.
To attain the first goal, Dante writes, men are led by the emperor, aided by philosophy—a mission described in the archetypal figure of the tempest and calm island.[66] To attain the
second goal, men are led by the pope, aided by the Scriptures.[67]
Odysseus leaves Phaeacia to reconstitute its values in this world
on his own terms as husband, father, and king; but Dante is
also sailing in the other direction—from Ithaca to Phaeacia and
beyond; from Penelope to Nausicaa; from Leah and Martha
to Rachel and Mary; and, as we shall see, from Matilda to
Beatrice. Without making the mistake of substituting the political treatise for the poem, this distinction would seem to explain why, in this Edenic garden at the summit of the peaceful
island, the poet chose to illustrate not the state of contemplative leisure but the perfection of the active life.

And yet, though one recognizes its (doctrinally) limited or
inferior status in the context of a poem whose last third proclaims the happiness of those who contemplate in the celestial
paradise, one is nevertheless drawn to this representation of
the active life in the terrestrial paradise, probably because, like
the dream of Leah, one would not normally regard it as "active"
at all. This starting point which seems so much like a stopping
place enjoys its own special irradiation of pastoral free time.
Activity here seems always to be near distillation into the
higher contemplative form. One of the key perceptions of
Erich Auerbach's splendid discussion of Dante was his recognition that the poet's awareness of religious ultimates tended
generally to heighten the concrete particulars of the secular
world.[68] To translate (and perhaps extend) that insight into the
terms of the sequence before us, we might say that the active
life acquires a character it would not have had in itself precisely because of its relationship (even though it is a subordi-
nate one) to the contemplative life. This characteristic perfec-

tion of the active life is its transformation into a higher state, where activity is eliminated. Yet this elimination is in every way an imaginatively realized perfection, a persuasive argument (to call it that) for the active life. Thus, for example, just before entering the sacred wood, Dante is instructed by Vergil to take "pleasure as his guide" from this point on. He is then "crowned and mitred" and enters that first garden as literally his own emperor and pope, the usual performance of these active offices being necessary only to fallen man (ll. 130–42). And yet, insofar as this poem is addressed to men in that fallen condition, this promise of the eventual withering-away of these authorities of state and church becomes the cogent justification for their continued administration.

This penetration and transformation of "unleisure" by leisure endows the twenty-eighth canto with its special radiance. Indeed, so suffused is the opening description of this famous *locus amoenus* with intimations of pastoral harmony and free time that this exquisite opposite to the dark and savage wood where the journey began may even strike the reader not as a "starting point" but as a most inviting "stopping place." The georgic achievement of the canto is that it gives us both of these meanings as one.

> *Un'aura dolce, sanza mutamento*
> *avere in sè, mi feria per la fronte*
> *non di più colpo che soave vento;*
> *per cui le fronde, tremolando, pronte*
> *tutte quante piegavano alla parte*
> *u'la prim'ombra gitta il santo monte;*
> *non però dal loro esser dritto sparte*
> *tanto che li augelletti per le cime*
> *lasciasser d'operare ogni lor arte;*
> *ma con piena letizia l'ore prime,*
> *cantando, ricevìeno intra le foglie,*
> *che tenevan bordone alle sue rime*
> (28. 7–18)

A sweet air that was without change was striking on my brow with the force only of a gentle breeze, by which the fluttering boughs all bent

> freely to the part where the holy mountain
> throws its first shadow, yet were not so much
> swayed from their erectness that the little birds
> in the tops did not still practise all their arts,
> but singing, they greeted the morning hours
> with full gladness among the leaves, which kept
> such undertone to their rhymes.

Like the condition which it nurtures, the atmosphere here is always still and still moving. The free and spontaneous movement of the boughs subtly betokens that this almost timeless scene is not quite free from time's imperatives: the night which has passed will come again, and the pilgrim must not be found here by the time the shadow to which the boughs now bend begins to lengthen in the other direction. So too, entrancing as is the blend of birdsong and the undertone of rustling leaves, the very occasion of the enchantment is a reminder of its impermanence; delicately it disallows an unqualified repose, such as the distraction into which Dante lapsed in listening to Casella sing, the first morning, at the foot of the mountain (2. 115–35). There need be no Cato here to remind the pilgrim of his journey's urgency; enjoyment and engagement have become one.

Following along the bank of a limpid stream, Dante next beholds a wondrous sight that "drives away every other thought":

> *una donna soletta che si già*
> *cantando e scegliendo fior da fiore*
> *ond'era pinta tutta la sua via.*
>   (28. 40–42)
>
> a lady all alone, who went singing and culling
> flower from flower with which all her way was
> painted.

As the language reminds us, the lady, called Matilda, is the fulfillment of the dream of Leah, the type of the active life. Indeed, in order to remind us of this message's relevance to man's present fallen condition, the poet will frame this blessed scene with allusions that presage its loss and iterate the consequent necessity of man's striving to regain it. Matilda will be com-

pared to Proserpina, as lovely as when "her mother lost her
and she the spring" (ll. 49–51), and, anticipating another seasonal myth of death and regeneration (ll. 64–66), to Venus,
struck by Cupid's arrow with a love for Adonis. The pastoral
irradiation of activity which was so striking in Leah's behavior
is even more luminous in this description of Matilda's "labor."[69] As her singing and the painted aspect of her path
suggest, work here has been raised to the level of art. This is
beautifully rendered in Matilda's response to Dante's request
that she come forward:

> *Come si volge con le piante strette*
> *a terra ed intra sè donna che balli,*
> *e piede innanzi piede a pena mette,*
> *volsesi in su i vermigli ed in su i gialli*
> *fioretti verso me non altrimenti*
> *che vergine che li occhi onesti avvalli;*
> *e fece i prieghi miei esser contenti,*
> *sì appressando sè, che 'l dolce sono*
> *veniva a me co' suoi intendimenti.*

> As a lady turns in the dance with feet close to-
> gether on the ground and hardly puts one foot
> before the other, she turned towards me on the
> red and yellow flowerets like a virgin that veils
> her modest eyes and gave satisfaction to my
> prayer, approaching so that the sweet sound
> came to me with its meaning.

With its details of disciplined steps and veiled eyes and yet its
final effect of liberation and revelation, the imagery of the
dance offers an unforgettable emblem of the perfection of the
active life, the transformation of labor into leisure by the fusion of work with art. And, one might add, with prayer. For
although Dante probably did not explicitly intend to illustrate
the Benedictine way of life, it seems doubtful that the theme
of *laborare et orare* has been so effectively dramatized anywhere else. Indeed, the movement of the lady hardly seems
like work or the active life at all; and, as her own response to
the beguiled pilgrim makes clear, this is because it is so much

like contemplative leisure: "You are new here," she says, "and
the fact that I am smiling in this place may prompt some doubt
and make you wonder. But the light of the psalm *Delectasti*
may dispel the clouds from your mind" (28. 76–81).

The psalm to which Matilda alludes is a song of praise and
gratitude which celebrates, as given, the pastoral beatitude
which Jesus was to demonstrate by the birds of the air and
the lilies of the field: "Lord, thou has made me glad through
thy works. . . . The righteous shall flourish like the palm tree,
he shall grow like a cedar of Lebanon" (Ps. 92).[70] In truth, to
quote Vergil again, it is a god who has given this free time,
and it is with a recognition of this parallel that Matilda's last
words salute the archetypal situation: Those who in ancient
times sang of the age of gold perhaps dreamed on Parnassus
of this place. Here the source of humanity is innocent. Spring
was always here (28. 139–43). Dante turns to look at "his poets,"
the author of the *Eclogues* and *Georgics* and him who was supposedly converted to Christianity by reading Vergil's Fourth
Eclogue.[71] Vergil and Statius, he writes, have listened to Matilda's last tribute *con riso*, with a smile. It is a propitious moment to bring this modest account of the medieval Christianization of civic leisure to a close.

Renaissance Transformations of Pastoral: Sacred and Secular Dimensions

Moving as is Dante's tribute to the active life, its claim to significance is still ultimately justified by the contemplative beatitude to which it leads, just as, in Auerbach's account, Dante's
secular world derives its considerable concrete importance from
its figural representation of the other world. Probably the best
way, generally, to introduce what Montaigne achieved is to
note his reversal of this Christian habit of mind: "Life on earth
is no longer the figure of the life beyond; he can no longer permit himself to scorn and neglect the here for the sake of a there.
Life on earth is the only one he has. He wants to savor it to the
last drop: *car enfin c'est nostre estre, c'est nostre tout.*"[72] Or, to

use the terms of the preceding discussion (which is simply to continue to explore the implications of Auerbach's remark), the accomplishment of Montaigne is the discovery that the condition of Matilda can have its own claim to celebration as a "stopping place" and not a "starting point." His characteristic exercise of the contemplative faculty is not to seek the vision of God but to contemplate, as an end in itself, the world once set aside for mere action and not contemplation.

Looked at in this way, Montaigne's alternative to Christian leisure provides a superb instance of the larger pattern of the secularization of European values which distinguishes the Renaissance from the Middle Ages. To do justice to the special Horatian quality of the *Essais*, however, a more exacting discrimination seems to be called for, one which would distinguish the focus of Montaigne from the more widely received Renaissance transformation of culture, from which (as from the medieval prospect) he may also be said to have retired. For it is necessary to recognize that the retired leisure of Montaigne involved a contraction in two dimensions, not only from the medieval-supernatural context but also from its Renaissance-secular alternative.

In various ways the following readings will all indicate the disintegration of the synthesis of action and contemplation, secular and supernatural, with which we concluded our discussion of Dante. We might begin by noting within the Western contemplative tradition an increasingly absolute emphasis upon mystical detachment from things mundane. For it would seem to be one of the fine ironies of intellectual history that the sense that man's "life on earth is the only one he has" was coincident with, if not precipitated by, the insistence that, so to speak, man's life in the next world is the only one he has. We have already considered this tendency within the origins of Christianity and Eastern monasticism. Today this may well be the commonly accepted notion of the contemplative experience in the West, but let us consider how this uncompromisingly pastoral celebration of the New Jerusalem triumphed over the georgic acceptance of and involvement with the sec-

ular order which has been observed in Augustine, Benedict,
Gregory, and Dante. One place to trace the progress of the new
Western, and yet older Eastern, emphasis would be the very
history of the Benedictine order, the evolution of which, "along
with the whole history of the religious life in the West," has
been called by the Benedictine historian "in large measure a
reaction against Benedict, a series of endeavors to restore the
elements of the older monachism which he discarded after
having made personal trial of them."[73] Thus, for example, in
the eleventh and twelfth centuries the contemplative leisure of
the Cluniac Benedictines so stressed the celebration of masses
and the singing of psalms and offices that there was no time left
in the day for manual labor.[74] There followed what might be
called a "georgic" reaction in the founding of the Cistercians
by Bernard of Clairvaux, who at least restored the dignity of
manual labor and service to others.[75] (Using the metaphor of
the soul's spiritual marriage to God, Bernard insisted that the
bliss of contemplative union must issue in the production of
"spiritual offspring," or good works.)[76] At the same time, however, the strenuously ascetic practices of the Cistercians (and,
even more so, of their own reformed branch, the Trappists)
have a certain resemblance to those austere features of Eastern
monasticism which are conspicuous by their absence in Benedict's *Rule*.[77]

Another way to describe the abatement of the georgic realization of Christian leisure would be to point to the increasing
influence of Pseudo-Dionysius' *Concerning Mystical Theology*
among the mystical theologians of the medieval West.[78] But,
however he may be said to have been anticipated, the climactic
example of this Western assimilation of the pastoral detachment of Eastern spirituality is the greatest mystical doctor of
the Renaissance, John of the Cross.

Significantly, he is also the author of what are, in the sense
already proposed, probably the greatest Christian pastorals,
The Spiritual Canticle and *The Dark Night*. As will be apparent from the discussion in the next section of this chapter,

these poems also owe a certain debt to the pastoral love poetry of the Renaissance.[79] They are first discussed here, however, because their central pastoral inspiration is from the Bible, specifically from The Song of Solomon and its use of such pastoral motifs as fragrant vineyards, laden fig trees, beds of spices, and gardens of lilies to endow the ecstasy of the "lovers" with symbolic life.[80] This richly detailed paradise will be John's way of representing the contemplative beatitude which Dante's Rachel, Mary, and Beatrice enjoy in the celestial paradise. Yet the difference between John's and Dante's paradises also illustrates the difference between the pastoral and georgic means of realizing the pastoral goal of Christian leisure. Even on earth, as John Frederick Nims astutely remarks, John is never far from heaven; Dante, even in heaven, is never far from earth: "As far as sixteenth-century Spain is concerned, John might as well have been writing at the very core of Dante's pearl-white moon."[81]

The impression is confirmed by an examination of the distinctively pastoral landscape which is the locale of John's poems. Even the restless quest of unfulfilled love which opens *The Spiritual Canticle* is enacted in a serene setting which, like the lilies of the field, is clothed in more majesty than Solomon and, like them too, pervasively invites the soul to be at ease and trust in the source of their beauty and joy.[82] These expectations are fulfilled in the poem's second movement, the celebration of the soul's "betrothal," giving all to her divine lover as she turns from the consideration of the creatures to the occupation of the saint, the exclusive enjoyment of contemplative leisure: "I no longer guard a flock, nor care for any other office. My only occupation is to love" (stanzas 18–19).

As Bernard had used the metaphor of the soul's mystical marriage to God in order to give a certain sanction to the activity necessary to produce "spiritual offspring," John invokes it to preclude all other attachments. To see how far we have come from the Western georgic resolution of work and leisure, consider the poet's introductory note to the next stanza:

For a very little of this pure love is more precious
. . . even though the soul appear to be doing nothing, than are all these works together. . . . Therefore
if any soul should have aught of this degree of solitary love, great wrong would be done to it, and to
the Church, if, even but for a brief space, one should
endeavor to busy it in active or outward affairs, of
however great moment. . . . I have said what I have
in order to explain this next stanza, for therein the
soul herself makes reply to all those that impugn this
her holy leisure and that desire her to be ever working, and making great display.[83]

The twentieth stanza itself is a haunting expression of the
absolute withdrawal necessary for this apprehension of the
timeless. Though he uses the language of exile, he is ecstati-
cally Vergil's Tityrus, not the alienated Meliboeus:

> *pues ya si en el exido*
> *de oy mas no fuere vista ni hallada*
> *direis que me he perdido*
> *que andando enamorada*
> *me hize perdidiza, y fui ganada.*

> If I'm not seen again
> in the old places, on the village ground
> say of me: lost to men.
> Say I'm adventure-bound
> for love's sake. Lost (on purpose) to be found.

The canticle's third movement celebrates the consummation
of the mystical marriage. Like the rest of the poem, it is sus-
ceptible to intricate allegorical explanation, but here, if anywhere, the lines make their first and deepest impress by the
immediate effect of the pastoral symbolism, and its erotic and
biblical implications, as the lover welcomes the bride:

> *Entrado se ha la esposa*
> *en el ameno huerto desseado*
> *y a su sabor reposa*
> *el cuello reclinado*
> *sobre los dulces bracos de el amado.*

> *Debaxo de el mancano*
> *alli comigo fuiste desposada*
> *alli te di la mano*
> *y fuiste reparada*
> *donde tu madre fuera violada.*

> (stanzas 27–28)

> She enters, the bride closes,
> soft, the enchanting garden dreams foretold her.
> Gracefully she reposes;
> my arms enfold her,
> her throat affectionate upon my shoulder.

> Under the apple tree
> the words of our betrothal and their spell:
> I took you tenderly,
> hurt virgin, made you well
> where all the scandal on your mother fell.

With their assurance of a paradise given again to one detached from worldly involvement, the lines lead us back to the scriptural resources of the Christian pastoral tradition and to its pristine expression in the monastic foundations of the desert. If they do not display the wide and complex range of experiences and responsibilities which characterize the georgic tradition of the medieval West, this very narrowness and simplicity may be said to generate their own kind of perfection. One does not find, perhaps, even in the celestial paradise of Dante, the same unqualified enjoyment of free time as is imaged here in the garden, to which, as the saint explains, God has been compared "by reason of the delectable and sweet repose which the soul finds in Him."[84]

At the same time, of course, there were other ways of conceiving "delectable and sweet repose" which were quick to emerge in those areas of experience from which the Christian pastoral vision had withdrawn and which, in his time, the Spanish mystic sought to recapture for Christianity. The secular renovation of the pastoral mode can be discerned in the celebration, as "given," of the values of romantic love or of poetry itself, the combination of which could be called courtly human-

ism or "courtesy." This redefinition of the form (which of
course also entailed the revival of the classical models) is glo-
riously evident in the Renaissance profusion of pastoral poetry,
which, if it is not the distinctive form of that era, was certainly
more widely sanctioned then than ever before or since. As the
very title of a representative collection like the "Muses Elizium" suggests, the pastoral landscape afforded a most congenial
symbolism for the imaginative quest for the happy island which
also bears a sovereign's name. In no other period was the pastoral mode more suited to poetry about the power of poetry:

> Decay nor age there nothing knowes,
> There is continuall youth,
> As time on plant or creature growes
> So still their strength renewth.
>
> The poets paradise this is,
> To which but few can come;
> The muses onely bower of blisse
> Their deare Elizium.[85]

Here we begin to realize that, like all poetry of its kind, this
is not a private alternative to the medieval vision of, say, Dante's sacred wood but the affirmation of certain new but still
publicly sanctioned values—even when "Eliza" is dead. What
we have, it will be seen, is something like the replacement of
one cult by another. The Renaissance pastoral is not merely
the revival of a classical form but the articulation of a novel
cultural ideal. The origins of this "paradise on earth" should
be looked for centuries earlier, even before Dante, in that revolution in attitude compared to which, as C. S. Lewis would
shock us into discovering, "the Renaissance is a mere ripple on
the surface of literature."[86] For the poetry of "courtly love" (or
whatever name we give this poetry) celebrated (among other
related results) an exciting new vision of free time, the pastoral
quality of which entertains any reader who enters the garden
(which is to say, "the court") of *The Romance of the Rose* and
observes the leisurely doorkeeper, Oiseuse:

> It seemed from her attire
> That she was little used to business,
> When she was combed, adorned, and well arrayed,
> Her daily task was done. A joyful time—
> A year-long, carefree month of May—was hers,
> Untroubled but by thoughts of fitting dress.
>
> . . . .
>
> Without another word
> The gate by Idleness was opened wide;
> I entered then upon that garden fair.
> When once I was inside, my joyful heart
> Was filled with happiness and sweet content.
> You may right well believe I thought the place
> Was truly a terrestrial paradise,
> For so delightful was the scenery
> That it looked heavenly; it seemed to me
> A better place than Eden for delight,
> So much the orchard did my senses please.[87]

Here, to use Dante's figures, we have a delinquent Matilda endowed with the happiness of a Beatrice; in this "better place than Eden" we have indeed a stopping place and not a starting point. "A god has granted this ease," and his name this time is Love. There is of course more to the poem than this excerpt, such as the disappointments and miseries of the lover, but one begins to understand why, during "the waning of the Middle Ages," as Huizinga demonstrates, the form of the classical pastoral became such a popular convention: "The lover or poet thinks himself a shepherd too, all contact with reality is lost, all things are transferred to a sunlit landscape full of the singing of birds and playing of reedpipes, where even sadness assumes a sweet sound. The faithful shepherd continues to resemble the faithful knight only too closely; after all, it is courtly love transposed into another key."[88]

As I have tried to suggest, however, an awareness of the origins of the Renaissance pastoral in the myth of love's young dream ought not lead to a deprecation of the form as "escapist," as even Huizinga seems to insinuate. On the contrary, this sin-

gularly artificial bucolic world loses "all contact" only with
those realities from which its culture, in its most civilized aspirations, would also be redeemed. A *locus classicus* for this interpretation of the civic quality of Renaissance pastoral poetry
would be a sequence such as the tenth canto of Spenser's sixth
book; there, amid the rural pleasance, and with characters
which might have inhabited the original allegory of love, the
poet finds the emblem of his civilization in the pastoral dance
of the Three Graces around his beloved:

> These three on men all gracious gifts bestow,
>   Which decke the body or adorne the mynde,
>   To make them louely or well fauoured show,
>   As comely carriage, entertainement kynde,
>   Sweete semblaunt, friendly offices that bynde,
>   And all the complements of curtesie:
>   They teach vs, how to each degree and kynde
>   We should our selues demeane, to low, to hie;
> To friends, to foes, which skill men call Ciuility
>   (*Faerie Queene* 6. 10. 23)

Though not always this explicitly, the Renaissance pastoral
of love and courtesy is a *public* celebration; it is escapist only
in the sense that the culture which nourishes the values it
idealizes can be called escapist.

Renaissance Transformations of Georgic:
Secular and Sacred Dimensions

It might be observed, however, that there were other cultural
values of a more pragmatically civil stamp and that even in the
sixth book of the *Faerie Queene* the pastoral vision of Mount
Acidale must yield to the overriding imperatives of the heroic
action which can subdue forces, like the Blatant Beast, against
which courtesy is powerless. As Harry Berger, Jr., puts it,
"poetry, having triumphed, must dissolve its triumph again
and again to show that it is still engaged in the ongoing process of life where experience is not yet ordered"[89] (Similarly,
one might recall that the House of Holiness in the first book

is by no means the immediate goal for the Red Cross Knight but rather, like Odysseus' Phaeacian experience, provides an incentive for his return to involvement and to earning through action the delights which are there prefigured.)

Just as the Homeric example served to introduce the "civic leisure" of the Greek *polis*, the Spenserian passages call to mind its Renaissance counterpart. For this new secular resolution of public responsibility and private recreation, action and contemplation, work and leisure, was, as might be expected, largely modeled upon a classical civic ideal. But this conception of "the state as a work of art" (to use the resonant Hegelian title of Burckhardt's first chapter) was by no means an automatic corollary of the classical revival. Within the frame of the present book, an interesting introduction to the civic leisure of the Renaissance is provided by the evolving reputation of that exemplar of the Roman civic and practical temper, Cicero. Cicero had lived in retirement, but only because of the pressures of the civil wars; indeed, his absence from our previous discussion of Roman civic leisure was dictated by what seemed to be (unlike Vergil's) his unequivocal distrust of free time. For Cicero, solitary leisure could be justified only by its public and active effects.[90] And yet, as Hans Baron has demonstrated in a truly fascinating study, "As a rule, the Cicero of the Middle Ages down to the twelfth century was disguised as a monastic scholar. The Roman citizen was doomed to be represented as a despiser of marriage and of woman, and of the cares of an active life."[91]

By the thirteenth century, in a development which Baron links to the growing importance of the civic order's claims, Cicero began to be recognized for what he was, a champion of the active life.[92] The crucial discovery took place in 1345 when Petrarch found the letters to Atticus in which the Roman statesman protested his unwillingness to retire and displayed his still feverish interest in politics. For Petrarch, who anticipated Montaigne in his retired humanism, the evidence was scandalous; but for the next generation of Florentine humanists, *Cicero Novus* (as he was called in the title of a book by Bruni, to distinguish him from the medieval figure) became a type of the

ideal union of political commitment and literary or philosophical recreation.[93] The state as a work of art was to be fulfilled in art as a work of state—an emergent ideal which (in
another place) Baron does not hesitate to compare to the civic
inspiration of the Greek *polis,* persuasively citing Bruni's 1428
Oratio Funebris as the Florentine equivalent of Pericles' famous tribute to Athens' assimilation of private interests into
public concerns.[94]

Fully to describe the proliferation of this secular ideal would
be to assess the rise of the modern state and the aspirations of
nationalist culture. Certainly among the classical literary genres
this vision of the good city irradiates that Renaissance form
which owes so much to Vergil's epic. In the revival of epic we
can also see the rediscovery of that classical "glory" which had
been transformed by Christianity: to contemplate it is to enjoy
the leisure of a new secular civic context. "The epic," writes
Thomas Greene, "is the poem which replaces divine worship
with humanistic awe. . . . It is the City of man, not of God,
which Tasso evokes in the last sentence of his discourse . . . ;
he saw the epic as 'Some very noble city full of magnificent
and royal dwellings, adorned with temples and palaces, and
with other royal and marvelous buildings.' "[95] This civic allegiance can be variously felt too in that distinctive genre of the
humanistic *paideia,* inspired by such works as Plato's *Republic,*
Cicero's *De Oratore,* and Quintilian's *Institutiones Oratoriae,*
which Greene in another place has aptly termed the "institute":
"Ideal portraits of a society or institution or occupation." In
his brilliant discussion of the humanistic "formation" or (more
transcendent) "transformation" of the self, Greene suggests the
range and complexity of this genre, inspired at the center by
the prospect of a new City of Man and often by a new vision
of what I have termed civic leisure, as it was variously brought
to imaginative life in "the portraits of an ideal society (More
and Bacon), of a family (Alberti), a prince (Pontano and Machi-
avelli), a courtier (Castiglione), a magistrate (Elyot), a gentleman (Della Casa and Spenser, in their very different versions),
a schoolmaster (Ascham), a poet (Minturno and any number

of other authors of *artes poeticae*), a lover (Ficino, Bembo, Leone Ebreo)."[96]

To conclude this account of the Renaissance transformation of earlier Christian versions of civic leisure, it is especially fitting to consider the "institutes" of two other authors whose writings radically redefine the traditions of the kinds of religious communities they had known in their lives: Erasmus and Rabelais.

The indictment of monastic culture is of course central to the urbane mischief of the *Praise of Folly*; but years before its publication, when Erasmus was scarcely twenty and a member of a community of Augustinian Canons Regular, he wrote in earnest a praise of that same folly, his *De Contemptu Mundi*, a work which shares more than its title with the imaginative world of a Bernard of Clairvaux but which, in retrospect at least, also heralds its transformation.[97] Written to persuade a young friend, Jodocus, of the vanity of worldly pleasures and the validity of contemplative joy, the work's double emphasis illustrates both its traditional and its novel character. In its seven chapters of repudiation of the world the book reads like a summary of many of the images and themes which have governed our previous discussions: the great world is likened to a sea in a storm, flight to a safe port is imperative, the example of Ulysses is lauded—especially when stopping up his ear to the sirens (*De Contemptu Mundi* 1. 1035–36). Most significantly, in a rich concentration of these images, the contemplative harbor which is urged upon the reader is epitomized in a quotation from nothing other than Vergil's Ninth Eclogue, lines 39–43: "Who (unless really deprived of vision) would not see that it is far more sure, more pleasant, and more delightful to stroll without fear through such lovely and green meadows than to be whirled with perpetual anxiety among so many images of death?" (2. 1036–37). Vergil's lines, to be sure, are an erotic invitation by Moeris to Galatea to enjoy a rosy spring, in contrast to the "perpetual" spring Erasmus offers his Jodocus. As Erasmus uses the playful source, he makes it even more Vergilian than Vergil himself, perfectly illustrating the Christian appropriation of civic pastoral: enjoying his perpetual spring, his speaker, unlike Vergil's more Theocritean Moeris, has the free time which the god had given Tityrus in the First Eclogue. And again true to the spirit of Vergilian pastoral, this perpetual spring is an emblem of the good city, the Jerusalem to which later we are exhorted to awaken from our sleep here in Babylon (8. 1044).

Erasmus devoted the second half of the book to the delights of that new world to which the solitary contemplative is admitted. Much of the argument seems quite traditional in its insistence that greater liberty, tranquillity, and pleasure are enjoyed out of the secular world than in it. Significantly, though, the pleasures of this new life receive a distinctive emphasis which will be the characteristic affirmation of this author long after he has ceased to depend on the monastic context. Not only Bernard but Epicurus, we are told, would prefer this life's superior joys, as we find them vividly imagined in a rapturous account of the contemplative's "paradise" that already seems to betoken a more humanistic potential. This is the paradise of poets and philosophers, we are told. Everything is full of delight: the meadow is green with grass, gleaming as if painted; gorgeous are the colors of the roses reddening, of the lilies glistening like snow, of the purple violet beckoning, while the tawny thyme breathes out sweet odors (11. 1052).

When the *De Contemptu Mundi* was finally published in 1521, a somewhat disenchanted Erasmus added an introduction and, especially, a twelfth chapter warning against the manifold potential for abuse of the monastic ideal.[98] The dream of a contemplative paradise, however, continued to exercise his imagination. It was to find its fullest realization not in the tradition of that early work but in a new vision of Christian leisure informed by a more sympathetic view of the secular, humanistic community. We have seen how Bernard of Clairvaux could celebrate the rural isolation of the contemplative as a means of apprehending the true Jerusalem; there is no better introduction to the distinctive achievement of Erasmus than his witty response to the letter of Bernard in which the saint promised wisdom in the woods to a contemplative who would learn from rocks and trees what no master could teach. Trees such as these, muses Erasmus, must surely be wise enough to sit in the professorial seat of the theologian or perhaps to be transformed, like Vergil's, into nymphs. "What can trees teach men?" he continues wryly. "Perhaps these are descendants of the Tree of Knowledge or of those which followed Orpheus: are they perchance philosophers imprisoned by some god in woodland shapes?" He then recalls the opening of the *Phaedrus*, where Socrates declares that he can learn nothing from fields and trees but learns from men in the city. "Why then did Bernard prefer to dwell among the oaks—unless, perhaps, France rejoices in trees more learned than any Greece has ever had?"[99]

In our discussion of Bernard and his tradition we tried to describe a certain kind of civic consciousness, if only because it would not seem apparent to a later reader—such as Erasmus. The city which Erasmus does envisage as the proper sphere of humane leisure is more like the familiar secular *polis* introduced in Baron's account of "civic humanism." So, Erasmus can insist, "No man is born to himself, no man is born to idleness. Your children are begotten not to yourself alone, but to your country; not to your country alone, but to God."[100] And yet the last dimension may also serve to illustrate the full complexity of Erasmus' vision of the good city: how much, we might say, it still owes to a Platonic and Christian model, which, to recall Socrates' response to Glaucon, is not to be found anywhere in this world but is the creation of a distinctive *paideia*. The republic of letters is the ultimate city of the great humanist. It is that special community, and not a mere cosmopolitanism, which, I believe, inspired Erasmus when, in the famous story, he rejected the citizenship of Zurich, declaring that he would rather be "a citizen of the whole world than of a single city."[101]

The most memorable affirmations of the city Erasmus sought can be found, appropriately, in the series of *Colloquia Familiaria* he wrote as an exercise to improve the Latin of school-

boys.[102] These festive dialogues recollect, concentrate, and renew so many of the motifs we have already noticed that one
begins to see how, in a culture to which those precedents were
more immediately available, such a book should have become
one of the most popular works of its age. If one had to choose
one work whose rehabilitation might be promoted in these
pages, it would be difficult to find one more engaging than this
neglected masterpiece.

The attraction of most of these vivacious "Colloquies" would
seem to be precisely their pervasive air of leisurely communion
in a public or transcendent context, their sense that there is
no such thing as a feast without gods—and that every humane
conversation can be a kind of feast. This is most evident, of
course, in the half-dozen *convivia* or *symposia* that enrich the
collection with their manifest celebration of the good city.
Thus "The Fabulous Feast" begins by choosing a master of
the revels:

> POLYMYTHUS: It's not right for a feast to be unregu-
> lated and lawless, any more than it's proper for
> a well-constituted state to be without laws and
> prince.
> GALASINUS: So heartily do I agree with this that I'll
> assent in the name of the whole people.

Similarly, in "The Sober Feast" the symposium begins in a
garden which blends the classical with the Christian dream of
ease:

> ALBERT: Ever seen anything more delightful than
> this garden?
> BARTHOLINUS: The Fortunate Isles have scarcely any-
> thing more pleasing, I dare say.
> CHARLES: Indeed I seem to see the paradise for which
> God appointed Adam guardian and gardener.

Significantly, too, that colloquy is literally a banquet of the
spirit, a feast of reason, for the characters soon compensate for
their lack of food and drink with the riches of their minds,

exchanging philosophical anecdotes instead of merely external delights.

This internalizing process is even more manifest in another conversation lacking an overt feast, this one between a Carthusian monk and a soldier. The soldier voices the familiar argument of the active as against the contemplative life. The monk's replies, however, are notable for their transformation of the medieval monastic life. We are not very far from the Abbey of Thélème. As Craig Thompson reminds us, the monk's talk is "more suggestive of a life given to quiet study than to devotional exercises, and he stresses the special pleasantness of monastic life rather than its strictness."[103] His cell is small, he admits, but, "Here's the whole world, to my imagination; and this map shows the entire earth, over which I wander in thought more enjoyably and safely than one who sails to the new islands" (p. 597). Despite the fact that the speaker belongs to an austere anchoritic tradition, pledged to silence, the life envisioned here is continually festive and rarely solitary. The ancient prophets and the pagan philosophers, poets, and astrologers sought solitude, the monk muses. And when solitude becomes tedious, there is always the conversation of friends— I have sixteen friends in everything I do. More friends come to visit me than I need. You call this a lonely life? As for the vow of silence, "Conversation is the more delightful for occasional interruptions" (p. 597). Significant, too, is the way in which this new vision of civic leisure still preserves enough of the older tradition to enjoy its sanction even as it transforms it. Even in solitude, says the monk, I enjoy wittier company than most boon companions:

> You see this book of the Gospels? In it one talks with me who long ago, as an eloquent companion of the two disciples on the road to Emmaus, caused them to forget the hardship of their journey but made their hearts burn most fervently in their wonder at his enchanting speech. In this book Paul speaks to me, in this Isaiah and the rest of the prophets. Here the honey-tongued Chrysostom converses

> with me, here Basil, here Augustine, here Jerome,
> here Cyprian, and other teachers as learned as they
> are eloquent. Do you know any other talkers so de-
> lightful that you would compare them with these?
> Or in such company, which never fails me, do you
> suppose solitude can become tedious? [p. 598].

To hear these names in this new light is to perceive what has
begun to happen to the values they stood for at the start of
this chapter. If, in the old saying, Socrates brought philosophy
down from heaven to earth, the Socratic achievement of Erasmus is surely to have transformed citizens of the heavenly
Jerusalem into the urbane, witty participants in these feasts
of reason. The city in the desert is becoming a republic of
letters. If in his *De Contemptu Mundi* Erasmus risked the
comparison of Christian beatitude to Epicurean happiness, it
is here accentuated to a contrast in which the former outdoes
the latter on its own terms: "There are no people more Epicurean than godly Christians"; and, as we proceed to discover,
"To the world they appear to mourn, but in fact they're joyful
and live agreeably, 'smeared all over with honey,' as the saying
goes: so that compared with these, Sardanapalus, Philoxenus,
Apitius, or any other famous voluptuary experiences a sad and
miserable life" (p. 751).

The one colloquy which draws all of these themes and images
together in a master image of the Erasmian vision of the new
leisure is the incomparable *Convivium Religiosum*, the "Godly
Feast." No work considered in this book will evoke and blend
so delicately so many of the classical and Christian motifs we
have discussed. No other selection offers such an inviting prospect of the new *polis* of Christian "humanism," in which, however paradoxically, each of those terms enforces the others.

So understood, the *Convivium Religiosum* is at once more
serious and more delightful than the Carthusian's more strenuous and more whimsical exercise in protesting too much, for
here Erasmus blends the reassertion of radical Pauline Christianity, which was the great inspiration of the Reformation,
with the humanistic recovery of the Renaissance, which to a

considerable degree provoked the reaction of the Reformation. While rejecting superstitious "works," Erasmus can still affirm the sacramental character of simple hospitality. With his radical Christology, ignoring the cult of the saints, he can still ask "Saint Socrates" to pray for him.

The appeal of the dialogue is readily apparent in the prologue, which provides the occasion for the feast itself. Eusebius and Timothy are walking in the fresh and smiling countryside, musing on how the smoky cities are enjoyed by such people as moneylenders and merchants and, for the same greedy reason, priests and monks, who are oblivious to the pastoral and georgic aspect of their faith. Freed from the crowded milieu "of the blind and their profit," the friends find that nature is not silent but speaks to them everywhere. Such language seems to recall the pastoral vision of Bernard, which we have seen Erasmus disdain, but it is important to see that he is not celebrating the landscape for his own sake but for the very thing he did not see in Bernard's rapture; that is, he celebrates it as the emblem of a new community, like the one Socrates and Phaedrus create outside Athens. With such companions as Socrates and Phaedrus, says Timothy, nothing could be more enjoyable than country life. "Would you care to try it?" Eusebius asks, and offers his modest country place for a luncheon meeting.

When, the next day, Timothy and his friends arrive at the estate of Eusebius, one is struck, even before the feast, by the kind of free time embodied here. They have come early, they say, in order to have leisure to walk around and look over (*otium lustrandi visendique*) this palace worthy of a man whose independence and contentment make him a king. As we soon discover too, the freedom enjoyed by Eusebius is not that of privacy and solitude but is the consummation of an expansive vision of the good community. This is manifest as early as his opening invitation to his friends to pluck some flowers from the outermost garden. "Don't be sparing, for I allow whatever grows here to be almost public property. The door of this courtyard is never shut except at night" (p. 673).

The civic quality of the house is even more manifest upon closer inspection of its architectural details: we find ourselves "hearing" as well as seeing its inscriptions and emblems. The house is literally a participant in the conversation of the friends. As much a rhetorical as an architectural delight, the estate embodies the Word, the divine Logos incarnate, and the analogous creating word of humanistic culture. Thus, as one enters into "salvation," the door from the world speaks its maxims in Latin, Greek, and Hebrew (p. 673), while an image of Jesus in the chapel not only points heavenward but, in the same languages, greets the guests with the glad tidings of his incarnation (p. 673). The fountain too speaks of a deeper reality, refreshing those who labor and are heavy burdened, as do the gardens, which must be Epicurean, Timothy surmises (p. 673). The whole place is designed for pleasure, says Eusebius, the host. It's not luxurious, but every aspect of the house is talkative, so that one never feels lonesome (p. 674). This *domus loquacissima* has even more to communicate when, proceeding more surely into the domain of art, the company notices the narrow channel of painted cement that looks like marble (and which in georgic fashion also performs the useful function of carrying off kitchen wastes), the garden's artificial hedges, and, finally, the three galleries with their painted gardens.

One garden outside is not enough to hold all the plants that we have here, Eusebius explains; besides, this one flourishes even in midwinter. The genius of nature is admired outside, and, inside, the imagination of the artist; "but in each [is admired] the goodness of God" (p. 674). Hence the paintings themselves are enjoyed as participants in the festive dialogue of a symposium, and the organic process illuminated is instinct with a georgic and ethical significance. For nothing is idle here, says the guest, Timothy; everything is doing or speaking something: the owl which tells us in Greek to be prudent, or the scorpion in the next gallery, announcing that God has found out the guilty, or the dolphin, the friend to man, in the third gallery, struggling against the crocodile.

Entertaining as they are, "these sights feast the eyes but don't fill the belly," and the guests are urged to hasten from the transformation of life into art to the feast and conversation that transform art into life (p. 675). Appropriately, the feast itself is introduced by one final garden, this time most specifically an emblem of the good city which is the "kingdom" of Eusebius. On one side are herbs, some for the table, some for medicines; on the other side is an open meadow with an orchard, in which Eusebius is domesticating many exotic trees. This georgic vista has its high point, appropriately, in an aviary, where even the birds most irreconcilable by nature have been trained to join in the conversation of Eusebius and his guests. Finally, at the end of the orchard, our last glimpse is of that familiar georgic model of the good society, the kingdom of the bees (p. 676). *Tu vincis vel ipsum Alcinoun*, says the chief guest Timothy, "you outdo Alcinous himself."

Just as our interpretation of Odysseus' Phaeacian experience tried to describe a concentric pattern of city, garden, and feast, so all these lovely details of the "talking" scene and house finally point inward and upward to the even more humanistic liberation of a symposium. Such a dimension is already felt in such a slight detail as the washing of hands before eating. The niceties of etiquette here are invested with a virtually sacramental significance, recalling the Last Supper (p. 676). "May he mingle with all our food and drink," says Eusebius, "so that everything taste of him, but most of all may he penetrate our hearts. . . . For so great a guest, you shall hear (if you don't object) a short passage from Sacred Scripture, but in such fashion that this won't interfere with your eating eggs and lettuce if you like" (p. 677).

The text selected for such communal entertainment is the first three verses of the twenty-first chapter of Proverbs. It is a passage our exegetes will compel the reader to recollect:

> The king's heart is in the hand of the Lord, as
>   the rivers of water:
> he turneth it whithersoever he will.
> Every way of a man is right in his own eyes;
> but the Lord pondereth the hearts.
> To do justice and judgment
> is more acceptable to the Lord than sacrifice.

As if they were beginning a parlor game, the group divides to interpret the text according to its three parts. That the speakers are not professional theologians is no accident, for what is most striking in their symposium is the general tendency away from external forms and restrictions to internal faith and liberation. Thus, explicating the first sentence, Eusebius begins with a discussion of the independence of a king's power from the criticism of his subjects: only God can judge him (p. 677). He extends the comparison with "rivers of water" to a plea for the proper education of a prince: just as a ruler's mind can be roused to fury like a large river, the best remedy is to shape his character by sacred teaching "while he's still a boy and doesn't realize he's a ruler" (p. 678). Deepening that perception, Timothy suggests a more radical Christian interpretation of the term "king," one which perfectly expresses the kind of insight Erasmus shared with the Protestant reformers. "King," he says, can be understood to mean

> the perfect man, who with his bodily passions under control, is governed solely by the Holy Spirit. . . . Moreover, to compel such a man to conform to human laws is perhaps inappropriate. Instead he should be left to his Master, by whose spirit he is led; he is not to be judged by those conditions through which the weak and simple are drawn, in one way or another, to true godliness. But if he does anything unrighteously, we ought to say with Paul, "God hath received him," "To his own master he standeth or falleth." Likewise: "He that is spiritual judgeth all things, yet he himself is judged of no man." Therefore nobody may prescribe to such men, but the Lord who set the bounds to sea and rivers has the heart of the king in his hand and directs it whithersoever he wills [p. 678].

It is regrettable that the distinguished American translation of the *Colloquies* does not indicate the sources of these quotations in Paul's Epistles (Rom. 14:3–4; 1 Cor. 2:15), for Erasmus alludes here not only to specific texts but to a more inclusive context of characteristically Pauline arguments on the radical nature of Christianity's liberation from the external limitations of the old Law, such as the prescriptions on clean and unclean food. Thus the first quotation stresses the king-like liberation of the Christian, answerable only to his transcendent "master" and not subject to the dietary laws which are the subject of the fourteenth chapter of the Epistle to the Romans. Indeed, if one were to choose an epigraph from that chapter that perfectly captures the Pauline character of the "godly feast," it would be the famous reminder that "the kingdom of God is not meat and drink but righteousness and peace and joy in the Holy Ghost". (Rom. 14:17). Jesus, one might say, has liberated the community Eusebius describes *from* foods *for* festivity.

The same vision of a new yet very old Christian civic leisure transforms the second quotation. Here the tribute to the freedom of one who judges spiritually (what later readers might call imaginatively) is the climax of Paul's contrast between the wisdom of this world and a faith that transcends mundane perception (1 Cor. 2:14).

The distinctive aspect of the matrix of these quotations is more explicitly stated in the interpretation of the other two sentences. Sophronius unabashedly exploits the Pauline potential in the second and intensifies the previous insistence on the deliverance of the individual soul from the bondage of external regulation, whether exerted by priesthood, celibacy or marriage, retirement or political action. Paul would have us be ourselves, says Sophronius, with only God above as judge. After all, in God's eyes, there are times when it is better to feast than to fast, to violate the rules of the Sabbath, to marry. The third scriptural sentence, with its even more manifest potential for similar interpretation, receives ample treatment from Theophilus (p. 679), who begins by invoking a parallel in Hosea—"For I desired mercy and not sacrifice: and the knowledge of God more than burnt offerings" (Hos. 6:6)—to introduce the exemplary instance of Jesus dining at the house of Levi, the publican, and answering the Pharisees with a justification of that feast that looks beyond the fulfillment of the Law: "I will have mercy and not sacrifice: for I am not come to call the righteous, but sinners to repentance" (Matt. 9:13). Asked to explain "mercy" and "sacrifice," Theophilus gives an extensive account of the dangers of substituting "corporeal rites" for an internal faith animated by charity. "Keeping the Sabbath," he says, "is a sacrifice; to be reconciled with your brother, an act of mercy." Jesus, after all, healed on the Sabbath and told those who reproached him that "the Sabbath was made for man, and not man for the Sabbath" (Mark 2:27). As these interpretations converge in a justification for radical Christian humanism, their relevance to this particular gathering of friends is also dramatized. Here, where brothers are reconciled, the authentic Sabbath is being celebrated. Their feast is a holy day because it is a holiday. That this is so is underscored by the continuing attention to the food after each interpretation (pp. 678–80): the eggs and greens that provide the "ovation" after the first discussion; next, the capon, whimsically contrasted to those who have made themselves eunuchs for the sake of the kingdom of heaven; and, finally, the invitation to the main course, of mutton, capon, and four partridges. For the central mystery of the dialogue (and perhaps of Erasmian humanism generally) is that the whole discussion of liberation *from* the laws regarding food has liberated the friends *for* the heightened enjoyment of their food. Thus, having just agreed that the Sabbath was but a mere "corporeal" rite, Eusebius can observe that, while they have been feasting their minds, they have been neglecting their bodies. Similarly, Timothy regards the luncheon as Epicurean or sybaritic, but Eusebius, whose little estate has provided most of the modest fare, ironically terms it *vix Carmeliticum*, scarcely enough for a Carmelite. The reader perceives that it is both of these together—indeed, the one because of the other, Epicurean because scarcely Carmelite.

This festive affirmation has its climax in the celebration of the wine, itself served in cups that, like the walls of the house, "speak" to the guests and appropriately prompt them to renew their conversation. In what is to be the climactic instance of scriptural exegesis, Eulalius produces his richly bound copy of Paul's Epistles and reads from the sixth chapter of First Corinthians: "All things are lawful unto me, but all things are not expedient: all things are lawful for me, but I will not be brought under the power of any." Though the immediate issue, again, is the law regarding food, Eulalius also sees the broader implications of the liberation, as, for example, in Paul's "being all things to all men that some might be saved" (1 Cor. 9:22; 10:33). It was permissible, therefore, to eat anything one liked, for "to the pure all things are pure" (*omnia mundi mundis*, p. 680). Erasmus presumed, of course, that his readers would recognize that classic text of Pauline theology from the letter to Titus (Tit. 1:15), here quoted in the Latin of Jerome's Vulgate. The famous phrase resonantly proclaims the liberty of the Christian from the Law, and that very freedom also suffuses the next and perhaps most engaging section of the symposium, the celebration of classical authors. Just as the friends are liberated for food and wine, they can delight in the leisurely contemplation of—and with—Cicero or Socrates. Speaking frankly among friends, Eusebius confesses that he can't read Cicero's moral discourses without sometimes kissing the book and blessing that pure heart, divinely inspired as it was. He would gladly let all of Scotus and others of his sort perish rather than one book of Cicero or Plutarch (p. 682).

What most commands the reverence of the friends is what might be called the Pauline aspect of the classical authors, their equivalent of the Christian liberation from the external works of the Law. Thus it is significant that Cicero's *De Senectute* is singled out for praise, especially that section where Cato declines to start life again as a child if he could. He will not complain of life, but he departs from it as from an inn, not a home: Nature gave us here a place to stop, not to settle down (p. 692). What Uranius appreciates most is the paradoxical affirmation that Cato nevertheless does make: "Nor am I sorry to have lived" (p. 682). Most Christians would say *that* only if at their deaths they could leave a pile of riches got by hook or crook, he says, but Cato left no such external treasure; his reason for thinking he had not lived in vain was his legacy of civic service: "He had been an honest, upright citizen of the republic and an incorruptible magistrate, and he left to posterity monuments of his virtue and industry" (p. 683).

The group is fascinated by how such affirmative enjoyment of life could coexist with the passage's overall insistence on detachment: "I depart as from an inn, not from a home." The analogies proliferate: Paul distinguishes a mere tabernacle, or *skēnos*, of the body from the soul's heavenly *oikia*, or home (2 Cor. 5:1–4), and that is why Jesus enjoins us to live as if we were soon to die (Matt. 25:42–44; Mark 13:31–32; Luke 21:36–37); and that reminds us of Paul's yearning to depart and be with Christ (Phil. 1:23). As with the discussion of the Pauline liberation from the dietary laws, the exchange has an immediate relevance to the theme and occasion of the present feast. If the mundane career of man is but an "inn," whence we must be prepared to depart, why, we might ask ourselves, does this most engaging of the *Colloquies* so invitingly dramatize the festive free time of that same transient situation? If we are never truly "at home" in this world, how can we account for the distinctive sense of homecoming in the inn-like hospitality of the elaborately detailed house of Eusebius?

Indeed, anyone who does hear the voice of Paul blending with that of Cicero's Cato might also realize that (as was even more the case with Cicero) a philosophic and religious detachment from the exigencies of time and history need not contradict an active and responsive involvement in those same currents. The quotation from Paul is itself but one half of the predicament he poses to himself; for not only does he desire to depart and be with Christ, but, as the next verse reminds us, "Nevertheless, to abide in the flesh is more needful for you. And having this confidence, I know that I shall abide and continue with you all for your furtherance and joy of faith" (Phil. 1:24–25).

To be "in" but not "of" the world sets up a tension as old as all those inviting stopping places that, we saw, were also starting points; Odysseus felt it in Phaeacia, Dante more recently in the Earthly Paradise. Yet, as in those earlier instances, what distinguishes the "inn," that is, the feast of Eusebius, is the degree to which it anticipates the liberation to be attained in the final city to which it summons its participants. What gives the community of this feast its unique character is the way its vision of civic leisure includes the very classical authors that a Jerome might have been tempted by—but, even more significantly, includes them for Jerome's reasons. Thus, more moving even than the works of Cicero's Cato, we are told, is the final speech of Socrates to Crito, with its manifest sense of the inadequacies of his own works, its radical commitment to a transcendent God. So at least Erasmus conceives of Socrates' deliverance from the secular city: "Diffident as he was about his own deeds, yet by reason of his earnest desire to obey the divine will, he conceived a strong hope that God in his goodness would accept them, because he had endeavored to live righteously" (p. 683). In this light, the following lines, the most famous of this colloquy, should be seen not so much as a slogan for a later and blander formulation of "Christian humanism" but as an insistence on a radical allegiance to the new city which transcends the classical *polis*:

> NEPHALIUS: An admirable spirit, surely, in one who has not known Christ and the Sacred Scriptures. And so, when I read such things of such men, I can hardly help exclaiming, "Saint Socrates, pray for us!"
>
> CHRYSOSTOM: As for me, there are many times when I do not hesitate to hope confidently that the souls of Vergil and Horace are sanctified.

It is poignant here to recall the exclusion of these authors, Vergil especially, from the rose-like City of Dante's final beatific contemplation, but it is even more important to see that they have been included here for reasons more radical than those that prompted Dante to exclude them. Cato and Socrates, Horace and Vergil, belong in the communion of saints celebrated at the feast of Erasmus because, in the context of Pauline Christianity, to revere them is to be liberated from "the

Law," which enjoins merely external and legalistic works and
ceremonies. That is why, more abruptly than a modern reader
might expect, the conversation immediately shifts from the
praise of classical authors to a criticism of the kind of external
observances that befuddle so many Christians when they should
in fact be more free even than Cato or Socrates. Chrysostom
complains that most Christians put too much faith in ceremonies, starting with the elaborate procedure of baptism, with
its exorcism, catechism, vowing, and abjuring before the child
is anointed, salted, and dipped. Soon he's anointed again in
confirmation, learns to confess, takes communion, learns to
fast and abstain. Next he either marries or takes orders and, in
either case, receives another sacrament. "All this I approve,"
says Chrysostom, "but their doing it from custom rather than
conviction I don't approve of." Most men trust to these ceremonies, he argues, and "lose no time in making money by hook
or crook and becoming enslaved to anger, lust, gluttony, ambition, until they come to death's door." There the ceremonies
are ready again: oils and the Eucharist, candles, crucifix, holy
water, indulgences, papal briefs, a lavish funeral. Surely, he
says, there must also be other more interior means of helping
us to depart this life with cheerfulness and Christian trust (pp.
683–84).

By now we can appreciate why this insistence on internal
liberation should paradoxically be fulfilled in the "external"
drama of the feast. "You preach piously and truly," responds
Eusebius, "but meanwhile nobody touches the food" (p. 684).
For the guests not only are freed from a dependence on merely
external ceremonies but themselves enact what might be called
the authentic ceremony—which is of course unceremonious.
Eusebius can offer nothing beyond a second course; there are
no exotic pheasants or woodcocks or Attic delicacies here, but
only the produce of the little garden previously surveyed. "You
see my hour of penury, not plenty," says the host; what he
offers is, he says, the kind of dish that would have overjoyed
"that good Christian monk Hilarion and a hundred companions of that age. For Paul and Anthony indeed it would have

been a month's provision." In the context of the present chapter, these allusions to the early city in the desert perfectly illustrate the evolution of the tradition we have been considering; equally interesting, however, and more characteristic of this feast, is the recovery of still earlier examples from the earliest Christian community. Timotheus declares that such a feast as theirs would not have been despised by Peter when he dwelt with Simon the tanner; nor would Paul have despised it, says Eusebius, when need compelled him to work nights as a tent-maker. "We owe this to God's goodness," responds Timotheus, "but I would rather go hungry with Peter and Paul, provided the lack of bodily nourishment were compensated by spiritual delights." Put so absolutely, such a preference prompts Eusebius to an answer (p. 684) that perfectly expresses the Pauline liberation of this new community from the limitations of mere external observance. "Rather let us learn from Paul," he says,

> both to abound and to suffer hunger. When there is lack, let us thank Jesus Christ for supplying us with means of self-control and patience; when there is plenty, we should thank the generosity of one who draws us by his gifts to love of himself. Enjoying in moderation what the divine goodness has provided, we ought to be mindful of the poor—who by God's will are without that in which we abound—in order that there may be occasion of mutual goodness by each to the other. . . . And well does this come to mind. Here, boy, tell my wife to send what's left of the roast to our Gudula. She's a neighbor who's pregnant and poor but blessed in spirit. Her husband, an idle spendthrift, died recently, leaving her nothing but a pack of children.

The homeliness of the last detail vividly captures the view of "good works" which the faith of Erasmus commends, in contrast to the merely ceremonial exercises which next provoke the scorn of Eusebius. Why should we adorn monasteries and churches at excessive cost, he asks, when meanwhile so many of Christ's living temples suffer want? He reports having seen in Britain the tomb of Saint Thomas covered with precious jewels. How much more preferable to give the jewels to the poor and decorate the tomb with branches and flowers! So too for the Carthusian monastery he saw in Italy, of solid marble. Why spend so much wealth in order for a few monks to sing in a marble church? All it does is attract a crowd for the wrong reasons (p. 685).

We notice too that, as in the previous discussions of scriptural texts, classical authors, and vain ceremonies, the abstract issue raised pertains to what is actually being dramatized at the feast. Here we have the alternative to the ornate tomb: the realm of branches and flowers, of charity not glory. (So insistent is Eusebius in his distrust of mere externals that he even advocates that gifts to the poor be distributed secretly.) We have been shown the valid alternative to the Carthusian monastery: the authentic contemplative community. For all its intricacy of symbolic detail, the house itself is not luxurious, Eusebius insists; after all, ironically, in these times "mendicants build more splendidly" (p. 685). Besides, the gardens daily pay tax to the needy, and every day he deprives his family of something in order to give it to the poor. The gardens were compared to those of Alcinous at the start of the dialogue, and that master image of civic leisure epitomizes the imaginative achievement of Erasmus here, where hospitality deepens into charity, nobility is humbled and therefore exalted, and the festive free time that Odysseus praised as the fairest thing there is flowers into interior liberation and communal contemplation.

In discussing the Christian transformation of Vergilian civic leisure, we found, in the Sermon on the Mount, the most memorable expression of the new vision of "the god who has granted this ease" to the humble and the dispossessed. This is why it is most significant that Eusebius should conclude his feast with a final scriptural explication of a passage from that discourse with which Matthew has Jesus begin his public ministry. Typically, the text is introduced (pp. 685–86) as something sweeter even than the choice desserts of the feast: "No man can serve two masters: for either he will hate the one and love the other; or else he will hold to the one and despise the other. Ye cannot serve God and mammon. Therefore I say unto you, Take no thought for your life, what ye shall eat . . . nor yet for your body, what ye shall put on. Is not the life more than meat and the body more than raiment?" (Matt. 6:24–25).

The lengthy discussion that follows, of why the first sentence's apparent tautology has the disjunctive "or," would hardly strike us today as a substitute for dessert, but its solution (opposing kinds of action, not persons) does illustrate a freedom from the letter of the law, a willingness to criticize creatively, and, in the best sense, "play" with the word because of a dedication to its spirit. In this symposium, exegesis and parlor game are one. So too, in the discussion of the second sentence, where the question is raised of reconciling its insistence on detachment with the later example of Paul working with his hands and rebuking the lazy (2 Thess. 3:8, 11–12). Timotheus offers two related responses, first, that the apostles were too busy preaching the gospel and could not be expected still to work as fishermen. Besides, he adds, "Christ did not forbid labor but anxiety." Nor is it said that the *sole* care of the Christian is the spreading of the gospel; it is simply his first and foremost care: "Seek ye first the kingdom of God and these things shall be added unto you" (Matt. 6:33). The host, Eusebius, however, offers a more radical challenge, concerned not with clothing but with survival: "Take no thought for your life what ye shall eat." His exegesis (p. 687) beautifully condenses the motifs we have been tracing. Committed to transcendence, he can simultaneously point to the heightened festivity which is the reward of the detached. Indeed, he need not even suggest the lilies of the field or the birds of the air; he need only notice the very feast at hand to find dramatic proof of the ease his God has granted.

> EUSEBIUS: . . . For if life is of great value, we should be the more zealous to preserve it.
> TIMOTHEUS: This argument does not dispel our uncertainty but adds to it.
> EUSEBIUS: But you misinterpret Christ's meaning. By this argument he increases our trust in the Father. If the benevolent Father gave freely and of his

own accord what is more precious, he will likewise
add what is more common. He who gave the soul
will not deny food; he who gave the body will add
clothing from somewhere. Relying on his kindness, therefore, we have no reason to be distracted
by anxiety over minor matters. What remains,
then, except to turn our whole care and zeal to
the love of heavenly things, using this world as
though we used it not; and, utterly rejecting earthly
riches, together with Satan and all his wiles, with
a whole and fervent heart serve God alone, who
will not forsake his children.

But meanwhile nobody touches the dessert.
Surely it's permissible to enjoy this, which is produced for us at home with no trouble at all.

By this time, as might be expected, the little community has
had enough to feast both their bodies and minds. Their final
rituals confirm the transcendent vision of Eusebius: washing
their hands as a symbol of an interior cleansing, and hearing
Eusebius conclude the hymn of thanksgiving from Chrysostom
with which the feast began. The human lord, whose "kingdom" has provided the feast which anticipates the joys of the
kingdom to come, next distributes parting gifts to the guests.
Like the estate and the feast, the gifts are modest in price but
rich in symbolic value; sometimes they are even enhanced with
a whimsical sense of their aptness to the particular guest: four
books (Solomon's *Proverbs*, Matthew's *Gospel*, Paul's *Epistles*,
and, significantly, Plutarch's *Moralia*), two clocks, a small lamp,
and a case of pens. The guests stroll through other parts of
the house not noticed in their opening tour, and it is again the
"talkative" or symbolic quality of the house that engages us.
In the summer courtyard, for example, not only do the sliding
windows save the inhabitants from the unpleasantness of the
seasons, but their paintings are at once pastoral and festive:
"When I lunch here, I seem to eat in a garden, not a house;
the walls too have flowers mingled with their green, and there
are quite good pictures. Here Christ keeps the Last Supper
with his chosen disciples." And here too are painted warnings

against those perversions of true festivity which also destroy the good city: Herod celebrating his birthday; Dives dining sumptuously while Lazarus is driven from the gates; Cleopatra swallowing a pearl; the Lapithae brawling; Alexander piercing Cletus. From the instructions of these pictures the guests proceed to the more usual place for such contemplation, the library, where Eusebius has "the main part" of his wealth. "Clearly," says Timotheus, "this place is hallowed, so radiant is everything" (p. 688).

What gives the library its special radiance is precisely that vision of the new city in which the Christian contemplative can enjoy the leisure of a citizen. In the center, a hanging globe puts all the world before our eyes, but we see it, and the regions painted on the walls, under the aspect of the other kingdom, represented by pictures of famous teachers and, preeminently, the triune divine teacher, who presides over the leisure of this community: "Christ seated on the mountain with his hand outstretched has the foremost place. The father appears above his head, saying 'Hear ye him.' With spreading wings the Holy Spirit enfolds him in dazzling light."

We begin to see why, in what might be supposed to be a mere interlude in their journey toward the attainment of that vision in the heavenly city, the guests and their host seem so at home in this "inn." What Bernard said of the pilgrim passing through his monastery might also be said of those at the house of Eusebius: they have found Jerusalem. In the same way, the final description of the galleries above the kitchen garden dissolves the limits of time and space and transports the contemplative into another country. In one the life of Jesus is related and illustrated: place names are added to enable the spectator to learn by which water or on which mountain an event occurred; captions speak forth the words of Jesus. Another gallery tells the same story but this time uses the appropriate figures and prophecies of the Old Testament. This contemplative prospect is the inmost revelation of this little community's gardens, rooms, feasts, and books. "Here I stroll sometimes," says Eusebius, "conversing with myself and meditating upon

that inexpressible purpose of God by which he willed to restore the human race through his son. Sometimes my wife, or a
friend pleased by sacred subjects, keeps me company." "Who
could be bored in this house?" replies Timotheus (p. 689),
rather like Telemachus marveling at Menelaus' house. There is
perhaps no finer example of the appropriation by the Christian
humanist of the monastic contemplative tradition of civic leisure.

And yet, as if cognizant of what we have termed the "georgic" awareness in that tradition, Eusebius has also included
reminders of a more active and mundane realm: along the tops
of the paintings are added, "as though supernumeraries," portraits of the popes and, across from them, portraits of the Cae-
sars, "to help one remember history." Indeed, at the very end,
in what is perhaps the most telling complication of the colloquy, Eusebius himself seems drawn to more active involvement
in the sphere of history. We sense this in the notice taken of a
small shed, where members of the household with contagious
diseases are isolated, and in the subsequent discussion of when
one should risk contact with the diseased. We hear it even more
urgently when the host invites the guests to stay and contemplate the house all day, while he departs. "Feast your eyes,
feast your minds," he says, "for I have business elsewhere" (p.
689).

The *neg-otium* which draws our Alcinous away from the
leisure of his festive estate is inspired by his allegiance to the
new city which his community already reflects in little. He is
"hunting," he says, not boars and stags, but friends, such as
one near death, whom he would counsel to depart as a Christian, or two who are quarreling, whom he would hope to
reconcile. In the most profound sense of the paradox of civic
leisure, Eusebius will do without leisure to have leisure. He
leaves his blessed island on a quest to make its promise come
true in a fallen world. In an unexpected but deeply relevant
reversal of the "inn" metaphor, it is the guests who are allowed
to linger at the house, freed for the moment from the pressures
of a return to time and anticipating their arrival "home." In

what is perhaps the most poignant detail in the colloquy, it is the saintly Alcinous, Eusebius, who must sacrifice his leisure and be so involved in his *negotia* that he cannot promise to return soon. "Not until I've tried everything," he says. "Hence I can't name a definite time. Meanwhile, enjoy yourselves with my things as with your own, and farewell" (p. 689). And yet in his very indifference to the *certum tempus*, his willingness to let his friends transfigure the festive moment *interim*, the *negotium* of Eusebius, like that described in earlier contexts of civic leisure, is itself still enlivened by the radical liberation which was at the center of the feast he had to leave in order to realize it more fully. This is perhaps the final significance of the quoted passages, in which Paul yearned for contemplative union with God yet still immersed himself in missionary work in the world from which he had been delivered. The friends at the feast pray that "the Lord Jesus will bless the going out and coming back of Eusebius," but it is equally important to see how both directions here are one. Eusebius can depart from the Phaeacian delights of his estate *tamquam hospitio*, as from an inn, because he is already and more profoundly living "at home" in the interior liberation of the god who has given this ease.

The *Convivium Religiosum*, so rich in its own right and so evocative of earlier works in this study, is yet so neglected that we have given it very full attention. Much less time need be devoted here to our other instance of the transformation of monastic civic leisure, the famous Abbey of Thélème in the *Gargantua* of Rabelais, who, like his contemporary, Erasmus, had his own personal experience of the religious orders. There is much in the majestic sprawl of his masterpiece that might be incorporated into the argument of this study, notably the humanistic *paideia* of Ponocrates and the robust heroism of that untypical monk, Friar John, in contrast to the bloodless self-seeking of Picrochole. Nevertheless, the Abbey of Thélème, built after the defeat of Picrochole to reward Friar John, and embodying the principles of Ponocrates, does provide us with a fascinating instance of what is happening to the civic or transcendental sanction for leisure, which Erasmus evoked in a new way. Most readers who know anything of the Abbey seem to remember it primarily as an attack on monasticism by means of an engaging reversal of monastic expectations. Thus, it is to be open, not enclosed; and conventional monks and nuns who trespass here will find that the ground they walk on is given the same ritual cleansing as the one that by custom follows a woman's entry into a monastery. The new monks and nuns, unlike the usual ones, who entered because of physical debility, will be beautiful and good-natured; and, instead of taking vows of poverty, chastity, and obedience, they will be allowed to be married, rich, and independent.[104]

But the parody of the monastic orders should not distract us from the enduring appeal of this description, namely, that it is a valid representation of an ideal of civic leisure that the orders in fact might be said to parody. Thus, for example, Gargantua dispenses with the canonical hours, and, indeed, with clocks and dials, so as to ensure the free time of personal duration instead of clock time: "For Gargantua said that the greatest waste of time he knew was the counting of hours— what good does it do?—and the greatest nonsense in the world was to regulate one's life by the sound of a bell instead of by the promptings of reason and good sense" (*Gargantua*, pp. 152–53). In that leisurely spirit, the motto of the Abbey (whose name is derived from the Greek *ethelō*, "I will") is, appropriately, *Fay ce que vouldras*—"Do what you will." Yet nothing could be more misleading than to overlook the shared *civic* consciousness of this community where each member rises when he pleases and drinks, eats, works, and sleeps when the fancy seizes him. Though they do not follow the Benedictine bell, these joyous folk celebrate in their own way a festive and communal dedication which animates the "wills" of all. "Making use of this liberty, they most laudably rivalled one another in all of them doing what they saw pleased one. If some man or woman said, 'Let us drink,' they all drank; if he or she said, 'Let us play,' they all played; if it was 'Let us go and amuse ourselves in the fields,' everyone went there" (p. 160).

The perfect embodiment of the civic inspiration of their leisure is of course the elaborately described Abbey itself, more magnificent than Bonnivet or Chambord or Chantilly, and containing 9,332 apartments, each one provided with an inner chamber, a closet, wardrobe, and chapel, and each one giving on a great hall. The contrast here with the godly feast of Erasmus is striking, not only in its gargantuan opulence but in its relative devaluation of those interior and transcendent values that had liberated Eusebius' guests from the bondage of the Law. If Erasmus complained of an all-marble monastery and offered instead a modest estate, vocal with invitations to transcend the external, Rabelais, we might say, delights in the all-marble structure (he would doubtless have more of it) and would simply replace the vulgar monks with inhabitants who could savor such surroundings. As the adornment of the house and the superb costumes of the inhabitants are lovingly described in details that swell chapters 55 and 56, we begin to understand why Thomas Greene should single out the praise of "civility" in the long inscription over the gate (p. 158) as distinctive of the freedom of the Abbey:

> *De civilité*
> *Cy sont les oustilz*
> *Compaignons gentilz*
> Here find civility
> Among your hosts will reign
> All worthy gentlemen

For, as Greene remarks: "Civility in the sixteenth century had to do with culture, cultivation, courtesy, urbanity, manners, with the graceful carriage of the body and the alert suppleness of the mind. It suggests all those appealing elements in human conversation which lead men to forsake their solitude and egoism and form a harmonious society."[105]

In their different ways, Erasmus and Rabelais could offer such images of a harmonious society, enjoying the fruits of civic leisure, by transforming what was once the imaginative world of the monastic contemplative. We could go on to find parallels to their achievement in English Renaissance celebrations of "civility," in that rather neglected group of poems which celebrates the great house in the country as an emblem of public order and festive communion—for example, in Ben Jonson's magnificent tribute "To Penshurst,"

> whose liberall boord doth flow,
> With all, that hospitalitie doth know!
> Where comes no guest, but is allow'd to eate,
> Without his feare, and of the lords owne meate:
> Where the same beere, and bread, and self-same wine,
> That is his Lordships, shall be also mine.

In its transformation of labor and its realization in history of a pastoral emblem of the civic order, its "Lordship," we might call such poetry profoundly Vergilian, and I hope soon in another book to consider its relationship to the more retired or Horatian English statements of that period. Here, however, let us return to the Continental Renaissance and consider the alternative, the private, focus, whose special quality can be gauged by its difference from the examples of pastoral, "institute," epic, or "georgic" adduced above. Could there be a vision of free time whose special quality would be its liberation from either amorous or religious or civic "Lordship"?

THE PRIVATE FOCUS

Petrarch and the Life of Solitude

One of the more interesting effects of the rise of civic humanism was a change in Dante's reputation which amounted to a recognition of such "georgic" qualities as I have tried to define. Once regarded as an aloof seer, he who had fought at Campaldino suddenly became a type of the civic activist. "When Dante returned from the battle," writes Bruni (the same humanist who penned that "Periclean" tribute to Florence), "he gave himself up to his studies more fervently than ever but nevertheless maintained all his social and civic intercourse. . . . And here let me say a word in reproof of the many ignorant folk who suppose that no one is a student except such as hide themselves away in solitude and leisure. . . . A great and lofty genius has no need of such inflictions."[106]

The attitude which the civic humanist censures here is precisely that of the poet's previous biographer, Boccaccio. While grossly misleading in its estimate of the poet's characteristic achievement, Boccaccio's disdain for Dante's martial and political involvement provides a fascinating introduction to the antifeminist and anticivic temper of retired humanism. We are told how, weary of the vulgar herd, Dante loved to withdraw to solitary spots to consider questions of cosmology or to compose a poem which might live forever. But involvement in love and the family distracted him, and this led to cares of state and the vain honors of civic office.[107] In a larger sense, Bruni's objection to those who "hide themselves away in solitude and leisure" might be directed against the retired humanism of Boccaccio's earlier and greatest production. For the framing story of the *Decameron* is nothing less than a charming renunciation of civic and religious engagement; with its seductive description of the retreat from the moribund and eschatologically minded city to the suburban villa whose watered gardens and shaded lawns betoken renewal and free time, the book proposes a way of life which is contemplative in every respect save the otherworldly context which sanctioned Christian withdrawal.

Even earlier than Boccaccio, however, the retired focus had found a celebrant in the very origins of Renaissance humanism. Indeed, if a civic humanist like Bruni may be said to have reacted against any one example of solitary leisure, it was surely that set by Francesco Petrarca.[108] When, in a letter to Atticus, Petrarch discovered the evidence of Cicero's political activism despite his retirement, the humanist "replied" to the statesman in a spirited letter which is charged with his own devotion to a life of solitary leisure. *O inquiete semper atque anxie,* he writes,

> O always restless and uneasy man—or to use your own words, "O impulsive and unhappy old man"— what did you hope to gain by these disputes and utterly profitless rivalries? Where did you abandon

that leisure so suited to your age and your profession
and your fortune? . . . O how much better would it
have been, especially for a philosopher, to have grown
old in rural tranquillity, "contemplating" eternity,
as you yourself put it somewhere, "and not this
slight earthly existence." O how much better if you
had never had the honor of the *fasces*, if you had
never gazed longingly after triumphs, or if no Cati-
lines had ever swelled your pride.[109]

Although he was the author of the great patriotic canzone,
Italia Mia, the advocate of Cola di Rienzi, and the crusader
against the "Babylonian captivity" of the papacy at Avignon,
Petrarch never celebrated the life of public involvement with
anything like the conviction of a Cicero or a Vergil, a Dante
or a civic humanist of his own time. Instead, his was the way of
Horace, or, later, of Montaigne, in insisting on the primacy
of what he called the "paradise" of solitude, such as he found
in retirement at Vaucluse.[110]

Petrarch first retired in 1337, the year after his ascent of
Mount Ventoux and his famous reading of a passage in Augustine's *Confessions* which reminded him, at the moment of his
triumph, how men admire the heights of mountains, the huge
waves of the sea, and the wheeling of the stars and yet ignore
themselves.[111] Seeking this center rather than simply the enjoyment of a sublime landscape, Petrarch abandoned the great
world of Avignon for Vaucluse. There he might be free from
the intrigues and ambitions of the city and free, too, from the
distractions of Laura.[112] For though some of Petrarch's most
haunting poems use the solitude of the lover to express the
poignancy of his passion, his retirement was essentially a repudiation of that "better place than Eden" advertised in the
garden of courtly love. He who would enjoy such love, writes
Petrarch, "must be banished from the paradise of solitude, for
the very same reason that the first man was expelled from the
paradise of delight" (p. 434).[113] Nothing could be further from
the ideal world represented by the Renaissance pastoral of
romantic love than this first emergence of what Renato Pog-

gioli has called the pastoral of solitude.[114] The critical question on the retired self remains the same as before: Given these exclusions and denials, what manner of affirmation is possible, how is a transfiguration to be achieved?

A likely answer, in Petrarch's case, would consider the Christian context. His withdrawal from the active life, even his anti-feminism, might be readily explained within the tradition of otherworldly detachment that we have briefly traced from the Eastern anchorites to the mystical pastorals of the Spanish Carmelite. Indeed, one need only turn the pages of Petrarch's *Vita Solitaria* to remark what seems to be its unmistakably Christian contemplative character, especially the long list of exemplary solitudes which make up most of the book's second half. Perusing this collection of instances, sacred and secular, ancient and modern, Eastern and Western, the reader may begin to wonder —perchance while reading of how Romulus, Achilles, and Hercules all loved solitude—if there is *any* man worthy of memory who was not in some respect a devotee of the solitary life (pp. 548, 550). One example which is more than a display of encyclopedic medieval exhaustiveness shows a real difference in temper from Dante's "georgic" affirmation of the active life, for the very Celestine V whom Dante scorned outside hell for his "great refusal" is commended by Petrarch for the same reason: citing a miracle supposedly performed by this ex-pope the day after his abdication, Petrarch insists that the withdrawal had the special sanction of God (pp. 474, 476).

And yet it would be misleading to see Petrarch's own retirement simply within this Christian context. The very absoluteness and "purity" of the Christian contemplative life as he defines it ignores large areas of secular experience which were assimilated into the more inclusive synthesis of Dante. In John of the Cross this quietist exclusiveness resulted in a pastoral statement of unexampled intensity; in Petrarch (and Montaigne) it would seem that a comparable tendency served only to isolate the life of religious contemplation and leave it less than relevant to his life. When, for example, Petrarch's brother Ghiardo became a Carthusian monk, the poet suffered from

what was perhaps his most typical tension; in the words of
E. H. Wilkins, "his religion was by no means in control of his
life; he felt that it ought to be, and that his brother had chosen
the better part, but the active life held so much for him that
he could not achieve renunciation."[115] What Petrarch could
not renounce (and this, it seems fair to say, is what Wilkins
means) was not the "active" life in its familiar sense but what
could be defined more precisely as the contemplative life secu-
larized. Yielding to Augustine's exhortation, on the summit of
Mount Ventoux, Petrarch retired from life's centrifugal whirl
to look within himself at Vaucluse, but he did so in a different
way from anything the saint might have conceived when he
pondered the example of Rachel and Mary. In the words of
Jacob Zeitlin, the translator of the *Vita Solitaria*, "There is
more in his attitude of Horace and Epicurus than of the moral-
ist or Christian mystic."[116]

It would seem to be in the Horatian and Epicurean tradition
that Petrarch found at Vaucluse a condition of leisure sanctioned by neither civic nor amorous nor religious circumstances, and it is for its articulation of this vision that the *De
Vita Solitaria* still deserves more attention than it has received.
But this is not to deny Petrarch's dramatized consciousness of
the monastic "city in the desert." Indeed, to understand the
transfiguration of retirement in his book, it is necessary to
perceive the rhetorical function of the most important context
which it tends to exclude, that of the Christian contemplative
tradition. For while it must be admitted that Petrarch's pervasive allusions to the mystical tradition do not exhaust the meaning of his book (there is more to it than there is, say, to his
De Otio Religioso), it seems equally misleading to dismiss these
allusions out of hand, as Zeitlin seems to do. The invocation
of the Christian contemplative tradition is part of the experience of the *Vita Solitaria*; to ignore it as mere lip service to
tradition is to reduce a work of rhetorical complexity to a
collection of anthology pieces in which Petrarch begins to
sound like Montaigne. There is a kind of "lip service" to tradition in his treatise, but this should only serve to underline

the imaginative purpose which is really served. Indeed, the pattern of Petrarch's manipulation of his allusions to the tradition of mystical detachment is perhaps the best introduction to Montaigne's Horatian transformation of that otherworldly civic leisure.

The rhetorical strategy of the *Vita Solitaria* can be reduced to two tactics: first, it invokes the context of Christian contemplation in order to repudiate the pressures of worldly involvement; second (and here one might find a parallel with the secularism of the skeptical fideist behind the "Apology for Raymond Sebond"), it exalts this religious tradition to so lofty a plane that it seems inaccessible to normal, limited human capabilities, becoming rather like those "transcendental humours" that frighten Montaigne like *lieux hautains et inaccessibles*. Characteristically, the author's modest "but as for me" signals the shift to the contemplation of this world, which follows the exaltation of the other world to a zenith of irrelevance. Thus, Petrarch tends to retire in two dimensions, first from the cares of this world to the joys of the next, second from the cares of the next world to the joys of this one.

A rather amusing instance of the first tactic can be found at the start of Book One, in the comparison of the lives of two men, one *occupatus* and *infelix*, the other *solitarius atque otiosus* and, of course, *felix*. The hues of the diptych are, as might be expected, black and white, even more so for the supernatural implications of the antithesis. Thus, for example, in describing the kind of dinner typical of each life, Petrarch not only accuses the busy man of perspiration and belching, gaping and gourmandizing, and having a kitchen whose spilled wine, smoke, fat, bones, and blood literally turn it into a slaughterhouse, but also leaves him on a couch which is his tomb and with a conscience that takes the place of hell (pp. 304, 306, 310). Compare to this the life of retired leisure, and notice too the otherworldly character of the praise: "His house is better suited for the feasts of angels than of men . . . ; there temperance rules as a queen, where the couch is chaste and untroubled and conscience is a paradise" (p. 310). Similarly, in their daily rounds, the busy man, bound by time, is impatient of delay, while the solitary man sees everything *sub specie aeternitatis* and does nothing hurriedly (p. 312). Or, while sleeping, the busy man is tormented for his sins by the Furies, while the other, "free from noxious food and superfluous care," is "solitary, silent, serene, almost like one of the angels" (p. 316).

Our author has used the imagery of angels and paradises to justify retirement from the world; now his tactic is, typically, to dissociate himself from the context in which this imagery has any validity. Thus, a few pages later, Petrarch finds himself in the position of having to admit that, while practically every busy man is unhappy, there have been worthy men who have led active lives and that, furthermore, the teachings of Christ and Cicero seem to counsel such engagement (p. 328). Petrarch's characteristic answer is to admit the perfection of such lives—but only for those for whom it is possible. He warns that such a life is more often talked about than actually practiced; moreover, he warns (in a parable that neatly turns the argument of Gregory's *Pastoral Care* upside down) that the shepherd may himself fall into the trap from which he would save the sheep (pp. 326, 328). Let those who will, attempt such hazards, Petrarch writes, and let those who can, be admired; but it is not his purpose to explain or promulgate the tradition which counsels so superior a course. Laced with a delicate irony, the author's disclaimer is a fine example of the rhetorical tactic noted above:

> But I am not so much proposing a rule for others as exposing the principles of my own mind. If it commends itself to anyone, let him follow its suggestion. Whoever does not like it is free to reject it, and, leaving us to our solitude, to embrace his own anxious cares and live to his own satisfaction in scorn of our rural retreat. I should not mind, I confess, to be of service to as many as possible or even, in Ovid's words, "to be a bearer of health to the entire world"; but the first is in the power of only a few, the last, of Christ alone. I would yield so far to persons of a con-

trary opinion as to admit that whoever is in a place of safety sins against the law of nature if he does not offer what aid he can to the struggling. *But for me, who have myself been struggling as in a great shipwreck, it is enough to pray for the aid of him who is alone able to provide aid in our need.* My prayers are far-reaching, but I shall be content if they are fulfilled to a moderate degree. I could wish to have everybody, or at least as many as possible, gain salvation with me. *But in the end, what do you expect me to say? It is enough for me, yea, a cause of happiness, if I do not perish myself.* But for those who profess themselves guardians of the helpless sheep, alas, how much I fear that they are wolves, eager to rend them alive [p. 328; italics added].

With its transformation of humility into egoism, of abnegation into indulgence, the passage perfectly illustrates the tendency which Charles Trinkaus has wittily summarized as "The Kingdom of God is within you. Its population numbers one."[117] How different, how much more solitary, this solitude is from "the city in the desert" of even the Egyptian anchorites. One cannot imagine a pilgrim stopping at Vaucluse on the way to Jerusalem and deciding, as Bernard declared at Clairvaux, that he had come to the Jerusalem of which he was genuinely a citizen. The acknowledgment of Christ's power seems, potentially at least, to dispense the writer from the communal responsibilities of being a Christian. As we shall see, the responsibilities that the Christian fideist does not presume to claim the secular humanist is happy to do without.

Turning from the repudiation of the active life to the contemplative life as Petrarch defines it, we find the same rhetorical strategy: the exaltation of the Christian context to a "lofty and inaccessible place" and the humble demurrer at the prospect of attaining it. Describing the mystical joys available to the Christian contemplative, Petrarch does not hesitate to compare them to the experience, in this life, of the life eternal: "though still confined to earth, he may hear the chorus of angels sing-

ing harmoniously in heaven and behold in an ecstasy of mind
what he is unable to express when he comes to himself" (p. 354).

The words are a moving exaltation of the contemplative life,
but their rhetorical function here is to be so exalted as to seem
irrelevant. As Petrarch's next words insist, his proper sphere
for contemplation is more human than supernatural, more literary than metaphysical: "But what can I know or say about
all these things, unhappy sinner that I am. . . ? My love of a
spot favorable to literary leisure springs, no doubt, from my
love of books; or perhaps I seek to escape from the crowd because of an aversion arising from a discrepancy in our tastes;
or it may even be that from a squeamishness of conscience I
like to avoid a many-tongued witness of my life" (p. 354).
There follows what is probably the best example of this rhetorical strategy and certainly the most memorable passage in the
Vita Solitaria:

> Therefore let us pass over these considerations, al-
> though, beloved Jesus, we have been created by you
> to the end that we may find our peace in you; for
> this we were born, and without it our life is un-
> happy and unavailing. How much value, my father
> [Philippe de Cabassoles, bishop of Cavaillon], do you
> set upon these common things: to live according to
> your pleasure, to go where you will, to stay where
> you will; in the spring to repose amid purple beds of
> flowers, in the autumn amid heaps of fallen leaves;
> to cheat the winter by basking in the sun and the
> summer by taking refuge in cool shades, and to feel
> the force of neither unless it is your choice! *To be-
> long to yourself in all seasons* and, wherever you are,
> to be ever *with yourself.* [Italics added.]

In this case the original will be of interest:

> *His igitur pretermissis—quanquam, bone Iesu, ad
> hunc finem creati abs te ut in te requiescamus, ad
> hoc nati et sine hoc inutiliter atque infeliciter nati
> sumus—quanti tandem, pater, extimes illa comunia,
> vivere ut velis, ire quo velis, stare ubi velis, vere*

> *inter purpureos florum toros, autumno caducarum*
> *inter frondium acervos acquiescere, apricatione hie-*
> *mem, umbris estatem fallere, neutram sentire nisi*
> *qua velis? In utraque tuum esse et ubicunque fueris*
> *esse tecum* [p. 354].

The section begins with a traditional reminder of where man
is destined to find repose, but, significantly, it is cast as an ad-
versative afterthought, kept in the background by *quanquam*.
The point of the previously quoted passage remains: *his igitur
pretermissis*, Petrarch is unworthy of mystical ecstasy. *Quanti
tandem, pater* announces the typical shift from the supernatural context to the natural, with the centripetal "but as for
me" implicit in the question: "I may be no mystic, but have
you ever noticed the ordinary human pleasures available to the
solitary?" *His igitur pretermissis . . . quanti tandem . . . ex-
times illa comunia?*

Even if the lines that follow did not contain a superb description of free time, they would be striking for their personal
and private quality. Here, just as in his earlier declaration that
he is not giving laws to others but is simply exposing the principles of his own mind, Petrarch recalls the dramatized self of
Horace and anticipates the fuller portraiture of Montaigne.
To gauge the intensity of this focus on the self one need only
compare the two uses of the second person in the passage. The
first, acknowledging Jesus, is almost perfunctory in tone, a far
cry from the plangent nostalgia of the lines of Augustine it
echoes: *quanquam . . . ad hunc finem creati abs te ut in te
requiescamus.* The second use of the second person is in fact
a generalized first person, tantamount to "one" or "we." The
focus is egoistic, and the tone, as registered in the mounting
intensity of the three similarly brief ending segments (*vivere
ut velis, ire quo velis, stare ubi velis*) and climaxed by the echo
in the conclusion of the last long periodic clause (*vere . . . nisi
qua velis*), is excited and exultant. By the time one begins the
next sentence, whose balance and chiasmus leave the sense of
all possible pleasures revolving around *tuum esse* and *esse
tecum*, the reader might well wonder what had happened to
that theme of a divine *te*, left behind in the *quanquam* clause.

This impression is accentuated by the vision of leisure, which is at the heart of the passage, as the special privilege of the retired self, that is to say, the self which has retired even from its Christian context. As in many of the depictions of free time already examined, the passage makes symbolic use of the seasonal cycle to express a condition free from seasonal extremes. By linking the springtime repose in the flower bed with that in the autumnal "heaps of fallen leaves," Petrarch establishes a sense of permanent free time which is nicely sustained by the mitigations of extreme change vividly imaged in the winter sunshine and the summer shade. And yet, if the lines suggest an abiding timelessness in a way that may remind us of the Vergilian rhythm of the countryside, a rhythm for which even Jerome yearned, their particular distinction would seem to be in their simultaneous insistence that the seasons *do* change. Indeed, their acceptance of becoming probably accounts more for their serenity than do their intimations of being. Petrarch's landscape does not intimate a celestial garden outside of time but only a personally timeless duration within the very process of time, as this world measures it. We saw such a liberating acceptance at the conclusion of our discussion of Horace; here, as there, Montaigne's declaration comes to mind: *Je ne peints pas l'estre. Je peints le passage.* And Georges Poulet's reading of that line, already cited in our discussion of Horace, might well apply to this affirmation by the earliest retired humanist of the Renaissance. By his acceptance of "becoming," Petrarch obtains communication with "being." In the flux of time he has discovered an island of free time, not in the feasts and gardens of the good city envisioned by his faith but by coming home to himself. It was not, to be sure, a haven in which his rich and anxious sensibility could always rest. Few of us, perhaps, can. The free time a god of some sort has granted will always provide the human imagination with the kind of mythic sanction it may need most deeply if it is to enjoy its freedom. But that is only to underscore the Horatian achievement of the author whose transfiguration of retirement, devoid of myth, is the subject of the next pages and the culmination of this book.

Ramenons à nous: *The Quest of Montaigne's* Essais

The Horatian achievement of Montaigne was to transform and appropriate to the Christian imagination the Vergilian kind of free time that a god had granted. While Petrarch's *Vita Solitaria* verged on this, it still depended on the tradition that began with the city in the desert. But every reader who opens Montaigne's *Essais* from the start finds himself warned of the provocatively new kind of *vita contemplativa* that the writing and the reading of this book entail. In the brief preface, "Au Lecteur," the reader is told that this book, written in good faith, "warns you from the outset that I have set myself no goal but a domestic and private one. I have had no thought of serving either you or my own glory." He has written it, he goes on to say, merely as a private convenience for relatives and friends who may wish to remember him after his death. If he had sought the world's favor, he would have appeared more stylish; but he wants to be seen in his simple, natural, ordinary fashion, with no contention or artifice—*car c'est moy que je peins.* The self he paints will not conceal his faults; indeed, had he been born among those primitive folk still enjoying the sweet freedom of nature's first laws, he would expose himself even more, *tout entier et tout nud.* And so, reader, he concludes, "I am myself the matter of my book; you would be unreasonable to spend your leisure on so frivolous and vain a subject. So farewell" (Thibaudet ed., p. 25; Frame trans., p. 2).

A dieu donq, de Montaigne. So on the first of March, 1580, at once cordial and impertinent, Montaigne leaves us to venture across well over a thousand pages with the promise of a rare discovery, one like that of the New World, whose natural liberty he cites as a model for his own kind of voyage of exploration; but he leaves us also with the warning that this is his private business and that we shall be wasting our time or, as he says more precisely, our leisure.

Both the promise and the warning are worth taking seriously in Montaigne's time and ours, for even to consider each is to consider the existential predicament of the modern condition of leisure which the *Essais* do so much to provoke and define.

The promise involves the Horatian transfiguration of Christian leisure, which is our final subject. It did not, apparently, come early or easily to its author, and that is why the warning deserves attention. Like Horace's spoof on the fantasized *Beatus ille* retirement of the daydreaming Alfius, Montaigne's preface cautions his reader that the experience of his book might well be *si frivole et si vain* as it doubtless has been for some readers. Such ironic self-deprecation may never win over the Pascals or the Sartres, but it is important to realize that, from the start, Montaigne reminds us of the hazards of the "domestic and private" game he has invented.

Writing now neither for the reader's "service" nor for his own "glory," Montaigne knew that for centuries terms like these had sanctioned the life of leisure, whether in a secular or sacred context. Writing an early essay, "Of Solitude," he will contrast his essentially Horatian vision with the kinds of civic leisure we have been considering. The leisure of the secular city will be reduced to the examples of Cicero and Pliny (T., p. 285; F., p. 182). As for Cicero's leisure, it is not even his frustrated political activism that disturbs Montaigne (as the discovery of his quite reluctant retirement outraged Petrarch), but, more significantly, the desire that his writings attain the glory of civic celebration. So too with Pliny, who, in a letter to his friend Cornelius Rufus, said: on this matter of solitude, leave the care of your retreat to your servants, devote yourself to writing, and attain "something that is all your own." But that something, Montaigne notes scornfully, is mere reputation, the kind of remembrance that Cicero sought. In the context of his letter Pliny has been urging a young poet to seek the one goal that will be his forever, while other possessions go from owner to owner. This is the immortality to be gained by singing of the triumphs of Trajan in the Dacian war, of rivers rechanneled and bridged, of a king driven from his city to pitch camp on craggy mountains. So the poet is exhorted to sing of georgic labor or epic quest, to give meaning to his leisure, as Vergil did, by celebrating, in the transformation of such toil, a reflection of the civic feast which will assure his glory as a "perpetual" possession, transcending time.[118]

Yet the author of these vain and frivolous essays will have none of this. To reverse the language of Christian leisure: Cicero and Pliny are not in the world, but they are of it. "Glory and repose," Montaigne insists, "are things that cannot lodge in the same dwelling. As far as I can see, these men have only their arms and legs outside the crowd; their souls, their intentions, are more than ever in the thick of it . . . ; they have only stepped back to make a better jump, to get a stronger impetus wherewith to plunge deeper into the crowd" (F., p. 182; T., p. 285).

As for the civic sanction of contemplative leisure in a Christian context, its norm has been implicit in this repudiation of the secular city, and its own case is easily, perhaps all too easily, presented. Those who seek solitude for religious reasons, Montaigne declares, are much more sane and consistent. They set before their eyes the image of God, infinite in goodness and power, capable of satisfying every desire of the soul, transcending affections and sufferings, and making death itself seem desirable. "Only this one goal of another life, happily immortal, rightly deserves that we abandon the comforts and pleasures of this life of ours. And he who can really and constantly kindle his soul with the flame of that living faith and hope, builds himself in solitude a life that is voluptuous and delightful beyond any kind of life" (F., pp. 180–81; T., p. 283).

We began our consideration of Christian leisure with language like this at the conclusion of the "Apology." If we are now in a position to perceive more fully the tradition that offered *une vie voluptueuse et delicate au delà de toute autre forme de vie*, we can also begin to appreciate the special significance of language like the characteristically contrasting and complementary passage from "Of Experience," with which we also began. For there seems to be in Montaigne's very reverence for the religious context of contemplative solitude a subtle but pervasive sense of its inaccessibility. *Cette seule fin d'une autre vie* that begins the first sentence becomes as remote as it is admirable compared to the concluding *commoditez et douceurs de cette vie nostre*. In the perspective of that homely *vie nostre*, the author and his reader can watch, with awe and a certain content, as the *Et ce qui peut* that begins the next sentence expands and rises, rhetorically and thematically, to the climactic *au dela de toute autre forme de vie*.

In what has long been the best single essay on Montaigne, Erich Auerbach offers a cogent insight into the kinds of *vie* we have just examined. Montaigne's debt to the "figural" tradition of the Middle Ages cannot be denied, writes Auerbach; "but it is also true that his creatural realism has broken through the Christian frame within which it arose. Life on earth is no longer the figure of the world beyond; he can no longer permit himself to scorn the here for the sake of a there. Life on earth is the only one he has. He wants to savor it to the last drop; *car en fin c'est nostre estre, c'est nostre tout*."[119] The French quotation is from another essay ("A Custom of the Island of Cea"), which deliberates the case for or against suicide in different situations (F., p. 254; T., p. 389). Its relevance to our concerns is even more compelling in its context, which also anticipates the language of the conclusion of "Experience" and the conclusion of the present book:

> For after all, life is our being, it is our all. Things that have a nobler and richer being may accuse ours; but it is against nature that we despise ourselves and care nothing about ourselves. It is a malady peculiar to man, and not seen in any other creature, to hate and disdain himself. It is by a similar vanity that we wish to be something other than we are. . . . A man who wishes to be made into an angel does nothing for himself; he would never benefit from the change [F., p. 254; T., pp. 389–90].

If, as a modern Catholic interpreter puts it, Montaigne had "the soul of an anchorite,"[120] lines like these illustrate how his achievement was to transform the anchorite's usual perspective.

Angels, traditionally, enjoy the perfection of Christian lei-

sure in the "beatific vision" of God; this is what religious contemplatives aspire to in this life, and, because of this, as our
quotation from "Solitude" stresses, death itself is desirable for
them as a passage to so perfect a state: *la mort, à souhait, passage à un si parfaict estat.* But Montaigne characteristically
will be concerned less with *passage à* than with the acceptance
and contemplative transfiguration of the flux of mundane existence—with *passage* as an end in itself. That is why, for example, in his essay "Of Glory" he will typically turn from the
concept of "glory," which in the classical world promoted the
civic celebration of reputation and which in the biblical world
became the visionary revelation of God's transcendence; the
first kind is exposed as but the wind and sound of empty language, the second kind deserves the valid celebration of God's
name among worshipers. "As our ordinary prayers say, *Gloria
in excelsis Deo, et in terra pax hominibus*" (F., p. 468; T., pp.
697–98). Montaigne is quoting the passage from Luke's gospel
(2:14) which first proclaimed the promise of Christian leisure to
the shepherds at Christ's birth; it also begins the major prayer
of celebration and praise in the Latin mass. In Montaigne's
hands, however, the *et* of the Latin will subtly take on an almost disjunctive force: let the angels enjoy giving God the
glory only He deserves, but let us settle for peace on earth.
Hence the quotation is introduced by a reminder that a starv-
ing man would be foolish to seek a fine garment rather than a
good meal, and the sentence following "our ordinary prayer"
dwells upon what we need on earth: *beauté, santé, sagesse,
vertu*; external ornaments can be sought after we have provided for these "necessary things." Years later Voltaire will
hail "the superfluous" as precisely the *chose nécessaire* in his
famous defense of the civilized luxury necessary to a life of
mundane leisure. To understand Montaigne's view, one must
go back centuries earlier, to the passage from the Sermon on
the Mount with which we also began to consider the pastoral
of Christian contemplation and which his language virtually
echoes even as it reorients it. Let us cite it this time in the
language Montaigne would have read:

> *Et de vestimento quid solliciti estis? Considerate lilia
> agri; quomodo crescunt; non laborant neque nent.
> Dico autem vobis quoniam nec Salomon in omni
> gloria sua coopertus est sicut unum ex istis. Si autem
> faenum agri, quod hodie est et cras in clibanum
> mittitur, Deus sic vestit, quanto magis vos modicae
> fidei? Nolite ergo solliciti esse dicentes: Quid man-
> ducabimus aut quid bibemus aut quo operiemur?
> Haec enim omnia gentes inquirunt; scit enim Pater
> vester quia his omnibus indigetis. Quaerite ergo pri-
> mum regnum Dei et iustitiam eius et haec omnia
> adicientur vobis* [Matt. 7:28–33].

Without denying the kingdom of God and his righteousness,
Montaigne will pursue the more modest quest of a new kind
of glory (*et in terra pax hominibus*) in an essay on that subject
that will return us to the new kind of solitude we have just
been considering. "All the glory that I aspire to in my life is
to have lived it tranquilly—tranquilly not according to Metro-
dorus or Arcesilaus or Aristippus, but according to me. Since
philosophy has not been able to find a way to tranquility that
is suitable to all, let everyone seek it individually" (F., p. 471;
T., p. 702). Or later: "It is not for show that our soul must
play its part, it is at home, within us where no eyes penetrate
but our own" (F., p. 472; T., p. 704). Or again: "I do not care
so much what I am to others as I care what I am to myself. . . .
As for me, I hold that I exist only in myself" (F., p. 474;
T., pp. 705–7).

This shift from the world of external celebration to one
selon moy . . . chez nous . . . en moy mesme . . . chez moy is
the final homecoming journey of this book. How resonant the
simple preposition *chez* will become in these essays! "If I am
not at home," he will say later, "I am always near it," *Si je ne
suis chez moy, j'en suis toujours bien pres* (F., p. 615; T., p.
907). "We have lived long enough for others," he says in the
most famous lines in the essay on solitude; "let us live at least
this remaining bit of life for ourselves. Let us bring back our
thoughts and plans to ourselves and our well being" (F., p. 178;

T., p. 279). *Ramenons à nous et à nostre aise*: it is a summons we shall hear again and again in the *Essais*. Though he seldom starts with himself, Montaigne always comes "to himself," as Herbert Lüthy says in his fine essay, "as he comes to the point."[121] It is the kind of odyssey proposed in the next lines of our passage from "Solitude": "Since God gives us leisure to make arrangements for moving out, let us make them; let us pack our bags; let us take an early leave of the company; let us break free from the violent clutches that engage us elsewhere and draw us away from ourselves" (F., p. 178; T., p. 279). Transforming the Christian counsel to be "in" the world but not "of" it, he warns us to love this and that but "be wedded only to ourselves," not to be so "joined and glued to things that we cannot be detached without tearing off our skin." "The greatest thing in the world," he concludes, "is to belong to oneself," *La plus grande chose du monde c'est de scavoir estre à soy* (F., p. 178; T., p. 280). For Montaigne, to begin to be *à soy* is to end a quest—and to begin one.

For if the purpose of solitude is "to live more at leisure and at one's ease," it is not a goal attained simply by retirement. Early in the essay we are warned that often men think they have left busyness when they have only changed it. "Furthermore, by getting rid of the court and the market place, we do not get rid of the principal worries of our life: *ratio et prudentia curas, / non locus effusi late maris arbiter aufert*" (F., p. 175; T., p. 276). Significantly, Montaigne is quoting the Latin of the Epistle to Bullatius, with which we began our discussion of Horace's final version. There, we recall, Horace reminds his friend that neither an odyssey through the famous Mediterranean resorts nor a retreat, forgetting and forgotten by friends, safe from Neptune's tumults, will give him what he seeks. Human fulfillment, Horace characteristically insists, is an internal and imaginative process, not the creation of external circumstances. As Montaigne's quotation puts it, "it is reason and wisdom that banish worries, not just a place commanding a wide vista of sea." It is this other quest within the self that liberates us from the anxiety of mere external idleness, which Horace acutely diagnosed as *strenua inertia*. Horace's final vision of that liberation led him, as we saw, to celebrate leisure in the acceptance of time or, as he says more concretely and pungently at the end of the epistle, to tell Bullatius that what he seeks is "here," at Ulubrae, among marshes and frogs. Montaigne, too, comes to this affirmation, and this is why he has already been quoted as a commentary on the *Epistles*; but it was not, apparently, an easy discovery in his life, and, more importantly, its apprehension is the particular challenge and reward of the quest which is the experience of reading the *Essais*.

Enforced by Montaigne's self-dramatization, the most influential criticism of this century has stressed the "evolution" of his sensibility. In the best modern editions the *Essais* are printed with the designations "a," "b," and "c" within the text to indicate: "a," material published before 1588, usually in the first, 1580 edition; "b," material published in the fifth edition of 1588 (some six hundred additions to books 1 and 2, as well as 3); and "c," material added by Montaigne in the "Bordeaux" copy of the latter edition so as to create a final, "sixth," edition before his death (about one-fourth of the total material). An awareness of the time of an essay's composition or of the various strata within it can elucidate many of the apparent inconsistencies and contradictions within the *Essais*, since they reveal an evolving transformation of attitude. This transformation has been variously described, most influentially by Pierre Villey, as a shift from a Stoic to a Skeptical to an Epicurean vision[122] —a shift reflected also in the transformation of the essay form from an impersonal to a personal statement or, in another way, by the replacement of Cato by Socrates as the author's ideal of behavior. In the best discussion of that evolution in English, Donald Frame's account, aptly subtitled "The Humanization of a Humanist," pays particular attention to the interest in the common man which marks the transformation of the apprehensive and aloof humanist into the *honnête homme*.[123] In the following pages we shall consider that "evolution" as being profoundly analogous to Horace's transfigurations of retirement as we saw it shift from an early summons to sail to the Isles of the Blest, to satiric detachment, to lyric celebration, to, finally, an acceptance of time as the final condition of free time.

At the same time, however, it is important to admit that the reader experiences the essays not as progress but as process. In Horace a certain pattern can be found as one kind of poetry, with its typical themes, follows another kind; but the very need for the "a," "b," and "c" designations reminds us that Montaigne did not delete or even separate his earliest statements. Instead, he left them in the text to complement, qualify, or contradict his later remarks, in the same way that the earlier essays do the later ones. We do not read the essays with an end in view; we need not even read them in any particular order. Encyclopedic in their absorption of the anecdotal phenomena of all times and places, they are themselves brashly uninhibited by any sense of history. So, too, the expressed consciousness of their author expands and celebrates itself omnivorously and inconsistently: he is large, he contains multitudes. A twentieth-century reader, less interested in the questions of particular essays ("Whether the Governor of a Besieged Place Should Go Out to Parley") but immersed in the ebb and flow of incident after incident, in what has aptly been called Montaigne's "oceanic prose,"[124] might begin to feel that he is reading something like *Finnegans Wake* as told by Walt Whitman. It is an impression confirmed by the fact that Montaigne is also the best introduction to the usual form and theme of such masters of seventeenth- and eighteenth-century English prose as Browne or Burton or Sterne. If we are to speak of Montaigne's "evolution," then, we must bear in mind that he "evolves" to an acceptance of *passage* itself more than to some specific reforming or even forming of the self. Hence, "Of Repentance" characteristically dismisses the concept of its title by beginning with a famous declaration that also captures the method and the matter of the essay:

> Others form man; I tell of him, and portray a particular one, very ill-formed, whom I should really make very different from what he is if I had to fashion him over again. But now it is done. Now the

limits of my painting do not go astray, though they change and vary. The world is but a perennial movement. All the things in it are in constant motion— the earth, the rocks of the Caucasus, the pyramids of Egypt—both with the common motion and with their own. Stability itself is nothing but a more languid motion. I cannot keep my subject still. It goes along befuddled and staggering, with a natural drunkenness. I take it in this condition, just as it is at the moment I give my attention to it. I do not portray being: I portray passing. Not the passing from one age to another, or, as the people say, from seven years to seven years, but from day to day, from minute to minute. My history needs to be adapted to the moment. I may presently change, not only by chance, but also by intention. This is a record of various and changeable occurrences, and of irresolute, and, when it so befalls, contradictory ideas: whether I am different myself, or whether I take hold of my subjects in different circumstances and aspects. So, all in all, I may indeed contradict myself now and then; but truth, as Demades said, I do not contradict. If my mind could gain a firm footing, I would not make essays, I would make decisions; but it is always in apprenticeship and on trial [F., pp. 610–11; T., pp. 899–900].

The lines were first cited in our discussion of Horace's *Epistles*; with them as both our point of departure and our destination, let us look more closely at the distinctive texture of the Horatian achievement of Montaigne.

"A Man Besieged": Centrifugal and Centripetal Images of the Public World

Montaigne's opening essay is appropriately entitled "Par Divers Moyens On Arrive à Pareille Fin," and we have only to turn the first page to read an early ("a") and seminal expression of the theme that our last quotation from "Repentance" exfoliates. "Truly man is a marvelously vain, diverse, and undulating object. It is hard to found any constant and uniform judgment on him" (F., p. 5; T., p. 29). If the lines are a caution to criticism of the "evolutionary" kind, one could answer that their full implications became progressively deeper and richer, not only in the author's life and later revisions but in the reader's experience of the whole collection; and this will eventually be the "evolutionary" aspect of our approach. At the same time, and this is the critical view of the next pages, the lines are an invitation to criticism of a phenomenological or even "spatial" kind that approaches the *Essais* as they themselves approach the action and thought of past history. Here, to risk one more comparison with that other great bedside book by Joyce, all past experience is seen not only as diversely rising and falling but all at once and as one in that very diversity. As the title and method of the first essay suggest, it is possible, without imposing an essentialistic "uniform and constant" judgment, to see a phenomenologically coherent "world" begin to take shape across all the essays.

Or rather, two such worlds can be seen: the public one, from which writer and reader withdraw, and then the new world, struggling to be born out of that retirement and to justify it. Dialectically related, the public world denied and the private world affirmed have a similar configuration. Each is shaped by centrifugal tendencies of expansion and flux as well as by centripetal tendencies of compression and limitation. There thus emerges a negative and a positive version of each of these kinds of phenomena.

Our interest is primarily in the pattern of affirmation in the private world, but we might begin with the pattern of negations in the great world. There is a certain evolutionary parallel here to beginning with Horace's *Epodes* and *Satires* before turning to his *Odes* and *Epistles*, but this is not to deny that Montaigne "evolved" into giving us all these attitudes together as one. We have already had a glimpse of Montaigne's resistance to the centrifugal tendency of the civic realm to draw us *hors de nous* to the spheres of political or angelic "glory."

Here we might also recall the insistence, at the very end of "Experience," that there seems to be a singular accord between this kind of centrifugal tendency and another, quite different kind, between "supercelestial thoughts and subterranean conduct": those who would change into angels, change into beasts (F., p. 856; T., p. 1256).

Long before we read these words, we have experienced their meaning as anecdote after anecdote from past and recent history has exposed how such public perversions of action and leisure as brute violence and empty fantasy, unspeakable mutilation and rhetorical decorations, have all too often been "in singular accord." And yet in singular accord, too, is another aspect of this centrifugal whirl of slaughter and ceremony: the peculiarly centripetal focus which so often enforces it. The slaughter is concentrated in a siege or tyranny, the ceremony conceals secrecy. As these extremes of expansion and compression define the public world, the reader will be confirmed in a retirement to a world that is at once more contracted and more open, more bridled and yet more free.

There is a personal and deeper dimension to these phenomenological worlds that is more than a matter of Montaigne's evolution, and it is nicely condensed in the (perhaps unintended) suggestiveness of a telling remark by his American biographer: "Altogether the early essays are not gay," writes Donald Frame. "Life is mostly bad; its chief facts are pain and death. . . . In his tower Montaigne is like a man besieged— not only by the things he fears but also by his own somber preparations for defense."[125] This "man besieged" lived through the French wars of religion that have their bloodiest memorial in the Saint Bartholomew's Day massacre; but it was another kind of onslaught that seems most to have prompted his retirement. In the decade before 1573 he had also lived through the death of his dearest friend, Etienne de La Boétie, the death of his father after long agony with the kidney stone that was to torment his son, the death of his brother, the deaths of all his children, and even his own apparent death after a riding accident.[126] Ultimately, then, the centrifugal and centripetal forces of the great world participate in the erosive flux of time and the final compression of death; in the figure of the man besieged we see the beginnings of a retirement which will eventually affirm a transformed vision of compression and flux.

The description I have just sketched is not, of course, intended to exclude the usual concerns of Montaigne studies in the history of ideas, like those masterfully presented in Hugo Friedrich's rich and definitive book or in the acute philosophical analysis of Philip Hallie; I wish rather to suggest how such themes as skepticism, naturalism, and self-discovery participate in the deepest structure of the characteristic texture of the *Essais*.[127] For example, the first essay not only illustrates its announced theme that "by diverse means" such as defiance or submission "we achieve the same end" of sympathy, but, moving back and forth over space and time, it also introduces a public world characterized by the kinds of centrifugal and centripetal tendencies I have outlined. There is first the world of Edward, Prince of Wales, who, having besieged and conquered Limoges, "could not be halted by the cries of the people and of the women and children abandoned to the butchery, who implored his mercy and threw themselves at his feet"; yet, going deeper and deeper into the city, he found and pardoned three Frenchmen still resisting the assault at the center (F., p. 3; T., p. 27). We begin to see what this world shares with that of Scanderberg pursuing a soldier, Conrad III besieging the duke of Bavaria, the Thebans accusing the defiant Epaminondas, Dionysus the Elder ordering that the resolute captive Phyto be stripped and dragged through the town, "whipping him very ignominiously and cruelly and in addition heaping on him slanderous and insulting words" (F., p. 4; T., p. 29). Soon the fact that such defiance can also arouse rage prompts the famous reflection on man as *merveilleusement divers et ondoyant*. Nevertheless, the conditions are still those of flux and siege, whether we are considering Pompey, pardoning the resistant Mamertines, or Sulla's army [at Praeneste], drawing no benefit from resistance.

The lesson Montaigne draws from the final anecdote, about Alexander, is directly contrary to his first examples, but the reader will also be struck by the resemblance of its centrifugal tendencies to the butchery and cries, whipping and insults, that whirled around the besieged figure in the opening anecdotes. Alexander, having fully conquered Gaza, comes upon the commander Betis, "now alone, abandoned by his men, his armor cut to pieces, all covered with blood and wounds, still fighting on in the midst of many Macedonians, who were attacking him from all sides." Captured, he infuriates Alexander by his silence and is grotesquely delivered back to the centrifugal whirl as the victor orders his heels pierced and has him thus "dragged alive, torn and dismembered behind a cart" (F., p. 5; T., p. 30). There was nothing to "bridle" the anger of Alexander, the essay concludes, not even when he conquered Thebes and massacred some six thousand heroic defenders. A day's revenge was not enough to satiate the conqueror, and the essay's last sentence matter-of-factly relates how "This slaughter went on to the last drop of blood that could be shed, and stopped only at the unarmed people, old men, women and children, so that thirty thousand of them might be taken as slaves" (F., p. 5; T., p. 31).

These instances are from but one brief essay—conveniently, the first one; but the kind of public action they describe will recur throughout the essays, whatever their ostensible topic. Again and again the flux of the uncontained life whirls violently around a central situation of siege, pursuit, enslavement, mutilation, or death. It is no accident, for example, that the essay discussing suicide ("A Custom of the Isle of Cea"), from which Auerbach selected the famous affirmation of the human condition as *nostre estre . . . nostre tout*, derives most of its examples from a figure subjected to such centrifugal forces, for example the old Jew Razis (Rasias in French), who was persecuted by Nicanor (2 Maccabees 14:37–46). With his gate burnt down and his enemies ready to seize him, Razis chose a noble suicide rather than a dishonorable capture. Unfortunately, the self-inflicted stroke of the sword was ineffective because of his haste. Razis then ran through his besiegers to the top of a wall and threw himself down so that he fell on his head. Still feeling some life in him, however, he picked himself up and ran all bloody through the crowd until, finally,

"He got to a certain steep, precipitous rock, where unable to do anything more, he plucked out his entrails with both hands through one of his wounds, tearing and mangling them, and threw them among the pursuers, calling down and attesting divine justice upon them" (F., p. 257; T., p. 393).

It is the sort of passage that reminds us of what Imbrie Buffum means when he stresses the importance of "horror" as one of the "baroque" aspects of Montaigne;[128] and the impression is confirmed by the discovery that Montaigne has added to his biblical source so as to make it more concrete ("through one of his wounds") and more grotesque ("tearing and mangling them"). Yet this is not so much a fascination with isolated details of horror for their own sake but rather an emergent vision of the pervasive horror of the world of unbridled public action. The added details point up the imagery already in the source, which itself is organically related to the characteristic imagery of other anecdotes of public activity, from the hare in the greyhound's teeth to the mob crushed under the wheels of the juggernaut.

Of course, as in the worship of the juggernaut, it is not only the violent flux of public activity which moves the reader to the centripetal focus of the *Essais*; the equally centrifugal whirl of public leisure or religious contemplation does so too, and it is typically conceived now as a world of empty rhetoric and mere ceremony, often concealing or enforcing the brutal depredations of the world of action: the singular accord of *les opinions supercelestes et les meurs sousterraines*.

We can now see the special relevance of an early essay's insistence that the governor of a besieged place should not go out to parley, for, as the next essay also illustrates, it is during peace talks that the danger of surprise and slaughter is greatest (F., pp. 16–19; T., pp. 47–50). So, too, the world of public ritual and festivity conceals sinister intrigue, whether of Lucius Cinna planning to murder Augustus during the performance of a religious sacrifice (F., p. 91; T., p. 156), or of Cesare Borgia planning to murder an enemy cardinal by carefully sending ahead a bottle of poisoned wine for their dinner (F., p. 162; T., p. 258). But these Machiavellian tactics only introduce the

deeper and more disturbing question of the very nature of the
civic or religious imagination that allows, or even encourages,
such perversions. Indeed, as early as the two essays preceding
the two warning against parley in siege, the reader has already
been warned of the perils of the unbridled myth-making faculty, the pursuit of fulfillment in a world beyond our grasp
where we are not at home. *Nous ne somme jamais chez nous,
nous sommes tousjours au dela* (F., p. 8; T., p. 34). *Au dela*
is that world of words which takes us out of ourselves even in
our own country. It is the world which Livy scorns when he
notes that "the language of men brought up under royalty is
always full of foolish ostentation and vain testimonies" (F., p.
9; T., p. 36). It is the world of "glory," of course, to which we
return to note one last instance of the repudiation of the civic
leisure which it introduced:

> Since men because of their inadequacy cannot be
> sufficiently paid with good money, let false be em-
> ployed too. This means has been practised by all law-
> givers, and there is no policy in which there is not
> some admixture either of empty ceremony or lying
> opinion to serve as a curb to keep the people in their
> duty. This is why most of them have their fabulous
> origins and beginnings, enriched with supernatural
> mysteries [F., p. 377; T., p. 711].

As he puts it, more psychologically and universally in the other
early essay that, with a telling coincidence, precedes the one on
"Whether the Governor of a Besieged Place Should Go Out
to Parley,"

> so it seems that the soul once stirred and set in mo-
> tion is lost in itself unless we give it something to
> grasp, and we must always give it an object to aim
> at and act on. . . . And we see that the soul with its
> passions will sooner deceive itself by setting up a
> false and fantastical object, even contrary to its own
> belief, than not act against something [F., p. 14; T.,
> pp. 42–43].

What we have just glimpsed is the centrifugal whirl of the civic or religious imagination; what we soon discover is its relation to the pattern of slaughter and siege with which we began this section but which we can now perceive to be a perversion not only of civic action but of civic leisure. Consider the grotesque festivity and even artistry of the holiday described in the essay "Of Cruelty," where Montaigne confesses his shock that

> there were souls so monstrous that they would commit murder for the mere pleasure of it: hack and cut off other men's limbs, sharpen their wits to invent unaccustomed torments and new forms of death, without enmity, without profit, and for the sole purpose of enjoying the pleasing spectacle of the pitiful gestures and movements, the lamentable groans and cries of a man dying in anguish [F., p. 316; T., pp. 476–77].

We have come a long way from Homer's affirmation of Odysseus' slaughter of the suitors, and what has been lost is the liberating sense of the end which such means once served; what is left is the substitution of means for ends and the futile voyeurism of a cultural acedia—the incapacity for leisure ironically registered in the *plaisant spectacle*. This could have been noticed before, most conspicuously in the degradation of the classical ideal of *scholē* in the bread and circuses of imperial Rome; but it was for Montaigne to see most vividly that *corruptio optimi pessima est*, that the Christian vision of imaginative leisure in a higher communion could degenerate into a bizarre and centrifugal civic fantasy of frustrated idleness, and that the myth of the god who gives ease can be parodied to sanction unholy feasts celebrating not the leisure of the contemplative but the desperate boredom of the ideologue. To choose one instance of "the pleasant spectacle" of this perversion of the Christian myth of civic leisure, one might consider the fate of George Sechel, leader of some crusading Polish peasants and defeated by the vaivode of Transylvania. While his men were given neither food nor drink, Sechel was bound naked to a wooden horse and subjected to every torture conceivable. While he was still alive, his captors gave his blood to his brother to drink and then "had twenty of his most favored captains feed on him, tearing his flesh with their teeth and swallowing the morsels. The rest of his body and the inner parts, when he was dead, were boiled and given to others to eat" (F., p. 530; T., pp. 786–87).

Across all the essays a master image of the centrifugal flux of the great world thus begins to take shape. Razis hurling out his entrails blends with Sechel devoured morsel by morsel. The unbridled violence of civic action blends with the unbridled fantasy of civic spectacle. Both swirl about the same central figure of the kind of victim who is, potentially, the victor in the *Essais*: the man besieged who shall find liberation by his very accessibility; deceived by rhetoric, he shall seem to expose himself artlessly; exploited by ceremony, he shall live into *Essais* that give leisure a new meaning.

From Idleness to Essaying: Transformations of Centrifugal and Centripetal Imagery

As the centerless striving of public action and leisure is more vividly apprehended, the contracted situation of the besieged or captured figure can begin to be seen not as a negative condition of retreat or stasis but as the beginning of a new kind of quest. We are now in a position to respond more fully to the summons of the essay "On Solitude," that we cease to live *hors de nous*, that we begin the voyage home, *chez nous*, to "repossess ourselves": "Since God gives us leisure to make arrangements for moving out, let us make them; let us pack our bags; let us take an early leave of the company; let us break free from the violent clutches that engage us elsewhere and draw us out of ourselves" (F., p. 178; T., p. 279). Even as it escapes the external flux of such *violentes pensées*, the retired mind, "wedded" to nothing but itself, must also begin an internal quest that will avoid the spiritual rapture of the kind of communion that gives fulfillment to a religious contemplative. It is a quest whose special urgency is poignantly apparent as early as the eighth essay of the first book, "Of Idleness," *De l'Oisiveté*. There, after seven essays exhibiting the centrifugal flux of public deeds and words, the reader is suddenly shocked to confront the same flux in the retired mind. One of the most powerful of the early essays, and one directly relevant to my sense of Montaigne's achievement, it is also brief enough to be quoted in its entirety:

> Just as we see that fallow land, if rich and fertile, teems with a hundred thousand kinds of wild and useless weeds, and that to set it to work we must subject it and sow it with certain seeds for our service; and as we see that women, alone, produce mere shapeless masses and lumps of flesh, but that to create a good and natural offspring they must be made fertile with a different kind of seed; so it is with minds. Unless you keep them busy with some definite subject that will bridle and control them, they throw themselves in disorder hither and yon in the vague field of imagination.
>
> *Sicut aquae tremulum labris ubi lumen ahenis*
> *Sole repercussum aut radiantis imagine Lunae*
> *Omnia pervolitat late loca, jamque sub auras*
> *Erigitur, summique ferit laquearia tecti.*
> (Aeneid 8. 22–25)
>
> as when in brazen bowls a flickering light from water, flung back by the sun or the moon's glittering form, flits far and wide o'er all things, and now mounts high and smites the fretted ceiling of the roof aloft.
>
> And there is no mad or idle fancy that they do not bring forth in this agitation:
>
>   *velut aegri somnia, vana*
> *Finguntur species.*
> (Ars Poetica 7)

Like a sick man's dreams
They form vain visions.

The soul that has no fixed goal loses itself; for as they say, to be everywhere is to be nowhere.

Quisquis ubique habitat, Maxime, nusquam habitat.

(Martial, 8. 73)

He who dwells everywhere, Maximus, nowhere dwells.

Lately when I retired to my home, determined so far as possible to bother about nothing except spending the little life I have left in rest and seclusion, it seemed to me I could do my mind no greater favor than to let it entertain itself in full idleness and stay and settle in itself, which I hoped it might do more easily now, having become weightier and riper with time. But I find—

variam semper dant otia mentem
(Lucian, 4. 704)

Ever idle hours breed wandering thoughts

—that, on the contrary, like a runaway horse, it gives itself a hundred times more trouble than it took for others, and gives birth to so many chimeras and fantastic monsters, one after another, without order or purpose, that in order to contemplate their ineptitude and strangeness at my pleasure, I have begun to put them in writing, hoping in time to make my mind ashamed of itself.

In earlier centuries the condition which Montaigne describes here would have been described by a religious contemplative as *acedia*, the ennui which is the sickness unto death, the desperate sloth which is the other side of work for its own sake. Here a richly related complex of agricultural, parturient, and equine imagery enforces the central insight that the peril of retirement is idleness, and idleness is the restless incapacity for true leisure. Idle land (*terris oysifs*) is not only wasted, it is overproductive; the crop of weeds is not only wild and useless but absurdly plentiful and variegated. To determine meaningful growth, what is needed even more than weeding is seeding. The same applies to women who otherwise produce shapeless masses and lumps of flesh and to minds that otherwise gallop unbridled *par-cy, par-la dans le vague champ des imaginations.* This last description recalls the teeming idle land of the opening line and also leads into the final concentration of all these in the nightmare centrifugal image of the retired mind as a runaway horse vexing itself and giving birth to chimeras and monsters. Having sought in retirement a centripetal focus of being, where the mind could "stay and settle in itself," Montaigne confesses that he still cannot escape the restless flux of becoming.

In earlier centuries these tendencies might have been absorbed or sublimated in a civic or religious tradition so that the mind could finally find leisure in something larger than itself—the restlessness of idleness being translated into action, which is itself a means to the goal of leisure. The very images of soil and horse and woman unite here to express a familiar georgic awareness of the simultaneous need for seed and bridle, generation and education, in the context of a communal reality. In contrast, Montaigne's own almost offhand response to the predicament of idleness is a radically personal version of the same process. Indeed, the fact that he does respond to it by writing about it, or, more precisely, by writing about writing about it, already illustrates his method and his theme: *et m'enfante tant de chimeres et monstres fantasques les un sur les autres, sans ordre, et sans propos, que pour en contempler à mon aise l'ineptie et l'estrangeté, j'ay commancé de les mettre en rolle, esperant avec le temps luy en faire honte a luy mesmes.* Of course the effect of this *mettre en rolle* will prove to be anything but the slyly announced purpose of putting an idle

mind to shame. Rather the writing—and implicitly the reading
—of these *essais* will transform idleness to leisure in a problematic and distinctively modern way.

It is a measure of what Horace gave us that, retrospectively,
we can think of so much of his best work as "essays" in self-
dramatization, whether written as satires, odes, or epistles.
Nevertheless, it is one thing to enact a retired and self-reflective alternative to the civic leisure of Augustan Rome and
another to venture the same private discovery in the context
of Catholic Rome and her ultimate city. This is why, for Montaigne and for those who read him and for all those since for
whom the old contexts will no longer be available, the discovery of the "essay" itself becomes so critically significant as both
the means and the goal of the imaginative achievement of the
new leisure, the feast without gods with its own reason for
being.

Ironically, the originality of Montaigne's conception of the
"essay" has been lost in the popularity and influence of his
work in the belles lettres of later periods and other cultures,
especially the English. What we need to recapture is precisely
that sense of the form (which we violate by calling it a form)
that is dramatized so pungently in this account of its genesis
in Montaigne's literally writing himself out of idleness. Or
rather "essaying himself": an awkward and unliterary phrase
that reflects the original sense of the word as a venture, an
experiment, a test, an assay. "To essay" is to create a provocatively new and private reconstruction of the life of action and
the life of leisure. In the language of the *Odyssey*, to essay is
to voyage out of Calypso's idleness and to experience the voyage itself as a homecoming to Phaeacian-Ithacan leisure. In the
language of the *Georgics*, to essay is to weed and seed and har-
ness and to experience that work as itself a harvest and liberation. The end is implicit in the means of "essaying," where
the process is itself its own product. In terms of the ends of
civic leisure or Christian contemplation, to essay is to enjoy the
free time of the citizen celebrating not the values of the *polis*

but his own act of celebration, contemplating not the vision of a god who has given ease but contemplating his own act of contemplation.

Let us admit that there is an infinite regress here in the celebration and contemplation of oneself celebrating and contemplating oneself celebrating and contemplating, but the predicament should be familiar to a twentieth-century reader as a characteristic strategy of the contemporary artist seeking to validate his work. A prime example is indeed the masterpiece of Montaigne's most distinguished twentieth-century admirer, André Gide. The distinction of *The Counterfeiters*, as Charles Feidelson points out in an illuminating analogy with the method of American symbolists, is just such an infinite regress:

> Thus the largest concept of the book is the making of the book. Its theme is a set of problems raised by its own creation. . . . While he is the advocate and practitioner of art, he calls his own method into question. The fictionality of the artifact, the transience of any resolution of the conflict that goes into its making, and the lawless variety of human creation are thoroughly taken into account by the structure of *Les Faux-monnayeurs*—by that very infinite regress which establishes creativity as the subject.[129]

And, of course, this is why Emerson, whose organic view of language and literature is the starting point of Feidelson's discussion, should himself have praised Montaigne as one of his representative men: "I know not anywhere the book that seems less written. . . . Cut these words and they would bleed; they are vascular and alive."[130] Indeed, as such a tribute reminds us, there is an ethical depth to the epistemological novelty of Montaigne's "essaying" of himself and his reader out of the flux of solipsistic idleness; it is the discovery of a new and innocent world of free time, proclaimed in the essay "Of Cannibals," translated into the vision "Of the Education of Children," and realized increasingly in the experience of the *Essais* themselves.

Hoc erat in votis: *"Of Cannibals," "Of the*
Education of Children"—The Natural Art

In these two essays, "Of Cannibals" and "Of the Education of
Children," which are among the most famous Montaigne ever
wrote, we can perceive an imaginative process profoundly akin
to the human or domestic recreation of those happy islands in
which we saw the vision of leisure emerge in the classical world.
What distinguishes Montaigne's, however, is its transformation
of that centrifugal and centripetal pattern which we began by
conceiving negatively. Now the world of natural flux and turbulence will be affirmed as the privileged perception of those
who disdain vulgar opinion and judge *par la voye de la raison,*
non par la voix commune (F., p. 150; T., p. 239) in contrast
to the centrifugal flux and violence of the centripetally petty
and rigid world we call civilization.

This contrast is powerfully expressed in the opening paragraph of the essay, before the New World of the cannibals in
South America is described directly. He begins casually, noting
the vanity of "civilized" opinion when a Greek general encounters the order and discipline of the Roman forces. " 'I do not
know what barbarians these are,' Pyrrhus is quoted as saying,
(for so the Greeks called all foreign nations) 'but the formation of this army that I see is not at all barbarous' " (F., p. 150;
T., p. 239). Here, reversing the pattern of siege and slaughter,
previously discussed in conjunction with rhetoric and ceremony, we have, so to speak, the emergence of the outsider as
victor, for every reader of the paragraph is reminded of the
massive historical triumph of "barbarian" Rome, which is his
inheritance, if he can see beyond "vulgar," superficially "civilized," opinion.

As we soon discover, that triumph was itself but the expression of a more elemental kind of triumph of natural forces.
For, in noting that he was acquainted for some ten or twelve
years with a native of the newly discovered continent, Montaigne speculates on other such continents, like Atlantis. Once
containing more land than Asia and Africa, Atlantis held in

subjection the breadth of Africa as far as Egypt and the length of Europe as far as Tuscany; indeed, it undertook to step over into Asia and subjugate all the nations that border on the Mediterranean, crossing Spain, Gaul, Italy, and Greece only to have its expansion checked by the Athenians. Then, almost anticlimactically, Montaigne reminds the reader that this sprawling, expanding world of civilized conquest was swallowed up in a flood (*mais que, quelque temps apres, et les Atheniens et eux, et leur isle furent engloutis par le deluge*, F., p. 150; T., pp. 239–40).

By this time, absorbed in the dialectical coordination of Greeks and Romans, "barbarian" order and "civilized" disorder, sprawling Atlantis and engulfing flood, the reader might well begin to wonder when the author intends to treat the subject announced in his title. And yet the very deluge, as it were, of this apparently disorderly and meandering style is profoundly what this essay is about. To encounter this oceanic prose is, from the start, to realize leisurely contemplation and naturalistic process, goal and journey, as one experience. For a moment, recalling Atlantis, our author will speculate on whether this New World might be the lost continent, but quickly he dismisses the possibility because of the remoteness of its location and, more importantly, because he cannot leave his contemplation of the flood, which paradoxically symbolizes what he is to celebrate in his new version of the blessed islands off in the West. For two paragraphs he meditates on the amazing changes wrought by the devastation of the waters on man's earthly habitations, violently separating Sicily from Italy, Cyprus from Syria, Euboea from Boeotia, but elsewhere joining lands that were divided, "filling the channels between them with sand and mud" (F., p. 150; T., p. 240). Appropriately, he cites Vergil's Helenus on the upheaval that created Sicily (*Aeneid* 3. 414–17) and Horace on the filling-up of a marsh, so that plows have replaced oars (*Ars Poetica* 65–66). And yet, Montaigne's view of the deluge will spring from deeper insights of each of these poets than these quotations suggest. Aeneas, after all, is being warned of the perils of navigating between Scylla and Charybdis as he seeks the goal of his storm-tossed odyssey. Montaigne's sense of the deluge's simultaneous dividing and uniting of lands expresses a more affirmative awe before the organic process of destruction and regeneration that might well remind us of the poem he regarded as *le plus accomply ouvrage de la Poesie*—Vergil's *Georgics* ("Of Books," F., p. 299; T., p. 451). Horace's allusion is to the mortality of human words and their speakers, despite our efforts to order nature. Beginning with the virtually Homeric comparison of the fate of words to the inevitable growth and fall of the leaves of trees, Horace somberly follows the lines that Montaigne quotes with the reminder that all mortal things will perish: *mortalia facta peribunt*. Words will fall and be reborn according to the cycles of usage (ll. 60–72). In this essay, as elsewhere, however, Montaigne will express an acceptance of natural process such as we saw in Horace's last *Epistles*. Indeed, the comparison of words to leaves will be transformed into a celebration of nature's organic art, which, like his own, is vascular and alive in contrast to empty ceremony and bloodless rhetoric.

Hence the meditation on the deluge continues, but this time closer to home. The movements, natural and feverish, of these great bodies are like those of our own, and Montaigne, looking down at the river Dordogne, reflects on how much ground it has gained over the past twenty years, eroding the foundations of several buildings. Were this to go on forever, the face of the world would be turned upside down (*la figure du monde seroit renversée*); but there are grounds for acceptance in the very fact of change, for the river overflows, now in one direction, now in another, and then again keeps to its course (F., p. 151; T., p. 251). Indeed, this author, whose first essay celebrated man as *merveilleusement vain, divers, et ondoyant* seems to find a sublime order, too, in the more disorderly inundations of the sea. In Médoc, his brother, the Sieur d'Arsac, can see the tops of some buildings of an estate of his buried in the sands. Resuming the martial imagery of the first paragraph, Montaigne now dramatizes the sea as the ultimate "barbarian," which, like the Romans against the Greeks, has a powerful discipline in its very wildness: "The inhabitants say that for some time the sea has been pushing toward them so hard that they have lost four leagues of land. These sands are its harbingers; and we see great dunes of moving sand that march half a league ahead of it and keep conquering land." Anticipating the opening affirmation in "Of Repentance"—that even the rocks of the Caucasus and the pyramids of Egypt share in the perpetual process, the *branloire perenne* of the world—the last sentence deserves special attention in the original for the blend of sublimity and naturalness which is its own form as well as its theme: *Ces sables sont ses fourriers: et voyons des grandes montjoies d'arène mouvant qui marchent d'une demi-lieue devant elle, et gaignent païs* (F., p. 151; T., p. 241).

When we recall that this study began by considering the sea as a virtually archetypal symbol of the flux of time, the special quality of Montaigne's affirmation becomes even more fascinating. Though "Of Cannibals" is usually related to Shakespeare's *Tempest* because of the echoes of its description of the culture of the cannibals in Gonzalo's naive utopian vision (*Tempest* 2. 1. 143–64), the deepest affinity between the two authors is perhaps best introduced by these opening paragraphs of Montaigne's and their kind of acceptance of a sea-change into something rich and strange, or, as Ferdinand proclaims at the end of the *Tempest*, "Though the seas threaten, they are merciful. / I have cursed them without cause" (5. 1. 178–79). Shakespeare, of course, defies simplification, by the very nature of dramatic characterization as well as by the rich and various complexity of his language and situations. (This is only Ferdinand speaking, and we must remember how Gonzalo's vision, like Miranda's "brave new world," has been undercut by subsequent events.) Nevertheless, perhaps the most thoughtful response to Auerbach's final and, one feels, reluctant assessment that Montaigne, alas, lacked the tragic sense of life might be the admission that he did, because his was another sense of life —one more like the vision of Shakespeare's final plays in their complex acceptance of life's tempests and time's flux.[131] As Polixenes says at the central festival of *The Winter's Tale*:

> Yet nature is made better by no mean
> But nature makes that mean: so, over that art,
> Which you say adds to nature, is an art
> That nature makes.
>
> *(Winter's Tale* 4. 4. 89–92)

The lines are about the grafting of flowers, but in their specific dramatic situation the reference to the marrying of a "gentler scion to the wildest stock" also alludes to union between the aristocratic Florizel and the (supposedly) base-born Perdita. The lines ask us to consider what it is that distinguishes the wild from the gentle, what those arts are that transform the one into the other. And they remind us (as the play will force their speaker to discover) that nurture and "great creating nature" finally are one:

> this grafting is an art
> Which does mend nature, change it rather, but
> The art itself is nature.
>
> (4. 4. 95–97)

So too, amid all the surprising revelations and reconciliations of the play's romance climax, we never lose sight of the triumph of time. The long-lost and now "revived" Hermione is presented first as a statue; but, as her transformed husband observes, the artifact shows the wrinkles of the sixteen years the "model" might have aged. "So much the more," responds Pauline, in a sentence that epitomizes the Shakespearean affinity with Montaigne, "our carver's excellence" (5. 3. 30). If the reader of Shakespeare's romances brings anything to Montaigne's essays, it is just this heightened consciousness that, as Frank Kermode says, transforming the language of Yeats, " 'whatever is begotten, born and dies' is nobler than 'monuments of unageing intellect'—and also, when truly considered, more truly lasting."[132]

Thus the essay "Of Cannibals" itself proceeds by linking the "march" of the sand dunes and the conquest of the sea to one other legendary place, as irrelevant as Atlantis, in one way, but just as relevant as that legend was in its affirmation of an emergent myth. The other reference in antiquity to this new world, he says, might come from Aristotle, who reports, in his little book *Of Unheard-of Wonders*, that certain Carthaginians discovered a "great fertile island, all clothed in woods and watered by deep rivers, far remote from any mainlands; and that they, and others since, attracted by the goodness and fertility of the soil," went to settle there with their wives and children" (F., p. 151; T., p. 241). If the fusion of art and wildness (*toute revestue de bois et arrousée de grandes et profondes rivières*) heightens the essays' earlier affirmation of "barbarian" invasions of natural forces, such as seas and rivers, that affirmation is confirmed by contrast with the rulers of Carthage, who, seeing their city depopulated, forbade anyone, on pain of death, to go to the fertile island and drove the new inhabitants from it, fearing that they might so multiply as to overrun the mother city. But of course this story does not apply to the new lands in America, Montaigne shrugs, having succeeded in further deepening his characteristic discrimination between one kind of expansion (positively, the landscape, the rivers, the "disorderly" population) and another (negatively, the "Seignieurs de Carthage" and their violence) and between one kind of contraction (positively, the island's remoteness from Carthage) and another (negatively, the strictness of the rule against migration).

And so, after some five paragraphs which have nothing and everything to do with the subject in their apparently "barbarian" disorder and naturalistic flux, we reach our destination: "that simple crude fellow" who, as the American translator conscientiously reminds the reader (who may well be still at sea himself), is the traveler who had lived in Brazil, whom Montaigne had spoken of at the beginning of the chapter. But, of course, the traveler, himself *simple et grossier*, points up the contrast between those whose words bear "true witness" and the *fines gens* who observe curiously but aim to report rhetorically and attractively. Like Montaigne and the savages who are his subject, the traveler is restricted in his expression but wide in his experience. The contrast irresistibly deepens again between the centripetal and centrifugal structures of the trav-

eler's (and Montaigne's) world and words and those of the map-
makers, who have seen only Palestine but would tell us of the
places they have never been—like those whose scrap of knowledge would encompass the whole of physics (F., p. 152; T., p.
242).

Here then is a blessed island in the West that is not presented
(like Horace's Sixteenth Epode) as a visonary alternative to our
fallen world but as one more down to earth than the illusions
of our culture, a place of serenity that is not so much removed
from the tempest but is the serene consummation of all that is
apparently tempestuous. In some of the most famous lines he
is to write, Montaigne draws together the reflections that have
led us through the opening paragraphs of our quest to the discovery, at once fabulous and naturalistic, that

> These people are wild, just as we call wild the fruits
> that Nature has produced by herself and in her nor-
> mal course; whereas really it is those that we have
> changed artificially and led astray from the common
> order, that we should rather call wild. . . . It is not
> reasonable that art should win the place of honor
> over our great and powerful mother Nature. We have
> so overloaded the beauty and richness of her works
> by our inventions that we have quite smothered her.
> . . . All our efforts cannot even succeed in reproduc-
> ing the nest of the tiniest little bird, its contexture,
> its beauty and convenience; or even the web of the
> puny spider. . . .
>   These nations, then, seem to me barbarous in this
> sense, that they have been fashioned very little by the
> human mind, and are still very close to their original
> naturalness. The laws of nature still rule them, very
> little corrupted by ours; and they are in such a state
> of purity that I am sometimes vexed that they were
> unknown earlier, in the days when there were men
> able to judge them better than we. I am sorry that
> Lycurgus and Plato did not know of them; for it
> seems to me that what we actually see in these nations
> surpasses not only all the pictures in which poets
> have idealized the golden age and all their inventions

in imagining a happy state of man; but also the conceptions and the very desire of philosophy. They could not imagine a naturalness so pure and simple as we see by experience; nor could they believe that our society could be maintained with so little artifice and human solder. This is a nation, I should say to Plato, in which there is no sort of traffic, no knowledge of letters, no science of numbers, no name for a magistrate or for political superiority, no custom of servitude, no riches or poverty, no contracts, no successions, no partitions, no occupations but leisure ones, no care for any but common kinship, no clothes, no agriculture, no metal, no use of wine or wheat. The very words that signify lying, treachery, dissimulation, avarice, envy, belittling, pardon—unheard of. How far from this perfection would he find the republic that he imagined: *Viri a diis recentes* (Men fresh sprung from the gods, Seneca, *Epistles* 90).

Hos natura modos primum dedit

[These manners nature first ordained, *Georgics* 2. 20.]

Ils sont sauvages, de mesmes que nous appellons sauvages les fruicts que nature, de soy et de son progrez ordinaire, a produicts: là où, à la verité, ce sont ceux que nous avons alterez par nostre artifice et detournez de l'ordre commun, que nous devrions appeller plutost sauvages. . . . Ce n'est pas raison que l'art gaigne le point d'honneur sur nostre grande et puissante mere nature. Nous avons tant rechargé la beauté et richesse de ses ouvrages par nos inventions, que nous l'avons du tout estouffée. . . . Tous nos efforts ne peuvent seulement arriver à representer le nid du moindre oyselet, sa contexture, sa beauté et l'utilité de son usage, non pas la tissure de la chetive arraignée. . . . Ces nations me semblent donq ainsi barbares, pour avoir receu fort peu de façon de l'esprit humain, et estre encore fort voisines de leur naifveté originelle. Les loix naturelles leur commandent encores, fort peu abastardies par les nostres;

*mais c'est en telle pureté, qu'il me prend quelque
fois desplaisir dequoy la cognoissance n'en soit venuë
plustost, du temps qu'il y avoit des hommes qui en
eussent sceu mieux juger que nous. Il me desplait
que Licurgus et Platon ne l'ayent eüe; car il me
semble que ce que nous voyons par experience en ces
nations là, surpasse, non seulement toutes les pein-
tures dequoy la poësie a embelly l'age doré, et toutes
ses inventions à feindre une heureuse condition
d'hommes, mais encore la conception et le desir
mesme de la philosophie. Ils n'ont peu imaginer une
nayfveté si pure et simple, comme nous la voyons
par experience; ny n'ont peu croire que nostre so-
cieté se peut maintenir avec si peu d'artifice et de
soudeure humaine. C'est une nation, diroy je à
Platon, en laquelle il n'y a aucune espece de trafique;
nul cognoissance de lettres; nulle science de nom-
bres; nul nom de magistrat, ny de superiorité po-
litique; nul usage de service, de richesse ou de pauv-
reté; nuls contrats; nulles successions; nuls partages;
nulles occupations qu'oysives; nul respect de parenté
que commun; nuls vestemens; nulle agriculture; nul
metal; nul usage de vin ou de bled. Les paroles
mesmes qui signifient le mensonge, la trahison, la
dissimulation, l'avarice, l'envie, la detraction, le pardon, inouies. Combien trouveroit il la republique
qu'il a imaginée esloignée de cette perfection:* viri a
diis recentes.

Hos natura modos primum dedit.

(F., pp. 152–53; T., pp. 243–44)

These last lines from the *Georgics* remind us of the civic
resonance of this description of a primitive folk that is at once
both Ithacan and Phaeacian, a culture where weapons and tools
of hard wood blend with frequent dancing, where fasting
blends with festive drinking, and where the ethical code can
be summarized in *la vaillance contre les ennemis et l'amitié a
leur femmes* (F., pp. 153–54; T., pp. 244–45). Cannibalism itself affords the possibility of heroism in defeat and, in victory,

provides Montaigne with his most outrageous affirmation of the centrifugal flux of the naturalistic world in contrast to the negative image, in the civilized world, of slaughter and ceremony, such as we have already glimpsed in the mutilation of a Sechelles. When the cannibals have taken their prisoners and have roasted and eaten them in common, the leftovers are sent round to absent friends. A grisly blend of the centripetal and centrifugal, there, to a common reader; but the same reader might perceive the more sinister implications of the centripetal/centrifugal imagery of the "civilized" alternative introduced by the Portuguese, which was to bury their prisoners up to the waist, shoot them full of arrows, and then hang them (F., p. 155; T., p. 247). Forcing the imagery to a grotesque extreme, forcing the reader to discriminate one savagery from another, Montaigne insists,

> I think there is more barbarity in eating a man alive than in eating him dead; and in tearing by tortures and the rack a body still full of feeling, in roasting a man bit by bit, in having him bitten and mangled by dogs and swine (as we have not only read but seen within fresh memory, not among ancient enemies, but among neighbors and fellow citizens, and what is worse, on the pretext of piety and religion), than in roasting and eating him after he is dead [F., p. 155; T., pp. 247–48].

Here, as the reader confronts the hideous kind of "feast" that the God of Christian piety has sanctioned, he begins to perceive that, though the ethos of the essay "Of Cannibals" is profoundly georgic, it is also peculiarly non-Vergilian. It uses the georgic myth of a rural emblem of the good community to enforce an alienation from the sacred and secular city of the historical moment. It is as if Vergil's rural workers had been transplanted to the prophetic isle of Horace's Sixteenth Epode. Unlike the georgic farmers of Rome's *Saturnia tellus*, these natives are themselves peculiarly retired; isolated by high mountains and the sea, they summon us not to a civic alle-

giance but to a redefinition of the good city and its free time
which will be, to use a barbarous locution, the *Georgics* Hora-
tianized or the *age doré* of the cannibals "essayed."

"Essayed" indeed, as they might be in the kind of natural art
which is his vision of the leisurely essence of liberal education
in his essay "On the Education of Children." In an anecdote
which perfectly illustrates the theme of this essay, Montaigne
tells how he met two teachers on the road; some distance behind them rode a count and his retinue. One of Montaigne's
men asked the first teacher "who that gentleman was, following behind." Unaware of the count, and thinking the question
referred to his companion, the teacher replied *plaisamment*,
"He is not a gentleman; he is a grammarian, and I am a logician." Outraged by such (literally) trivial distinctions, Montaigne's next sentence is savagely sarcastic and abrupt: "Now
we, who are trying on the contrary to make not a grammarian
or a logician, but a gentleman, let us allow them to misuse
their free time: we have business elsewhere" (*Or, nous qui
cherchons icy, au rebours, de former non un grammarien ou
logicien mais un gentil'homme, laissons les abuser de leur loisir: nous avons affaire ailleurs*, F., p. 125; T., p. 204).

The distinction organizes the essay, and it is worth noting
at the start that, unlike those who "abuse their leisure," the
gentleman's affinity is with the natural man, even the savage
as previously defined, more than with the scholar, just as, in
the opening argument, Montaigne announces his preference
for *un habil homme* to *un homme sçavant*. Montaigne opens
the essay's central imaginative vision of the goal of liberal education with the engaging instance of Socrates to exemplify the
value of the "gentleman," who is of course also a "barbarian"
in his way (and hence superior to the pedant, whose values
recall previous cases of whirling words and violence that spring
from constricted and rigid systems). Reworking the early pro-
treptic anecdote on the detachment of Anaxagoras, Montaigne
has someone ask Socrates where he is from. His reply is at once
more solitary and more inclusive: "not Athens," he answers,
but "the world." For, seen in this perspective, it is the civic

activist who is really huddled and concentrated in himself (like the seigneurs of Carthage who forbade migration). It is the solitary sage, rising above vulgar civic opinion, who has been vouchsafed the more inclusive vision: "He, whose imagination was fuller and more extensive, embraced the universe as his city, and distributed his knowledge, his company, and his affections to all mankind, unlike us who look only at what is underfoot" (F., p. 116; T., pp. 190–91).

But this imagination, *plus plaine et plus estanduë*, is possible only because of the philosopher's withdrawal and acknowledgment of his own limitations. This simultaneous expansion and contraction is movingly phrased a few lines later:

> But whoever considers as in a painting the great picture of our mother Nature in her full majesty; whoever reads such universal and constant variety in her face; whoever finds himself there, and not merely himself, but a whole kingdom, as a dot made with a very fine brush; that man alone estimates things according to their true proportions [F., p. 116; T., p. 191].

In themselves these two exalted statements read like nothing if not a justification of the life of otherworldly detachment. Their truly remarkable quality, however, is that they use such language to advance a radically different goal, closer to that of the essay "Of Cannibals": that of the *habil homme* instead of the *homme sçavant*. Whether or not Montaigne was aware that his parable of Socrates had a parallel in the story of Anaxagoras, his version of it is symptomatic of his transformation of the contemplative life from an exercise in metaphysical speculation to the mundane pursuit of self-scrutiny. This is especially evident in the next lines, which turn from the objective and transcendental language of the universe as one's city and of the great picture of Nature to the subjective and humanistic implications of a mirror in which we recognize ourselves as our true book (F., p. 116; T., p. 190). It was a medieval commonplace that in addition to the Scriptures there existed a "book of the creatures" (which by a nice coincidence was also

the subtitle of Sebond's *Natural Theology*) and that, by using
this book for contemplation of created things, man might ascend to God. In the mirror-like book that Montaigne proposes
here, however, no such ascent is promised. The student is to
contemplate nothing more than the human condition, and he
is to find nothing less than himself.

This substitution of a radically humanistic for a metaphysical justification of the contemplative life is particularly evident
a few lines later, in a discussion of the proper priority of subjects in the curriculum. The first lessons, Montaigne insists,
should be those that teach ethical behavior, those "that will
teach him to know himself and to die well and live well" (F.,
p. 117; T., p. 192). But what strikes any reader aware of the
traditional dictum that, like the contemplative leisure of the
gods, liberal knowledge is its own end is Montaigne's audacious
labeling of this pragmatic instruction (or even "servile work")
as a liberal art, indeed as the most liberal: "Among the liberal
arts, let us begin with the art that liberates us. They are all
somewhat useful for edification and service of our life, just as
everything else is somewhat useful. But let us choose the one
that is directly and professedly useful for it" (F., p. 117; T.,
pp. 192–93). The first two authorities cited to support this are
Socrates, because of his contempt for any knowledge that is not
humanly useful, and Horace, because of a quotable injunction
from the Epistle to Lollius Maximus which was to become
Goethe's motto for the Enlightenment: "Dare to be wise—and
start right away" (*Sapere aude, / incipe*, line 40). Aside from
Horace, few authors have been able to dramatize what I have
called the liberations of contentment, suffusing the moderation
of the contained life with the celebration of free time. What
is needed would seem to be some equivalent of the Christian
pastoral reward for those who accept a yoke which therefore
seems sweet and a burden which therefore seems light. Such
a discovery is the climax of this essay, the transformation of
mundane moral education into an authentic condition of contemplative leisure which shares in the liberation of Socrates and
the cannibals and of the author and reader of the *Essais*. To

turn a page here is to behold the difference between being told what is most liberating and seeing it come to imaginative life:

> It is a strange fact that things should be in such a pass in our century that philosophy, even with people of understanding, should be an empty and fantastic name, a thing of no use and no value, both in common opinion and in fact. I think those quibblings which have taken possession of all the approaches to her are the cause of this. It is very wrong to portray her as inaccessible to children, with a surly, frowning, and terrifying face. Who has masked her with this false face, pale and hideous? There is nothing more gay, more lusty, more sprightly, and I might almost say more frolicsome. She preaches nothing but merry-making and a good time [F., p. 118].

> *C'est grand cas que les choses en soyent là en nostre siecle, que la philosophie, ce soit, jusques aux gens d'entendement, un nom vain et fantastique, qui se treuve de nul usage et de nul pris, et par opinion et par effect. Je croy que ces ergotismes en sont cause, qui ont saisi ses avenues. On a grand tort de la peindre inaccessible aux enfans, et d'un visage renfroigné, sourcilleux et terrible. Qui me l'a masquée de ce faux visage, pasle et hideux? Il n'est rien plus gay, plus gaillard, plus enjoué, et à peu que je ne dise follastre. Elle ne presche que feste et bon temps* [T., p. 194].

> The surest sign of wisdom is constant cheerfulness; her state is like that of things above the moon, ever serene. It is *Barroco* and *Baralipton* that make their disciples dirt-caked and smoky, and not she; they know her only by hearsay. Why, she makes it her business to calm the tempests of the soul and to teach hungers and fevers to laugh, not by some imaginary epicycles, but by natural and palpable reasons. She has virtue as her goal, which is not, as the schoolmen say, set on the top of a steep, rugged, inaccessible mountain. Those who have approached virtue maintain, on the contrary, that she is established in a

beautiful plain, fertile and flowering, from where, to be sure, she sees all things beneath her; but you can get there, if you know the way, by shady, grassy, sweetly flowering roads, pleasantly, by an easy smooth slope, like that of the celestial vaults [F., p. 119].

La plus expresse marque de la sagesse, c'est une es-jouïssance constante; son estat est comme des choses au dessus de la Lune: tousjours serein. C'est "Bar-roco" et "Baralipton" qui rendent leurs supposts ainsi crotez et enfumés, ce n'est pas elle: ils ne la connoissent que par ouïr dire. Comment? elle fait estat de serainer les tempestes de l'ame, et d'appren-dre la fain et les fiebvres à rire, non par quelques Epicycles imaginaires, mais par raisons naturelles et palpables. Elle a pour son but la vertu, qui n'est pas, comme dit l'eschole, plantée à la teste d'un mont coupé, rabotteux et inaccessible. Ceux qui l'ont ap-prochée, la tiennent, au rebours, logée dans une belle plaine fertile et fleurissante, d'où elle void bien souz soy toutes choses; mais si peut on y arriver, qui en sçait l'addresse, par des routtes ombrageuses, gazon-nées et doux fleurantes, plaisamment et d'une pante facile et polie, comme est celle des voutes celestes [T., p. 195].

In these two unforgettable passages the difference between Philosophy as she appears to most men and Philosophy as she "really" is might epitomize all of the differences I have been trying to explore between the Greek and the "savage" Roman, the pedant and the gentleman, the metaphysician and the mor-alist. What distinguishes the description of authentic philos-ophy, however, is a veritably visionary transformation of an abstract conception or personification into a fabulous presence personally encountered. What gives the latter its peculiarly mythic effectiveness would seem to be the rich and inviting profusion of festive and (in the second quotation) pastoral imagery which enacts its promise of free time. In its imme-diate context, the description of Philosophy—which, as Mon-taigne means it here, might be called "Wisdom"—is as expansive as the lines on Socrates' "city of the universe" or "the great picture" of mother nature in which man is lost; at the same time, it is as intimate as the "mirror" or "book" in which man finds himself. Looked at in terms of the preceding essays, this vision of *un feste et bon temps* offers a convivial and expansive center to the stoic fugitive of *De la Solitude*. With *une belle plaine fertile et fleurissante* it reveals the transformation of *De l'Oisiveté*'s idle fields and weeds by the discovery of *une autre semence*, creative leisure instead of *acedia*. At the same time, to return to this chapter's point of departure, transcendental humors frighten him here, too, "like lofty and inaccessible places," and one thinks of him, even near Dante's Mountain of Purgatory, happy enough at the foot of the hill, enjoying Casella's song, or, in the *belle plaine fertile et fleurissante* of the sacred wood, content to contemplate for its own sake what is only the starting point for a more exalted and dizzying contemplation in Dante's poem. Montaigne does not seek a handful larger than the hand, but his contraction contains an unmistakable expansion, just as, to use his own figure, the deep valley at the foot of the inaccessible mountain reflects and, as it were, assimilates the grandeur of the altitude it opposes. The "descent," to contemplate the human condition, is thus its own kind of ascent. The natural implicates the supernatural reality which it displaces, just as the *routes ombrageuses, gazonnées et doux fleurantes* of the smooth, sloping descent remind the author of nothing more than *les voutes celestes*.

Finally, looking back to "On Cannibals," we see that Montaigne's vision of education not only proposes a renovation of the Christian contemplative or pastoral tradition but also assimilates the naturalistic myth of the essay on the cannibals and renders it into a civilized ideal by the liberal "art" which "itself is nature." One cannot sail off to the blessed isles—or to Brazil—but one can at least recreate those dreams in human terms, as Horace did on a Sabine farm and as Montaigne proposes in this essay.

There is an instructive irony in the coincidence that the quotation from Plato's *Laws* which, following Pieper, I have already quoted to defend the festive leisure of Phaeacian civilization should become in Montaigne's hands a way of justifying that natural nurture by which man might attain to the artless *age doré* of the cannibals. In both Plato and Montaigne the target is much the same: for Plato, it is a Lacedaemonian severity, a simple-minded moralism and civic pragmatism; for Montaigne, it is the discipline of the schools:

> They might have erred less harmfully by leaning toward indulgence. They are a real jail of captive youth. They make them slack, by punishing them for slackness before they show it. Go in at lesson time: you hear nothing but cries, both from tortured boys and from masters drunk with rage. . . . How much more fittingly would their classes be strewn with flowers and leaves than with bloody stumps of birch rods! I would have portraits there of Joy and Gladness, and Flora and the Graces, as the philosopher Speusippus had in his school. Where their profit is, let their frolic be also. Healthy foods should be sweetened for the child, and harmful ones dipped in gall.
>
> It is wonderful how solicitous Plato shows himself in his *Laws* about the gaiety and pastimes of the youth of his city, and how much he dwells upon their races, games, songs, jumping, and dancing, whose conduct and patronage he says antiquity gave to the gods themselves: Apollo, the Muses, and Minerva [F., p. 123].

> *On eust faily à l'adventure moins dommageablement, s'inclinant vers l'indulgence. C'est une vraye geaule de jeunesse captive. On la rend desbauchée, l'en puissant avant qu'elle le soit. Arrivez-y sur le point de leur office: vous n'oyez que criz et d'enfans suppliciez, et de maistres enyvrez en leur cholere. . . . Combien leurs classes seroient plus decemment jonchées de fleurs et de feuilles que de tronçons d'osier sanglants. J'y feroy pourtraire la joye, l'allegresse, et Flora et les Graces, comme fit en son eschole le philosophe Speusippus. Où est leur profit, que ce fust aussi*

> *leur esbat. On doit ensucrer les viandes salubres à*
> *l'enfant, et enfieller celles qui luy sont nuisibles.*
>
> *C'est merveille combien Platon se montre soigneux*
> *en ses loix, de la gayeté et passetemps de la jeunesse*
> *de sa cité, et combien il s'arreste à leurs courses, jeux,*
> *chansons, saults et danses, des quelles il dit que l'an-*
> *tiquité a donné la conduitte et le patronnage aux*
> *dieux mesmes: Apollon, les Muses et Minerve* [T.,
> p. 200].

What especially arrests the attention here is how the rhetorical forces of that vivid image, *leurs classes . . . jonchées de fleurs*
et de feuilles, transcends its logical and grammatical function
as a preferable but hypothetical alternative to *tronçons d'osier*
sanglants. The classroom strewn with leaves and flowers becomes in itself a profoundly suggestive symbol of nature as
nurture, domesticating the pastoral ideal of the cannibals and
concretely embodying the idyllic situation of this essay's virtue,
logée dans une belle plaine fertile et fleurissante. It is the perfect alternative to the earlier essay's horror of natural exuberance springing from the *terres oisives* of unleisurely idleness.
The passage from the *Laws* which Pieper cites in declaring that
there is no such thing as a feast without gods thus becomes an
occasion for Montaigne to declare that there are no such things
as gods without a feast. In the same way, one notices that the
gods evoked by this humane vision are distinctively anthropo-
morphic. Like his Philosophy, which preaches nothing but *feste*
et bon temps, Montaigne's Joy and Gladness, Flora and the
Graces, are personifications of human qualities, images of man's
own leisure transfigured as opposed to divine authorities by
whom it is sanctioned or "nurtured." Like Shakespeare's Perdita, a princess mistaken for a commoner dressed up as a queen
in a harvest festival, Montaigne's classroom strewn with flowers
and leaves—the container and the thing contained each absorbing and being absorbed by the other—tells us beyond paraphrase
that the art itself is nature.

As the quotation from Plato's *Laws* reminds us, this reading
of *De l'Institution des Enfans* has so far been concerned with
the public aspect of the essay, suited to its being a letter of

advice to a noble lady with children to educate. To demonstrate the distinctively retired quality of the essay, it will be useful for a moment to consider its affinity with the proposals of two of Montaigne's countrymen in the eighteenth century, both of whom shared his interest in a naturalistic utopia and in the improvement of education: Rousseau and Voltaire. For unless one posits an irreconcilable conflict between the pedagogy and politics of Rousseau (that is, between *Emile* and *The Social Contract*), his program—despite its withdrawal from society —must, I think, be seen as the formulation of a new doctrine of civic leisure, conceived in Romantic and naturalistic terms. "Rousseau's plan of education," as Cassirer writes, "by no means rules out Emile's education to citizenship, but it educates him exclusively to be a 'citizen among those who are to be.' "[133] More like Montaigne, it would seem, is the disposition of Voltaire's Candide: cast out of the bogus Eden of his childhood's civilization, he finds in El Dorado a deistic utopia which proves unavailable to him in any practical public way. According to this interpretation, therefore, the famous conclusion becomes an image of the hero's recreation in his private circumstances of the ideal he found in South America.[134] In the same way it might be said that just as Montaigne's naturalistic dream in "Of Cannibals" is translated into the educational vision of "On the Education of Children," so this vision can be realized by him only in a most private way. For Montaigne, to contemplate "Nature" or "Virtue" is to contemplate himself; to "cultivate his garden" is to compose the *Essais*.

As Montaigne describes it in "On the Education of Children," the personal nature of the statement he is making—and the kind of education he is enacting as well as preserving— opposes the derivative or public one in much the same way as his "artless" style opposes elaborately wrought rhetoric or his "natural" and liberating view of education opposes the formal and restrictive one. In writing the essays he disdains to do as others have done, "covering themselves with other men's armour until they don't even show their fingertips." Instead, his essays will be artless and personal:

However that may be, I mean to say, and whatever
these absurdities may be, I have had no intention of
concealing them, any more than I would a bald and
graying portrait of myself, in which the painter had
drawn not a perfect face, but mine. For likewise
these are my humors and opinions; I offer them as
what I believe, not what is to be believed. I aim
here only at revealing myself, who will perhaps be
different tomorrow, if I learn something new which
changes me [F., pp. 108–9].

*Quoy qu'il en soit, veux-je dire, et quelles que soyent
ces inepties, je n'ay pas deliberé de les cacher, non
plus qu'un mien pourtraict chauve et grisonnant, où
le peintre auroit mis, non un visage parfaict, mais
le mien. Car aussi ce sont ici mes humeurs et opinions; je les donne pour ce qui est en ma creance, non
pour ce qui est à croire. Je ne vise icy qu'à découvrir
moy mesmes, qui seray par adventure autre demain,
si nouveau apprentissage me change* [T., p. 180].

Non un visage parfaict, mais le mien—the portrait of the
author exhibited in Montaigne's essays is the living record of
his transformation of otherworldly contemplative leisure into
the study of himself, and, regarding it in that light, one can
begin to understand Pascal's indignation at *le sot projet qu'il
a de se peindre.* Yet, as I have tried to demonstrate, the project
had its precedents in Horace. That Montaigne was directly influenced by Archilochus and Alcaeus is unlikely, but it seems
clear, as Villey suggests, that here, if anywhere, one can detect
the influence of the Latin poet whom the essayist quotes most
often: "Guidé par Horace," writes Villey, "Montaigne dégage la
morale qui convient à son tempérament, il devient lui-même,
il vient à nous sans faire toilette."[135] So vivid is Montaigne's
peinture de moi that the reader of the essays may well feel that,
in the fullest sense of the cliché, he knows Montaigne as well
as he knows himself. Certainly the features of his character
which the author has selected for bold delineation create the
effect of an uncommonly intimate revelation, *sans faire toilette.*

The most notable is doubtless his confession of his experiences with the kidney stone, how he lived in horror of death from it, such as his father suffered, but how gradually he came to accept it. There are, however, many other details, less momentous but telling in their cumulative effect. In the present essay, for example, Montaigne's views of education are colored by the recollection of his own experience of the process he is describing—of how, for example, his father had him awakened every morning to music or how, as a child, he learned Latin "naturally" as his native tongue (it was spoken to him by a tutor who could not speak French). In chapter 3 I have suggested how the tutelage of his father and the free time of the Grove of Academe function in Horace's poetry as symbols of an ideal to be recaptured on a Sabine farm—or even "at Ulubrae." In the same way, Montaigne's own self-portraiture becomes the best example of his theory of education. The essayist's condition now is the mature recreation in a problematic world of an early state of innocent leisure.

What needs special emphasis, however, is that the essayist's condition is very much the condition of being an essayist. To see the full significance of the self-portrait of Montaigne, one must see more than the portrait of a man with certain amiable personal habits: one must see the portrait of a man composing a portrait. It is this self-critical quality of the author's dramatized consciousness that informs Montaigne's contemplation of the mundane rather than the sacred with a complexity that is, in the best sense, modern. Montaigne yields more than the worldly wisdom of a Sancho Panza shrugging off idealism, because he offers within his centripetal secular realism a kind of idealism which, if it is contradictory or "evasive" of the norms of Christian humanism, nevertheless defines the possibility of another kind of humanism, albeit not a simple one. There is more involved in what I have described as Montaigne's personal secularization of the contemplative life than simply the focus on this world rather than a supernatural one, more even than the focus on the self in all its idiosyncrasies. The "critical" and, I suspect, distinctively modern quality of Montaigne's humanism is its self-reflective character: for him to contemplate this world or himself is first and essentially to contemplate his own act of contemplation as much as, perhaps even more than, the particular object to be contemplated. That Montaigne's father had awakened him to music might be interesting in itself, but what is interesting in the essay—and what interests the author—is his own savoring of the recollection. What matters is the recapturing more than the thing recaptured, the contemplating more than the thing contemplated, or, as Montaigne put it in a later statement, informed by the very form-content dualism which he reverses, it is the "fashioning" rather than the "furnishing" of his mind which occupies him (in the contemplative freedom from occupation):

> I would rather fashion my mind than furnish it. There is no occupation that is either weaker or stronger, according to the mind involved, than entertaining one's own thoughts. The greatest minds make it their profession, "to whom living is thinking." Thus nature has favored it with this privilege, that there is nothing we can do so long, and no action to which we can devote ourselves more commonly and easily. It is the occupation of the gods, says Aristotle, from which springs their happiness [F., p. 622].

> *J'aime mieux forger mon ame que la meubler. Il n'est point d'occupation ny plus foible, ny plus forte, que celle d'entretenir ses pensées selon l'ame que c'est. Les plus grandes en font leur vacation, "quibus vivere est cogitare."* Aussi l'a nature favorisée de ce privilege quil n'y a rien que nous puissons faire si longtemps, ny action à la quelle nous nous addonons plus ordinairement et facilement. C'est la besongne des Dieus, dict Aristote, de laquelle nait et leur beatitude et la nostre [T., pp. 915–16].

*Cicero, *Tusculan Disputations* 5. 38.

Here the emphasis, characteristic of Montaigne and so different from Aristotle's justification of the contemplative life,
is on becoming rather than being, on process rather than direction, on form rather than content. More precisely, to use the
language of the habit of mind which Montaigne is literally
turning inside out, the insistence is on form as its own kind
of content, process as its own direction, becoming as its own
intimation of being. The classic example of contemplative leisure which Montaigne cites, the timeless beatitude of the gods,
is seen as a possibility within time. To return to the excerpt
cited by Auerbach: even though he may regard this life as
nostre estre, nostre tout, Montaigne does not contemplate it
the way angels enjoy the beatific vision or Christian contemplatives find intimations of "paradise." They do not contemplate themselves contemplating their object. And they do not
write "essays." Unfortunately, since Montaigne first assigned
it to his collection of jottings, the currency of the formal literary meaning of the word "essay" has tended to obscure its original connotations of experimentation, trial, and incomplete-
ness which are so apposite to Montaigne's way of redefining
contemplative leisure. For just as Montaigne contemplates himself in the act of contemplating, the "personal" quality of the
essays, which seems to have been least appreciated, resides in
the extraordinary extent to which their subject is their own
composition. The essays not only enact the process of Montaigne's contemplative leisure but are themselves the objects
of his contemplation. The essays are assays of themselves.

This interpretation of Montaigne's portrait or contemplation of himself and the personal and self-critical character of
the essays might be summarized by the last sentence of the essay
on the education of children: "By dint of whipping, they are
given their pocketful of learning for safekeeping; but if learning is to do us any good, we must not merely lodge it within us,
we must espouse it" (*On leur donne à coups de foület en garde
leur pochette pleine de science, laquelle, pour bien faire, il ne
faut pas seulement, loger chez soy, il la faut espouser,* F., p.
131; T., p. 213). *Il la faut espouser:* if the marriage metaphor
reminds us of a similar injunction in "Of Solitude" (*n'espouser*

rien que soy) the difference in the present instance is even more striking. In the earlier essay the emphasis is on a negative withdrawal from entanglement and process, connotations more suitably suggested here by the image of "the pocketful of learning for safekeeping," the mere *loger chez soy*. In the present case the metaphor expresses a creative projection of the self, a "seeding" of idleness that will come to fruition in leisure, in the discipline of the "philosophy" that preaches nothing but *feste et bon temps*. For what Montaigne says of the education of children applies also to his transformation of *acedia* into leisure. It is not enough to be *chez soy*; one must also be *espousé*, which is to say, if one is Montaigne, one must write essays. That is why probably the best commentary on the essay's final image of a mind married to learning is the first sentence's confession of the author's parental love for his "offspring":

> I have never seen a father who failed to claim his son, however mangy or hunchbacked he was. Not that he does not perceive his defect, unless he is utterly intoxicated by his affection; but the fact remains that the boy is his. And so I myself see better than anyone else that these are nothing but reveries of a man who has tasted only the outer crusts of sciences in his childhood, and has retained only a vague general picture of them: a little of everything and nothing thoroughly, French style [F., p. 106].

> *Je ne vis jamais pere, pour teigneux ou bossé que fut son fils, qui laissast de l'avoüer. Non pourtant, s'il n'est du tout enyvré de cet' affection, qu'il ne s'aperçoive de sa defaillance; mais tant y a qu'il est sien. Aussi moy, je voy, mieux que tout autre, que ce ne sont icy que resveries d'homme qui n'a gousté des sciences que la crouste premiere, en son enfance, et n'en a retenu qu'un general et informe visage: un peu de chaque chose, et rien du tout, à la Françoise* [T., pp. 176–77].

We recall how, in the essay "Of Idleness," the image of deformed "offspring" from an unseeded ground or woman was charged with the author's perturbation at his failure to find the stasis he had sought in merely doing nothing. In the lines before us, however, the employment of the comparable image of the *teigneux ou bossé . . . fils* expresses the author's acceptance of his own "deformity" and "disorder" as the conditions of the self-knowledge and growth which define his own education and which are reflected in the form of the essays themselves—*un peu de chaque chose, et rien du tout, à la Françoise.*

Similarly, a few lines later, in describing his particular abilities and preferences, of which the essays are assays, Montaigne admits:

> As for the natural faculties that are in me, of which this book is the essay, I feel them bending under the load. My conceptions and my judgment move only by groping, staggering, stumbling, and blundering; and when I have gone ahead as far as I can, still I am not at all satisfied: I can still see country beyond, but with a dim and clouded vision, so that I cannot clearly distinguish it [F., p. 107].

> *Quant aux facultez naturelles qui sont en moy, de-quoy c'est icy l'essay, je les sens flechir sous la charge. Mes conceptions et mon jugement ne marche qu'à tastons, chancelant, bronchant et chopant; et, quand je suis allé le plus avant que je puis, si ne me suis-je aucunement satisfaict: je voy encore du païs au delà, mais d'une veue trouble et en nuage, que je ne puis desmeler* [T., p. 177].

Again, in "Of Idleness" the author had spoken ruefully of the tendency of the unbridled mind to sport in the vague fields of imagination, to gallop off like a runaway horse lacking a fixed goal (*but estably*). The lines just quoted define and exemplify an equivalent of this fixed goal but without the static "bridling" which the author of the earlier essay seems to have meant by the term. For, unlike most goals, this one exists not in some country *au delà*; rather, the process of self-study is autotelic. To reiterate the remark of Jacques Perret, quoted apropos of Horace's *Epistles* but most relevant to this aspect of

Montaigne, "There is no port: these gropings are wisdom itself. . . . Wisdom is that extending of oneself that is always new even although in a continuous line, always unfinished although always in progress."[136] Nor, as this appreciation reminds us, can Montaigne's "goal" properly be called "fixed' or *estably*. Instead, as the asyndetic flow of the syntax and the present-participial quality of the verbal adjectives describe it (*ne . . . qu'à tastons, chancelant, bronchant et chopant*), the movement of his mind is as random and wayward as it is linear and progressive. Likewise, while the next two segments are more hypotactic in structure, their very conclusions are still, so to speak, inconclusive (*si ne me suis-je aucunement satisfaict . . . que je ne puis desmeler*).

Christians speak of seeing now as in a glass darkly, but they are assured of finally seeing God face to face, and this beatific vision is their "fixed goal." In these lines Montaigne is vouchsafed no such ultimate revelation, and yet his *veue trouble et en nuage* might be said to have its own title to being regarded as a *bios theōrētikos*, a life devoted to seeing. It is the kind of "seeing" which leaves the seer "dissatisfied . . . , unable to distinguish" the country which lies beyond his own clouded range of vision. It is the seeing that comes with groping, staggering, stumbling, and blundering which is being "essayed" on this very page, *de quoy c'est ici l'essay*. For Montaigne himself is forming "not a grammarian or a logician" but a man, an *honnête homme*, one who is to contemplate not unchanging truths but a changeable self in the very act of contemplation, one whose free time will be found not in the timeless realms of pure being but in this world of flux and becoming, one who is to be not an angel but a man: one who makes "essays."

Je peins le passage: *The* Essais *as Continuing Quest and Transformation*

It was, appropriately, Montaigne who best articulated what I have been trying to say about his transformation of the contemplative life. These famous words, already invoked in the

reading of Horace's *Epistles* and invoked again as a point of
departure for the present discussion, may now perhaps be savored with a fuller appreciation of their constellation of his
central images and themes.

> Others form man; I tell of him, and portray a par-
> ticular one, very ill-formed, whom I should really
> make very different from what he is if I had to fash-
> ion him over again. But now it is done. Now the
> lines of my painting do not go astray, though they
> change and vary. The world is but a perennial move-
> ment. . . . Stability itself is nothing but a more
> languid motion. I cannot keep my subject still. It
> goes along befuddled and staggering, with a natural
> drunkenness. I take it in this condition at the mo-
> ment I give my attention to it. I do not portray
> being: I portray passing. Not the passing from one
> age to another, or, as the people say, from seven years
> to seven years, but from day to day, from minute to
> minute. My history needs to be adapted to the mo-
> ment. . . . If my mind could gain a firm footing, I
> would not make essays. I would make decisions; but
> it is always in apprenticeship and on trial [F., pp.
> 610–11].

> *Les autres forment l'homme; je le recite et en repre-*
> *sente un particulier bien male formé, et lequel, si*
> *j'avoy à façonner de nouveau, je ferois vrayement*
> *bien autre qu'il n'est. Mes-huy c'est fait. Or les traits*
> *de ma peinture ne forvoyent point, quoy qu'ils se*
> *changent et diversifient. Le monde n'est qu'une bran-*
> *loire perenne. . . . La constance mesme n'est autre*
> *chose qu'un branle plus languissant. Je ne puis as-*
> *seurer mon object. Il va trouble et chancelant, d'une*
> *yvresse naturelle. Je le prens en ce point, comme il*
> *est, en l'instant que je m'amuse à luy. Je ne peints*
> *pas l'estre. Je peints le passage: non un passage d'aage*
> *en autre, ou, comme dict le peuple, de sept en sept*
> *ans, mais de jour en jour, de minute en minute. Il*
> *faut accommoder mon histoire à l'heure. . . . Si mon*

*ame pouvoit prendre pied, je ne m'essaierois pas, je
me resoudrois: elle est tousjours en apprentissage et
en espreuve* [T., pp. 899–900].

To leave Montaigne at this point, with many of his greatest
essays unexamined, is, borrowing his own terms, to leave his
book "fashioned" but not "furnished"—an inconclusive procedure, perhaps, but one which can claim at least to reflect its
subject. It is to leave him, as he says here, without a firm foothold—and therefore writing essays. For this if anything is the
key to Montaigne's transfiguration of the retired focus. If Montaigne sought anything in the first versions of the earlier essays,
it was just such a firm foothold, secure from the centrifugal
flux of the uncontained self from within and the ravages of
time from without. But now, to recall Poulet's great insight, "by
dint of portraying passage, Montaigne obtains communication
with being."[137] In the lines before us and throughout the great
later essays, the unique accomplishment of Montaigne's transformation of traditional contemplative leisure is his centripetal
affirmation of free time, not in some "lofty and inaccessible
place," but in the centrifugal flux of time, the vouchsafing to
personal duration of the "now that fills eternity" previously
reserved for the divine timelessness.

Man is as much a god, he writes, quoting from Amyot's Plutarch on the last page of the last essay, as he recognizes himself
to be a man. It is his last declaration of the expansion within
contraction which is generated simply by contraction, "the
handful larger than the hand" held by the very relaxation and
diminishment of the grasp. "It is an absolute perfection and
virtually divine," says the man who seldom uses such language,
"to know how to enjoy our being rightfully" (*C'est une absolute perfection, et comme divine, de sçavoyr jouyr loiallement
de son estre*; F., p. 857; T., p. 1257). To enjoy our being rightfully is to perceive the georgic dignity of the peasants accepting
death in the fallen world of the civil wars in "Of Physiog-
nomy." In "Of Experience," it is to accept the excruciating
pain of the kidney stone, which, by the very nature of the
affliction, finds relief in the natural process of erosion which

is simultaneously a reminder of our mortality, like the sea at
the opening of the essay on cannibals. As a result, his body
itself enacts the georgic process of decay and regeneration,
finding its regeneration literally in the *passage* of the stone.

At the conclusion of *As You Like It*, Jacques, the "Monsieur
Melancholy," whose characterization may owe something to the
Montaigne of the early essays, announces that he will visit the
usurping duke, who has been converted to a life of religious
retirement. His farewell to the company is a veritable catalogue of the larger contexts of leisure, religious, civic, and
amorous, from which the solitary withdraws:

> To him will I. Out of these convertites
> There is much matter to be heard and learned.
> You to your former honor I bequeath;
> Your patience and your virtue well deserves it.
> You to a love that your true faith doth merit;
> You to your land and love and great allies;
> You to a long and well-deserved bed;
> And you to wrangling, for thy loving voyage
> Is but for two months victualled. So, to your
>   pleasures:
> I am for other than for dancing measures.
>   (*As You Like It*, 5. 4. 184–93)

This chapter began with the example of the "convertite"
Charles V and the announcement of Montaigne that, so to
speak, he was "for other than dancing measures." Beginning
with the announcement of Christ's birth to the shepherds and
his later teachings to a band of fishermen, we have traveled
through many imaginative landscapes, pastoral and georgic, to
which, for religious, civic, and amorous reasons, men have long
flocked, "fleeting the time carelessly as they did in the golden
world." From these celebrations, none "without gods," there
was, one hopes, "much matter to be heard and learned," but
perhaps nothing of more importance than to appreciate the authentic "dancing measure" which Montaigne may truly be said
to have found within the centripetal focus of his retirement.

When I dance, I dance; when I sleep, I sleep; yes, and when I walk alone in a beautiful orchard, if my thoughts have been dwelling on extraneous incidents for some part of the time, for some other part I bring them back to the walk, to the orchard, to the sweetness of this solitude and to me. . . . We are great fools. "He has spent his life in idleness," we say; "I have done nothing today." What, have you not lived? [F., p. 850].

Quand je dance, je dance; quand je dors, je dors; voyre et quand je me promeine solitairement en un beau vergier, si mes pensées se sont entretenues des occurrences estrangieres quelque partie du temps, quelque autre partie je les rameine à la promenade, au vergier, à la douceur de cette solitude et à moy. . . . Nous sommes de grands fols: Il a passé sa vie en oisiveté, disons nous; je n'ay rien faict d'aujourd'huy. —Quoy, avez vous pas vescu? [T., pp. 1246–47].

To which we may add, What, have you not written essays? Or been reading them?

NOTES

PREFACE

1. Marcus Tullius Cicero, "Pro Sestio" 45. 98 (*The Speeches, "Pro Sestio" and "In Vatinium,"* ed. R. G. Gardner [Cambridge, Mass., 1958], pp. 168–69). As we shall see, Cicero's sense of "cum dignitate" is far more civic than the "poet's dignity" of Pope's private station. See Jean-Marie André, "Ciceron et le drame de la retraite impossible," *L'Otium dans la vie morale et intellectuelle romaine* (Paris, 1966), pp. 279–334.

CHAPTER ONE

1. Jean-Paul Sartre, *Nausea*, trans. Lloyd Alexander (Norfolk, Conn., n.d.), p. 116. I was reminded of this passage by Remy G. Sausselin, "From Montaigne's Tower to the Fox-Hole," *Symposium* 14 (1960): 27. On Montaigne and existentialism see W. G. Moore, "Montaigne's Notion of Experience," in *The French Mind: Studies in Honour of Gustave Rudler* (Oxford, 1952), pp. 34–52.

2. Matthew Arnold, "On the Modern Element in Literature," *Essays* (Oxford, 1914), pp. 471–72.

3. Matthew Arnold, *On the Study of Celtic Literature and On Translating Homer* (New York, 1924), pp. 245–46. Cf. Lionel Trilling, *Matthew Arnold* (New York, 1955), p. 10.

4. Friedrich Nietzsche, *Human, All Too Human*, in *Complete Works*, trans. Paul V. Cohn (London, 1911), vol. 8, pt. 2, pp. 241–42.

5. Robert Lee, *Religion and Leisure in America: A Study in Four Dimensions* (New York, 1964), p. 19. I am pervasively indebted to Lee's research.

The study of leisure at the present time is a fascinating blend of sociological and economic method with humanistic and imaginative values. See, for example, Ida Craven's article "Leisure" in the *Encyclopedia of the Social Sciences* or Sebastian de Grazia's *Of Time, Work, and Leisure* (New York, 1962); for an interesting dissent, cf. Joffre Dumazedier, "Leisure," *International Encyclopedia of the Social Sciences* (New York, 1968), and his earlier *Vers une civilisation du loisir* (Paris, 1962). There is a "Preliminary Bibliography on Leisure" by Reuel Denney and Mary Lee Meyersohn in the *American Journal of Sociology* 62 (1957) and a bibliographic essay by Marjorie Casebier, *An Overview of Literature on Leisure* (San Anselmo, 1963). Alasdair Claire has written perhaps the most provocative recent book, *Work and Play* (New York, 1974).

6. Charles Lamb, "The Superannuated Man," *The Last Essays of Elia*, in *The Complete Works and Letters*, ed. Saxe Commins (New York, 1935), pp. 174–75.

7. Ibid., p. 175.

8. Aristotle, *Nicomachean Ethics* 10. 7. 177b5–6. This and subsequent references to Aristotle in English are to *The Basic Works*, ed. Richard McKeon (New York, 1941). The Greek text is from the Loeb edition of the *Politics*, ed. H. Rackham (London, 1932).

9. Bertrand Russell, "In Praise of Idleness," in *Socialist Humanism*, ed. Erich Fromm (Garden City, 1965), p. 234.

10. Johan Huizinga, *Homo Ludens: A Study of the Play Element in Culture* (Boston, 1964). Huizinga quotes the Vulgate version because of its greater emphasis on play.

11. Thomas Aquinas, *Expositio super Boethium "De Hebdomadibus,"* ed. P. Mahonnet (Paris, 1927), p. 165.

12. Gregory Nazianzen, *Carmina* 1. 2. 2. 589–90 (*Patrologia Graeca*, vol. 37, col. 624a). I was led to this and the previous reference by Hugo Rahner in *Man at Play* (New York, 1967), pp. 1–25.

13. Heraclitus, frag. 52 (my translation), in Hermann Diels, ed., *Fragmente der Vorsokratiker*, 6th rev. ed. by W. Kranz (Berlin, 1954), vol. 1, p. 162; Plato, *Laws* 644d–e; Nietzsche, "Philosophy during the Tragic Age of the Greeks," trans. Maximilian A. Mugge, in *The Complete Works*, ed. Oscar Levy (New York, 1924), vol. 2, p. 108. At the conclusion of *The Birth of Tragedy* the same Heraclitean description is of course celebrated as "Dionysian" (trans. William A. Haussmann, *Works*, vol. 1, p. 184).

14. Mircea Eliade, *The Sacred and the Profane: The Nature of Religion*, trans. Willard Trask (New York, 1959), p. 92. All of Eliade's chapter 2, "Sacred Time and Myths," pp. 68–113, pertains to the terms of this discussion.

15. Josef Pieper, *Leisure: The Basis of Culture*, trans. Alexander Dru (New York, 1954), pp. 56, 40. Pieper's thesis illuminates what I shall term "civic" leisure, but it has also prompted me to consider the imaginative achievement of those, like Horace or Montaigne, whose vision of leisure transcended mere idleness without the sanction of a public or supernatural cult. It is interesting to discover that an early review challenged Pieper's categories precisely with the example of Montaigne (C. F. Hovde, *The Nation* 175 [1952]: 362). For further development of ideas akin to Pieper's, see Jean Danielou, *Prayer as a Political Problem*, ed. and trans. J. R. Kirwan (New York, 1967), Roman Guardini, *The Spirit of the Liturgy*, trans. Ada Lane (New York, 1935), and Karl Rahner, "Theological Remarks on the Problem of Leisure," *Theological Investigations*, vol. 4, trans. Kevin Smith (Baltimore, 1966). For similar views in the Protestant and Jewish traditions, see Harvey Cox, *The Feast of Fools: A Theological Essay on Festivity and Fantasy* (Cambridge, Mass., 1969), and Abraham Heschel, *The Sabbath* (New York, 1951). For a specific reply to Pieper, see E. J. Hobswam, *Laboring Men* (New York, 1965), pp. 182–88, and, for a cogent Protestant restatement of the ethic Pieper disputes, see Karl Barth, *Church Dogmatics*, trans. J. W. Edwards, O. Bussey, and Harold Knight (Edinburgh, 1958), p. 228.

16. For the largest implications of the theory of play see Jacques Ehrmann, "Homo Ludens Revisited," trans. Cathy and Phil Lewis, in *Game, Play, Literature*, Yale French Studies, vol. 41 (1968). "To define play is at the same time and in the same movement to define reality and to define culture" (p. 55).

17. Eugen Fink, "The Oasis of Happiness: Toward an Ontology of Play," trans. Ute Saine and Thomas Saine, in *Game, Play, Literature*, p. 21.

18. Huizinga, *Homo Ludens*, pp. 180–81.

19. Northrop Frye, "The Archetypes of Literature," *Fables of Identity* (New York, 1963), p. 18.

20. Plato, *Republic* 592a–b, trans. Paul Shorey. (This and subsequent Plato quotations are from *The Collected Dialogues*, ed. Edith

Hamilton and Huntington Cairns [New York, 1963]). See also
Northrop Frye, "Varieties of Literary Utopia," *Daedalus* 94 (Spring,
1965): 332, 335–36.

21. Northrop Frye, *The Modern Century* (Toronto, 1967), pp.
89, 92, 102–3.

22. Charles Augustin Sainte-Beuve, "Qu'est-ce qu'un classique?"
in *Causeries de Lundi*, 4th ed. (Paris: Garnier Frères, n.d.), vol. 3,
pp. 51–52. This *causerie* took place on 21 October 1850.

Chapter Two

1. See *Iliad* 6. 138; *Odyssey* 4. 805; cf. *Iliad* 24. 525–26. These
and subsequent line references are to the Greek texts in the Loeb
editions, edited by A. T. Murray (London and Cambridge, Mass.,
1957 [*Iliad*]; 1953 [*Odyssey*]).

2. Hannah Arendt, *The Human Condition* (Garden City, 1959),
pp. 103–4.

3. Aristotle, *Nicomachaean Ethics* 10. 6. 1178b. Norman Went-
worth DeWitt suggests the Homeric passage as a source of Epicurus' detachment (*Epicurus and His Philosophy* [Minneapolis,
1954], p. 75).

4. Friederich Schiller, *On the Aesthetic Education of Man*, trans.
Reginald Snell (New Haven, 1959), p. 80.

5. Virginia Woolf, "How One Should Read a Book," *The Second
Common Reader* (New York, 1932), p. 245.

6. The Homeric translations in this chapter are from Richmond
Lattimore's *Iliad* (Chicago, 1961) and Robert Fitzgerald's *Odyssey*
(Garden City, 1963). Both employ Greek transliterations, but I have
referred to characters by their familiar Latinate names, e.g., Mene-
laus rather than Menelaos. The line numbers refer to the Loeb
Library editions, cited above.

7. Simone Weil, "The *Iliad*, or the Poem of Force," in *The
Proper Study*, ed. Quentin Anderson and Joseph Mazzeo (New York,
1962), p. 5. Originally published by the Pendle Hill Press, n.d.

8. Charles H. Taylor, Jr., ed., *Essays on the Odyssey* (Blooming-
ton, Ind., 1963); see Taylor's "The Obstacles to Odysseus' Return,"
pp. 87–99 (reprinted from *Yale Review* 50 [1961]: 569–80), and
William S. Anderson, "Calypso and Elysium," pp. 73–86 (reprinted
from *Classical Journal* 54 [1958]: 2–11).

9. George Dimock, "The Name of Odysseus," *Hudson Review* 9
(1956): 52–70 (also in Taylor's *Essays on the Odyssey*, pp. 54–72).

10. J. Gwyn Griffiths, "In Search of the Isles of the Blest," *Greece and Rome* 15 (1946): 122–26. For other versions of the Isles see Hesiod, *Works and Days*, ed. H. G. Evelyn White (Loeb) (London, 1957), p. 167; Pindar, *Odes*, ed. Sir John Sandys (Loeb) (London, 1957), *Olympian* 2. 68–76.

11. Werner Jaeger, *Paideia: The Ideals of Greek Culture*, trans. Gilbert Highet (New York, 1945), vol. 1, p. 18. More than any other classical scholar, Jaeger has emphasized the issues I raise in this chapter, and much of what I say here about the relationship of civilization to contemplation is but a slight effort to refine certain of his great insights.

12. Thomas M. Greene, *The Descent from Heaven* (New Haven, 1963), p. 55.

13. George deF. Lord, "The *Odyssey* and the Western World," *Sewanee Review* 62 (1954): 406–27, reprinted in Taylor, ed., *Essays on the Odyssey*, pp. 36–53; see esp. p. 46. Though my reading draws from Lord's insights, it will try to envision the poem's image of the good life in terms less Vergilian or Christian.

14. M. I. Finley, *The World of Odysseus* (Cleveland, 1962), p. 135.

15. Notice, however, that, as Athena warns Odysseus (*Od.* 7. 30–33), the hospitality of the Phaeacians is not uncritically naive. The paradox that distrustful scrutiny should be the condition of festive acceptance was a historical necessity; see Finley, *The World of Odysseus*, pp. 105–7. Nor does the competitive behavior at the games (*Od.* 8. 143–233) seem seriously to vitiate the ensuing dancing and singing.

16. Plato, *Laws* 653c–d, trans. A. E. Taylor.

17. On Penelope's knowledge see Anne Amory, "The Reunion of Odysseus and Penelope," in Taylor, ed., *Essays on the Odyssey*, pp. 100–121, and Philip Whaley Harsh, "Penelope and Odysseus in *Odyssey* XIX," *American Journal of Philology* 71 (1950): 1–21.

18. Lewis Mumford, *The City in History* (New York, 1961), p. 37; cf. pp. 46–47.

19. *Republic* 390b.

20. *Politics* 1338a.

21. *Ibid.*, 1271b. The argument begins with Plato, *Laws* 625e, 630.

22. *Politics* 1333a–b.

23. Ibid., 1334a. See Werner Jaeger, *Aristotle*, trans. Richard Robinson (Oxford, 1960), pp. 73, 280.

24. *Politics* 1338a–b.

25. *Nicomachean Ethics* 10. 6. 1178b. But see Jaeger's insistence on the practical difference between Aristotle's *phronēsis* and more purely theonomic and apolitical justifications (such as Plato's) (Jaeger, *Aristotle*, chap. 9, esp. pp. 236–43, and chap. 10, esp. pp. 280–82). Cf. F. Sohnsen, "Leisure and Play in Aristotle's Ideal State," *Rheinisches Museum* 7 (1964): 193–220.

26. Sebastian de Grazia, *Of Time, Work, and Leisure* (New York, 1962), p. 21. Cf. *Politics* 1253a.

27. *Politics* 1325b; 1329a.

28. Ibid., 1338a–b.

29. Arendt, *The Human Condition*, pp. 9–21. Her view of the nonpolitical aspect of *scholē* is stated succinctly in her note 10, p. 303.

30. *Scholia Graeca in Homeri Odysseam*, ed. William Dindorf (Oxford, 1855), vol. 2, p. 408.

31. *Epicurus: The Extant Remains*, ed. Cyril Bailey (Oxford, 1926), p. 86. Subsequent quotations from Epicurus are from this edition.

32. See Thucydides, *The Peloponnesian War* 2. 2, trans. Rex Warner (London, 1954), p. 119. See also Alfred Zimmern, *The Greek Commonwealth* (Oxford, 1961), chap. 8, "The Ideal of Citizenship: Happiness or the Rule of Love." Still interesting to read is Numa Denis Fustel de Coulanges's classic account of how total was the public absorption of the typical Athenian's daily round of civic leisure; see his *The Ancient City* (Garden City, n.d.), pp. 334–36. Cf. Aristotle, *Politics* 1253a.

33. See Jaeger, *Paideia*, vol. 1, pp. 111, 444 (n. 45); vol. 3, p. 11. For the invidious (i.e., "privative") connotations of "private," see also Arendt, *The Human Condition*, pp. 35, 53.

34. So to abbreviate Jaeger's thesis is not, I hope, to oversimplify it. For the high points of his exposition, see *Paideia*, vol. 1, pp. xxvi, 78, 410; vol. 2, pp. 4, 73–74, 272–74, 356.

35. This is still quite concisely described by Eduard Zeller, *Outlines of the History of Greek Philosophy* (New York, 1960), pp. 225–27.

36. Jaeger, *Paideia*, vol. 1, chaps. 5–6. Bruno Snell, *The Discovery of the Mind: The Greek Origins of European Thought*, trans. T. G. Rosenmayer (New York, 1960), p. 64.

37. Archilochus, frag. 8, in *Elegy and Iambus*, ed. J. M. Edmonds (Loeb) (London, 1931), vol. 1, p. 100. Subsequent references are to this text.

38. Archilochus, frag. 6 (cf. Horace, *Odes* 2. 7). See also C. M. Bowra, *Early Greek Elegists* (Cambridge, Mass., 1938), pp. 8–13.

39. Archilochus, frag. 63.

40. Archilochus, frag. 25. The Greek version reiterates the negative particle more emphatically.

41. Aristotle, *Rhetoric* 1418b.

42. Snell, *Discovery of the Mind*, p. 65.

43. Alcaeus, frag. 157, in *Lyra Graeca*, ed. J. M. Edmonds (Loeb) (London, 1928), vol. 1, p. 416. Subsequent references are to this edition.

44. Nicely epitomized by Anacreon: "I like not him who at his drinking beside the full mixing-bowl tells of strife and lamentable war, but rather one that taketh thought for delightsome mirth by mingling the Muses and the splendid gifts of Aphrodite," (Anacreon, frag. 116, in *Lyra Graeca*, ed. J. M. Edmonds, vol. 2, p. 197). Edmonds' appendix (vol. 3, pp. 583–679) provides a useful survey of the forms and themes of the sympotic lyric (see esp. pp. 651–56). The classic account is Richard Reitzenstein's *Epigramm und Skolion* (Giessen, 1893), esp. pp. 13–24.

45. Alcaeus, frag. 161; cf. Horace, *Odes* 3. 13. 9–12. See C. M. Bowra, *Greek Lyric Poetry* (Oxford, 1961), pp. 158–62.

46. Alcaeus, frag. 73. The lyric's abdication from public responsibility is treated, rather unsympathetically, by Denys Page, *Sappho and Alcaeus* (Oxford, 1955), pp. 193–95, and, more appreciatively, by C. M. Bowra, *Greek Lyric Poetry*, pp. 152–57, 161–62.

47. See Jaeger, *Paideia*, vol. 1, p. 201.

48. Theognis, 53–60, in Edmonds, *Elegy and Iambus*, vol. 1, p. 234. (Subsequent references are to this edition.) Cf. 683–86, 817–18, 945–46, and 149–50. See the discussion in Jaeger, *Paideia*, vol. 1, pp. 201–12, 463.

49. Theognis, 499–502. The lines say more than "in vino veritas"; see Snell, *Discovery of the Mind*, p. 68.

50. Theognis, 985–88.

51. Id., 973–78.

52. Id., 879–94.

53. See Herodotus, *The Histories*, trans. Aubrey de Selincourt (London, 1954), p. 82; Plato, *Seventh Epistle* 1574–98 (trans. L. A. Post, in *Collected Dialogues*).

54. *Republic* 519c–d, 751–52.

55. I draw here from the impressive survey in Jaeger's Appendix II, "On the Origin and Cycle of the Philosophic Ideal of Life," *Aristotle*, pp. 426–61.

56. Horace, *Epistles* 1. 12. 12. Cf. Diogenes Laertius, *Lives of Eminent Philosophers*, ed. R. D. Hicks (Loeb) (London, 1938), vol. 2, p. 36.

57. Diogenes Laertius, *Lives*, vol. 1, p. 7.

58. The most influential source of the allegory, supposedly deriving from Heraclides of Pontus, is Cicero. See his *Tusculan Disputations* 5. 3, ed. J. E. King (Loeb) (Cambridge, Mass., 1966). For the background, see Jaeger, *Aristotle*, pp. 92, 432.

59. Jaeger, *Aristotle*, p. 430.

60. A. E. Taylor, *Plato, The Man and His Work* (Cleveland, 1952), p. 295. Cf. André M. J. Festugière, *Contemplation et la vie contemplative selon Platon* (Paris, 1936). Festugière's description of Plato as, essentially, the first Hellenistic philosopher is the best account of the predicament described here. Cf. his *Personal Religion among the Greeks* (Berkeley, 1954), and see also note 80, below.

61. *Seventh Epistle* 1574–1603, esp. 1575–76; Jaeger, *Paideia*, vol. 2, pp. 73–74, 83.

62. *Republic* 496–97a; cf. 497c, 519c.

63. *Republic* 614b–621d. Cf. Jaeger, *Paideia*, vol. 2, p. 370. In the original, Odysseus' choice is *bion andros idiōtou apragmonos*. The translation here is not Shorey's but is mine, somewhat closer to Jowett's. "*Apragmonos* characterizes the quiet man who is not a busybody, litigant, or a politician looking for trouble" (Paul Shorey, *Classical Philology* 15 [1920]: 301).

64. Snell, *Discovery of the Mind*, p. 293. Significantly, Snell cites the example of Plato's withdrawal as a kind of prelude to pastoral poetry's "Discovery of a Spiritual Landscape." Cf. Jaeger, *Paideia*, vol. 2, p. 274; Jaeger, *Aristotle*, p. 429.

65. Plato, *Thaeatetus* 173d–e, trans. F. M. Cornford.

66. Adam Parry, "Landscape in Greek Poetry," *Yale Classical Studies* 15 (1957): 3–29.

67. Plato, *Phaedrus* 230d–e, trans. R. Hackforth.

68. Parry, "Landscape," p. 17.

69. *Phaedrus* 230b–c.

70. Alberto Grilli, *Il Problema della Vita Contemplativa nel Mondo Greco-Romano* (Milan, 1953), pp. 361–64. See esp. listings under such seasonal (or navigational) terms as *aithria, galēnē, eudia,*

limēn. Especially in the defining of a parent metaphor, my debt to Grilli's survey is enormous (certainly it should be translated into English).

71. Seneca, *Ad Lucilium Epistulae Morale* 41.4, ed. Richard M. Gummere (Loeb) (London, 1934), vol. 1, p. 273 (my italics); see also no. 59. Subsequent references are to this edition. English translations are from this edition.

72. Lucretius, *De Rerum Natura* 2. 1–135, ed. Cyril Bailey (Oxford, 1947). English translations are from this edition.

73. See, for example, Seneca, *Epist.* 19: *In freto viximus, moriamur in portu*; see also no. 68.

74. *Epist.* 23; see also no. 92.

75. Grilli, *Il Problema*, pp. 33–86.

76. *Epicurus*, ed. Bailey, p. 115 (see n. 31, above). See Grilli's discussion of *mē politeuesthai* in *Il Problema*, pp. 59–64.

77. *Epicurus*, p. 86.

78. Ibid., p. 113.

79. Ibid., p. 121.

80. Ibid., p. 115. The best discussion of Epicurean friendship and freedom is by André M. J. Festugière in his *Epicurus and His Gods*, trans. C. W. Chilton (Cambridge, Mass., 1956), chap. 3.

81. Lucretius, *De Rerum Natura* 2. 29–33.

82. George Santayana, *Three Philosophical Poets* (Garden City, n.d.) (originally published in 1910), p. 63.

83. Renato Poggioli, "The Oaten Flute," *Harvard Library Bulletin* 11 (1957): 150. The parallel between Epicurus and Theocritus, suggested by Thomas G. Rosenmeyer (*Classical World* 57 [1963]: 102), confirmed my early speculations, and his ampler and provocative treatment of the pastoral mode from this perspective in *The Green Cabinet: Theocritus and the European Pastoral Lyric* (Berkeley, 1969) might be considered alongside my view of the "transformations" of Theocritus in my later chapters.

84. A. S. F. Gow, *Theocritus* (Cambridge, 1960), vol. 2, p. 127. Subsequent line references are to the Greek text in Gow's first volume.

85. Here and later I use the translation by Barriss Mills, *The Idylls of Theocritus* (West Lafayette, Ind., 1961).

86. In a notable recent reading of the poem, Gilbert Lawall accentuates the privacy of the encounter between Simichidas and Lycidas—as if, indeed, the latter were the pastoral *persona* of the former; see Lawall's *Theocritus' Coan Pastorals: A Poetry Book*

(Washington, D.C., 1967), pp. 77–80. Here, as in his later reading of the festival as a personal "harvest" of the first seven poems (pp. 106–7), Lawall offers a complementary interpretation to mine.

87. In a perceptive aside, Poggioli suggests a link between the *epyllia* (such as Theocritus also wrote) and pastoral poetry in a common recoil from the tragic and heroic dimensions ("The Oaten Flute," p. 150). See also Gow, *Theocritus*, vol. 2, p. 144, for the Alexandrian literary milieu. Here as elsewhere I am indebted to Gow's volume of commentary.

88. Cf. Lawall, *Theocritus' Coan Pastorals*, p. 87. He also notes a parallel to the First Idyll.

CHAPTER THREE

1. Eduard Fraenkel, *Horace* (Oxford, 1959), p. 43. My view of the early poems of Horace is greatly indebted to this classic study.

2. In another early poem, Horace cast this doomed vision of Roman destiny in the language of an original contamination, the fratricidal blood guilt of Romulus. See *Epodes* 7, esp. ll. 17–20.

3. *Satires* 1. 6. 71–75. See Fraenkel, *Horace*, pp. 2–3, and his first chapter, "Vita Horatii," for a thorough review of much of the following information.

4. *Epodes* 2. 2. 45–48. Tenney Frank entitles his seventh chapter "Horace the Republican," in his *Catullus and Horace: Two Poets in Their Environment* (New York, 1928).

5. *Epodes* 2. 2. 49–51. Fraenkel (*Horace*, p. 13) suggests an analogy with the threatened expropriation of Vergil's estate, an analogy which I develop at some length in the next section of this chapter.

6. *Sat.* 1. 6. 52–56; Fraenkel, *Horace*, pp. 14–16.

7. I have dealt more extensively with this poem and the sense of time and history in pastoral poetry in "Woods Worthy of a Consul," in John H. Dorenkamp, ed., *Literary Studies: Essays in Memory of Francis A. Drumm* (Worcester, 1973). For an interesting interpretation of the poem's rhetorical structure see John B. Van Sickle, "The Fourth Pastoral Poems of Vergil and Theocritus," *Atti e Memorie dell'Arcadia* (1969), vol. 5. The classic account of the poem's significance is by Jerome Carcopino, *Virgile et le mystère de la IV*ᵉ *Eclogue* (Paris, 1930). For a more general discussion of these issues, relevant also to my use of Vergil, see Renato Poggioli, "Naboth's Vineyard, or the Pastoral View of the Social Order," *Journal of the History of Ideas* 24 (1963): 23–24.

8. L. P. Wilkinson, *Horace and His Lyric Poetry* (Cambridge, 1945), p. 65. This is not to deny that, chronologically, Vergil may have preceded Horace. See Bruno Snell, "Die 16. Epode von Horaz und Vergils 4. Ekloge," *Hermes* 73 (1938): 237–42. While the question was not conclusively settled by Snell's argument (based on echoes of Theocritus), the priority of Vergil is now more strongly urged. See the bibliography compiled by G. E. Duckworth (*Classical World* 51 [1957–58]: 125) and Fraenkel's review of recent research (*Horace*, p. 51). Carl Becker's "Vergils Eklogenbuch," *Hermes* 83 (1955): 314–49, is a persuasive restatement of Snell's view.

9. This view of the complexity of the First Eclogue's conclusion might be applied to the sequence of the *Eclogues* as a whole. Brooks Otis has extensively outlined such a pattern in his *Virgil: A Study in Civilized Poetry* (Oxford, 1964), esp. pp. 128–31. Yet, sensitive as Otis is to the contrast between "Roman" and "Theocritean" eclogues and to the relationships between particular eclogues within these categories (i.e., contrasting eclogues 1 and 9, 2 and 8, 3 and 7, 4 and 6, 5 and 10), his "spatial" view of the arrangement does not suggest why Vergil never seems to give us his poems in the right order. Why, if the First is "obviously constructed as a counterpart" to the previously composed and less optimistic Ninth Eclogue, is it not equally "obviously" in the more ultimate position in the book? Because, as my reading of the First tries to indicate, its optimistic theme is weighted by a sense of loss as well as gain. The same complexity may account for the relatively unclimactic situation of the Fourth Eclogue and its curious relation to the song of man's decline sung by Silenus in the Sixth. If the apocalyptic poem is not placed in the ultimate position, it may be a measure of the author's sense that the wondrous epiphany is not yet quite accomplished.

10. This view of the rural scene as the nursery of peculiarly Roman virtues—what might be called the Cincinnatus myth—was of course a venerable tradition. See A. L. Keith, "Vergil and the Soil," *Classical Journal* 37 (1938): 523–24. On the other hand, as M. L. Clarke points out, "the antiquarianism of the new age," especially its reverence for the rural deities (*sacra deum sanctique patres*, *Georgics* 2. 473), stands out in marked contrast to the attitude of the previous age: "It is significant that Vergil, proclaiming his love of the country, probably in conscious opposition to Lucretius, expresses it in terms of religion: 'fortunatus et ille, deos qui novit

agrestis / Panaque Silvanumque senem Nymphasque sorores' "
(*Georg.* 2. 493–94) (Clarke, *The Roman Mind* [Cambridge, Mass.,
1956], p. 81).

11. See L. P. Wilkinson, "The Intention of Vergil's *Georgics*,"
Greece and Rome 19 (1950): 21. There are acute perceptions in
Wilkinson's version of the poem's "political intention"; see especially his treatment of "the beating of swords into ploughshares"
and the recurrent leitmotif of "splendid slow stability," *agricola
incurvo terram molitus aratro* (*Georg.* 1. 494). For an ampler treatment of many of the issues in this article, see the same author's *The
Georgics of Virgil: A Critical Study* (Cambridge, Eng., 1969).

12. Clarke, *The Roman Mind*, p. 90.

13. T. S. Eliot, "Vergil and the Christian World," *On Poetry
and Poets* (London, 1957), p. 126.

14. Kenneth Clark, *Landscape into Art* (Boston, 1961), p. 54.

15. In addition to Wilkinson, I draw here from the interpretation of Heinrich Altevogt, *Labor Improbus: Eine Vergilstudie*
(Muenster, 1952), and the commentary in Will Richter's edition,
Georgica (Munich, 1957). "Die Arbeit des Bauern," writes Richter,
"ist die einzige die ursprünglich nicht an den Übeln der Welt teil-
hatte, und steht daher dem goldenen Zeitalter am nächsten" (p. 40).

16. See Eric A. Havelock, *The Liberal Temper in Greek Politics* (New Haven, 1964), pp. 36–37.

17. "Er empfindet die Vertreibung aus dem Paradies," writes
Richter, "als Segen, als Verjüngung der Menschheit" (*Georgica*,
p. 157).

18. Wilkinson, "The Intention of Vergil's *Georgics*," p. 25.

19. Tibullus 1. 3 in *Catullus, Tibullus, and Pervigilium Veneris*,
ed. F. W. Cornish, J. P. Postgate, and J. W. Mackail (Loeb) (London, 1950), p. 206.

20. Altevogt, *Labor Improbus*, p. 8.

21. See, for example, the epigraph to Samuel Smiles's interesting
manifesto of the gospel of work, *Life and Labour*; I owe this information to a note by Ian Watt in "Robinson Crusoe as a Myth,"
Eighteenth-Century English Literature, ed. James L. Clifford (New
York, 1959), p. 177.

22. When Jean-Marie André speaks of Vergil's "travail joyeux,"
he captures this note precisely, though in doing so he ignores the
negative connotations of *improbus* (*L'Otium dans la vie morale et
intellectuelle romaine* [Paris, 1966], p. 505). Otis, on the other

hand, tends to reduce the *variae artes* to the fallen condition of *labor improbus*: "man's civilization has a curse on it" (*Vergil*, p. 157).

23. See the very detailed table and structural summary by Otis, *Vergil*, pp. 148–54. My dialectical interpretation seeks to deepen the implications of what Otis does recognize to be, for example, the "reciprocal relationship" between books 1 and 2 (p. 169).

24. See ibid., p. 164. Cf. D. L. Drew, "The Structure of Vergil's *Georgics*," *American Journal of Philology* 50 (1929): 242–54.

25. Wilkinson, "The Intention of Vergil's *Georgics*," p. 26; Otis, *Vergil*, p. 164.

26. W. F. Jackson Knight, *Roman Vergil* (London, 1946), p. 119.

27. Otis, *Vergil*, p. 186.

28. Ibid., pp. 181–86.

29. Drew, "The Structure of Vergil's *Georgics*," p. 246; W. B. Anderson, in "Gallus and the Fourth Georgic," *Classical Quarterly* 27 (1933): 36–45, has denied that any substitution took place, but his argument is more historical than critical. Cf. the detailed structural analysis by Otis, *Vergil*, pp. 190–92. But the contrasts he notes can yield a more creative relationship.

30. "Vergil and the Christian World," p. 126. If I understand Eliot (or Benedict) correctly, the analogy has not really been apprehended by those who challenge it—for example, Wilkinson: "The text of Vergil's *Georgics* was not *laborare et orare* [*sic*], as some have suggested, but *laborare et vivere*" ("The Structure of Vergil's *Georgics*," p. 24). In fact, *laborare* et *orare* meant *laborare est orare*, as Carlyle stressed: "True work *is* worship" (*Past and Present*, chap. 12).

31. Eliot's lines are also quoted by Smith Palmer Bovie in the introduction to his fine translation of the *Georgics* (Chicago, 1956), pp. xxv–xxvi.

32. The special nature of Horace's treatment of these motifs is evident if one compares Vergil's *Georgics* 2. 461–66.

33. The allusion to "excision" is not entirely metaphorical; as Wilkinson points out, the conclusion was frequently not printed in Renaissance versions ("The Structure of Vergil's *Georgics*," pp. 165–67).

34. Ibid., p. 54.

35. Fraenkel, *Horace*, p. 60. The quoted remark is from Paul Shorey's annotated edition of the *Odes and Epodes* (Boston, 1898).

See also W. Y. Sellar, *Horace and the Elegiac Poets* (Oxford, 1924), p. 130.

36. While the following interpretation of the Second Epode is relatively novel, there is a certain precedent for it in Heinze's insistence that the opening descriptions parody "die Schwärmerei des Städters für des Bauernleben, das er nur als Sommerfrischler kennen gelernt hat" (quoted by Fraenkel, *Horace*, p. 61).

37. One might compare the similar strategy in the reversal of tones from the grandiloquent to the playful at the end of *Odes* 1. 22 (*Integer vitae*). A modern reader might recall Frost's poem in praise of New Hampshire which ends "At present I am living in Vermont." I was reminded of this by Rosenmeyer's complementary discussion of the epode in his *Green Cabinet*, p. 177.

38. Wilkinson, *Horace*, p. 166.

39. G. L. Henderson, "Are the Letters of Horace Satires?" *American Journal of Philology* 18 (1897): 313–24; B. L. Ullman, "Satura and Satire," *Classical Philology* 8 (1913): 172–94; cf. Alvin Kernan, "A Theory of Satire," *The Cankered Muse* (New Haven, 1959), pp. 1–36. Kernan distinguishes between Horace's kind of satire, which "verges on the comic," and Juvenal's kind, which stands "on the threshold of tragedy" (pp. 28–29). Cf. my own account of the difference, pp. 88–89.

40. Blaise Pascal, *L'Apologie de la religion chrétienne* in *Oeuvres Complètes*, vol. 3, ed. Fortunat Strowski (Paris, 1931). The indictment is a perfect description of Horace's self-portraiture: "Le sot projet qu'il a de se peindre et cela non pas en passant et contre ses maximes, comme il arrive à tout le monde de faillir, mais par ses propres maximes et par un dessein premier et principal. Car de dire des sottises par hasard et par faiblesse, c'est un mal ordinaire; mais d'en dire par dessein, c'est ce qui n'est pas supportable, et d'en dire de telles que celle-ci" (p. 17). Cf. Fraenkel, *Horace*, p. 88.

41. Maynard Mack, introduction to his edition of Henry Fielding, *Joseph Andrews* (New York, 1948), p. xxiv.

42. This and subsequent quotations of Juvenal are from Juvenal and Persius, *Satires*, ed. G. G. Ramsey (Loeb) (London, 1957).

43. See, for example, Juvenal, *Sat.* 3. 15–20, 203–11. Notice that while a retired scene (Cumae) is Umbricius' destination in that poem, its enjoyment is not presented as realized but as dramatically unavailable within the poem. (See also lines 190–91, 223–31.)

44. The likelihood of some reference to Lucilius' *Iter Siculum* is, of course, important as a clue to Horace's debt to Lucilius, but

it seems too large a claim for the poem's imitative fictionality to deny it any basis in fact. See W. S. Anderson's "Reply" to H. A. Musurillo's "Horace's Journey to Brundisium—Fact or Fiction?" *Classical Weekly* 48 (1954–55), in the same journal, 49 (1955–56): 57–59.

45. Fraenkel (*Horace*, p. 112) notes even a certain verbal resemblance; cf. *nil me paeniteat sanum patris huius* (*Sat.* 1. 6. 89) with the last line in the quotation: *nil ego contulerim iucundo sanus amico* (1. 5. 44).

46. V. D'Anta suggests a parallel with the conference of Antony and Octavian at Tarentum in "Il Viaggio di Orazio da Roma a Brundisi," *Rendiconti della Academia Napoletana* 24–25 (1949–50): 235–55. Anderson (see n. 44, above) uses D'Anta's suggestion to insist on some factual basis for the trip. In my own reading, the parallel would exemplify a typical way of regarding the movers and shakers of the great world in the festive perspective of the friends.

47. Lucretius, *De Rer. Nat.* 1. 82.

48. Niall Rudd, *The Satires of Horace* (Cambridge, Eng., 1966), p. 105.

49. Fraenkel, *Horace*, p. 105.

50. Ibid., p. 15.

51. See Steele Commager, "Nature as a Moral Metaphor," *The Odes of Horace* (New Haven, 1962), pp. 235–37. Cf. J. W. Duff, *A Literary History of Rome* (London, 1953), p. 540: "he loved the external aspects of nature for their own sake."

52. See the openings of *Odes* 8, 11, 17, 18, and 28 of the first book; 2, 11, 12, and 18 of the second book; and 1 of the third book.

53. See the openings of *Odes* 6, 23, and 31 of the first book.

54. For a different interpretation, see André's arrangement of these occupations in the light of traditions—whose structures (to me) do not inhere in the ode (*L'Otium dans la vie romaine*, pp. 466–67). More inclusively, here, as in his interpretation of the *Odes* generally, André stresses a more civic tendency than I find. "La grandeur romaine" (as in the treatment of Maecenas here) is never the final reason one reads Horace—despite his presumed intentions. See also Viktor Pöschl, "Horaz und die Politik," *Sitzungsberichte der Heidelberger Akademie* (1956), pp. 5–29.

55. The best introduction to my own approach to the *Odes* would probably be *Velox amoenum saepe Lucretilem* (1. 17) as it has been interpreted by Commager: "Most of Horace's invitations are

haunted by a kind of nostalgia for the impossible, for a lasting world of sweet wine, beautiful women, and ever-fragrant flowers. His banqueters achieve what is in effect a state of secular grace, but in the Ode to Tyndaris, for almost the only time, that state becomes more than a possibility of the moment. No *dum licet* boxes the occasion; the banqueter's usual garland of 'too brief roses' has become the poet's wreath. Here is the timeless world of art, of creativity, and of order—and of the peace possible within it" (*The Odes of Horace*, p. 352). The sensitivity of the reading here would make any parallel treatment in this essay superfluous. My interpretation of other poems could be described as an attempt to prove that this is not "almost the only time when that state becomes more than a possibility of the moment."

56. See Wilkinson, *Horace*, p. 43.

57. Cf. Fraenkel, *Horace*, p. 177.

58. Commager, *The Odes of Horace*, pp. 271–72.

59. Ibid., p. 272.

60. See the Oxford edition, textual note to line 15. For a brief survey of the history of this interpretation, see J. P. Elder, "Horace's *Carmen* I. 7," *Classical Philology* 48 (1953): 1, 7 (n. 1). For a typical instance see C. H. Moore's complaint at line 15: "The only connection between the preceding and that which follows is *Tiburis umbra tui* . . . . It must be acknowledged that the connection is very slight. We may have here in reality a combination of two 'fragments' which Horace never completed" (*Horace: Odes and Epodes* [New York, 1902], p. 79).

61. Cf. Commager, *The Odes of Horace*, p. 343.

62. Pindar, *Pythian* 1. 41–45, in *The Odes*, ed. Sir John Sandys (Loeb) (London, 1957), p. 158.

63. In view of this, it seems almost presumptuous to announce that these "autobiographical" lines not only can be integral to this ode but may even be characteristic of Horace's retired imagination. Fraenkel (who provides an amusing anthology of the complaints of learned readers of the poem) goes so far as to speculate that the average Roman reader would have been "even more startled than we are when he found that the solemn invocation of the first stanza and the inspired vision of the second are followed by a scene in which not only the very ordinary name of Horace's nurse appears but also the names of three townlets in the district of Venusia, the existence of which was presumably unknown to anyone who had not lived in that part of far-off Italy" (Fraenkel, *Horace*, p. 274).

64. It is curious that Fraenkel, whose sensitivity to the self-portraiture of the *Satires* is so acute, should not have drawn a parallel in his reading of this ode, which is probably the most telling defense of it which has appeared. My own account, which attempts to demonstrate the parallel with the movement of mind in the poet's other poems, finds its point of departure in Fraenkel's superb conclusion (*Horace*, pp. 284–85).

65. See Elder, "Horace's *Carmen* I. 7," pp. 5–7. Horace's tendency to address some of his finest odes to other figures of questionable respectability was noted by W. Y. Sellar, *Horace and the Elegiac Poets,* p. 175.

66. Commager, *The Odes of Horace*, p. 175. See also Elder, "Horace's *Carmen* I. 7," p. 7.

67. In ascribing these lines to Bullatius, I must stress that I use the Latin text of the Oxford edition instead of that of the Loeb edition, p. 322. I have likewise added quotation marks to Fairclough's rendering in the Loeb.

68. Fairclough defends his version, which would give the lines to Horace, as follows: "Why may we not suppose that this lonely sea-side place, which Horace had probably visited when he served with Brutus, appealed strongly to the poet?" (Loeb ed., pp. 322–23). The lines, as M. Courbaud insisted, are "le clef de la pièce"; his explanation of why one may not accept them as Horace's is outlined in my paragraph (see Edmond Courbaud, *Horace: Sa vie et sa pensée à l'époque des Epîtres* [Paris, 1914], p. 366).

69. See Courbaud, *Horace: Sa vie,* p. 144. Courbaud's entire discussion of the epistle (pp. 133–47) has been most useful.

70. On the other hand, viewed in this tradition of abstract moralizing, Horace's *Epistles* are equally remarkable. As Perret puts it, "there appears a man engaged in this adventure. We can no longer feel or grasp the generalities except through him, for they have become interior to the fellow-feeling and interest that he arouses in us, and are intermingled with his own particular adventure. It is no longer life in the country that we see, but Horace in the country, trying to become better" (Jacques Perret, *Horace,* trans. Bertha Humez [New York, 1964], p. 112).

71. *Boswell in Holland, 1763–64,* ed. Frederick A. Pottle (New York, 1952), p. 229.

72. This was the general thesis of Courbaud's influential study; see *Horace: Sa vie,* pp. 1–60. For an intelligent review of the ques-

tion of Horace's Stoic, Epicurean, or eclectic tendencies, see Commager, *The Odes of Horace*, p. 255.

73. Perret, *Horace*, pp. 118–19.

74. Georges Poulet, *Studies in Human Time*, trans. Elliott Coleman (New York, 1959), p. 48.

75. Ibid., p. 49.

76. Montaigne, *Essais* 3. 2 (Thibaudet ed., p. 907). See Perret, *Horace*, p. 115. The emphasis on a sense of "continuity" in the *Epistles* is well proposed. One might continue the argument even further, perhaps, with a text such as *an secretum iter et fallentis semita vitae* (*Epist.* 1. 18. 103), where the suggestion of contraction and seclusion (*secretum . . . fallentis*) is extended in time and even space (*iter . . . semita*). The line, incidentally, was the motto over Pope's grotto.

77. Carl Becker, *Das Spätwerk des Horaz* (Göttingen, 1963), pp. 34–37. I draw from this fine treatment in most of my remarks in this paragraph.

78. Fraenkel, *Horace*, pp. 336–37.

79. Ibid., p. 336.

80. For a sensitive account of the tact of this (and other) refusals see Raymond T. Ohl, "Ironic Reserve in Horace," *Classical Weekly* 43 (1949): 35–40, esp. 37. Ohl points out that Maecenas' relations with Augustus display the same qualities of independence and tact as do Horace's with him.

81. Cf. Courbaud, *Horace: Sa vie*, p. 169. With this general estimate and my appreciation of the following lines (in the terms of this particular poem and of the argument of this book), compare the judgment of E. P. Morris on Horace's treatment of the countryside: "there is no sufficient justification for the description of the farm at the beginning of Epistle XVI" ("The Form of the Epistle in Horace," *Yale Classical Studies* 2 [1931]: 110).

82. The possibility that Horace may have drawn from the *Pentheus* of Pacuvius instead of Euripides' *Bacchae* has been suggested by H. J. Rose, "Horace and Pacuvius," *Classical Quarterly* 20 (1926): 204–6. According to this interpretation, the stranger before Pentheus is not necessarily Dionysus; at the same time, it is more likely that the *moriar* refers to an external threat of death (p. 206). Rose's interpretation forgets the probability that Horace's (and even Pacuvius') audience would associate the very mention of Pentheus and a stranger with the story of Euripides' *Bacchae*.

83. Courbaud, *Horace: Sa vie*, p. 186.

84. William Arrowsmith, introduction to *The Bacchae*, in *The Complete Greek Tragedies*, vol. 4: *Euripides*, ed. David Grene and Richmond Lattimore (Chicago, 1960), p. 537.

85. Despite its length and its affinity with the first book, the Second Epistle of the second book was ignored by Courbaud. Fraenkel uses it mainly as a source for his biographical chapter, "Vita Horatii." Becker's reading is concerned largely with its thematic and chronological relation to the other *Epistles* (*Das Spätwerk des Horaz*, pp. 54–63).

86. Marie Borroff, "Wallace Stevens: The World and the Poet," introduction to *Wallace Stevens: A Collection of Critical Essays* (Englewood Cliffs, 1963), p. 10.

CHAPTER FOUR

1. The Latin, aside from the dates, reads: "Mich. Montanus, servitii aulici et munerum publicorum jamdudum pertaesus, dum se integer in doctarum Virginum recessit sinus, ubi quietus et omnium securus [quant] illum id tandem superabit decursi multa jam plus parte spatii, si modo fata duint, exigat istas sedes et dulces latebras avitasque libertati suae tranquillitatique et otio consecravit." See Donald Frame, *Montaigne: A Biography* (New York, 1965), pp. 112–15, for the circumstances of his retirement; the Latin text is in the note to page 115 on page 353. On Montaigne's public career, the fifteenth chapter of Frame's distinguished biography is especially interesting.

2. The best discussion of the question is still probably Maturin Dréano, *La Pensée religieuse de Montaigne* (Paris, 1936).

3. On the translation and Sebond's doctrines see ibid., pp. 91–110; Frame, *Biography*, pp. 103–12, who also cites Joseph Coppin, *Montaigne, traducteur de Raymond Sebond* (Lille, 1925).

4. Donald Frame, "Did Montaigne Betray Sebond?" *Romanic Review* 38 (1947): 297–329; *Biography*, pp. 162–80. See also Dréano, *La Pensée*, pp. 243–95.

5. The letters (a), (b), and (c) refer, respectively, to the three strata normally distinguished in the publication of the *Essais*: material published before 1588, material published in 1588, material published after 1588, based on the revisions and additions of the "Bordeaux copy." Their significance throughout the *Essais* is discussed above, pp. 242–43.

6. For the state of the issue since Dréano, along with some remaining questions, see Donald Frame, "What Next in Montaigne Studies?" *French Review* 46 (1963): 583–85.

7. This is the position of Clement Sclafert, *L'Ame religieuse de Montaigne* (Paris, 1951); see, for example, pp. 236, 239, 176, 178.

8. Hannah Arendt, *The Human Condition* (Garden City, 1959), pp. 10, 18–21.

9. The second etymology is the most common one in the dictionaries; the first is preferred by A. J. Vermeulen, *The Semantic Development of "Gloria" in Early-Christian Latin* (Nijmegen, 1956), p. 29. The following discussion owes a considerable debt to this fascinating study.

10. As a glance at a concordance will reveal, and as Vermeulen points out, the Vergilian usage of the term is not usually so clearly defined in a patriotic sense, perhaps because of Vergil's pacific and melancholy sensibility (*"Gloria,"* pp. 24–25). Typically, the problem of the *Aeneid* is resolved in the *Georgics*: e.g., *divini gloria ruris*, 1. 168; cf. 3. 102; 4. 205. Horace reserves the word for the patriotic odes but seems more concerned with the concept of the glory of the poet's triumph, the *monumentum aere perennius*. See Vermeulen, *"Gloria,"* pp. 35–36.

11. Augustine, *Civitas Dei*, in *Patrologia Latina*, ed. J. P. Migne (Paris, 1857–86), hereafter cited as *P.L.*; the quotation is from volume 91, col. 77. I quote the translation of Gerald G. Walsh, S.J., Demetrius B. Zema, S.J., Grace Monahan, O.S.U., and Daniel J. Honan (New York, 1951). Notice that the quotation within (not noted in Migne) is to the speech of Aeneas over his slain allies, including the "martyred" Pallas: *quae sanguine nobis hanc patriam peppere / suo* (*Aeneid* 11. 24–25).

12. Vermeulen, *"Gloria,"* pp. 5–27. It is interesting to find such manifestations of glory likewise associated with contemplation and divine "play." Citing the vision of the fabulous creatures and chariot wheels of the first chapter of Ezekiel, Romano Guardini finds a model for the "playfulness of the liturgy": "How 'aimless' they are! How discouraging for the zealous partisan of reasonable suitability for a purpose! They are only pure motion, powerful and splendid, acting according to the direction of the Spirit, desiring nothing save to express Its inner drift and Its interior glow and force" (*The Spirit of the Liturgy*, trans. Ada Lane [New York, 1935], p. 178).

13. See Vermeulen, *"Gloria,"* pp. 202–6, on the transformation of the *gloria Christi*.

14. "So, according to St. Ambrose, *gloria* is not something natural, but a garment which gives man a new appearance and envelops him in a new lustre. . . . This garment is nearly always referred to as a vestment of light, of an outward, blinding, resplendent light. Besides *videre Deum* and man's transformation into the glory and light of God, St. Ambrose also mentions the *requies pura, lux immortalis, gratia perpetua, hereditas animarum, pia et secura tranquillitas,* and the *vitae aeternae beatitudinem,* all of them elements derived partly from Stoic ideas" (ibid, pp. 177–78); references are to the *Corpus Scriptorum Ecclesiasticorum Latinorum* (Vienna, 1866), vol. 32, pt. 1, p. 751, and vol. 64, pt. 10, pp. 16–18. The standard treatment of the subject is P. J. Couvée, *Vita beata en Vita eterna bij Lactantius, Ambrosius, Augustinus* (Utrecht, 1947).

15. Especially fascinating is the fusion of garlands and martyrs' wreaths with a halo-like symbol of triumph. See for example, Vermeulen's plates (*"Gloria,"* opposite p. 118), comparing two sarcophagi, one showing the magi offering their gifts to the infant, the other showing Peter and Paul offering their wreaths to an enthroned Christ.

16. T. S. Eliot, "Virgil and the Christian World," *On Poetry and Poets* (London, 1957), p. 126.

17. On the pastoral imagery of Christianity see, for example, Northrop Frye on "Lycidas," *Anatomy of Criticism* (Princeton, 1957), pp. 99–100. Cf. Ronald Knox, "The Shepherds at the Crib," *The Pastoral Sermons,* ed. Philip Carman, S.J. (New York, 1960), pp. 361–63.

18. Many of the religious works first cited in chapter 1, in the preliminary discussion of contemplation and leisure, are relevant here. Hugo Rahner's slim *Man at Play* (New York, 1967) is especially pertinent. Describing "The Playing of God," Rahner refers to a poem by Gregory Nazianzen that is a memorable fusion of the pre-Socratic "aeon that plays on high" with the playful god in the Book of Proverbs: "The Logos on high plays" (*Paidzei gar Logos aipus*), writes Gregory, "stirring the whole cosmos back and forth, as he wills, into shapes of every kind" (*Carmina* 1. 2. 2 [pp. 589–90 in *Patrologia Graeca,* vol. 37, col. 624 A; hereafter cited as *P.G.*). But, even more than in creating the world, such a god, by freely becoming incarnate in (unworthy) man, performed what might be called the ultimate act of play. "Indeed," writes Rahner, "there is an even better reason for calling this [the Incarnation] a game

than for applying that term to the Creation, for in this game of grace Christ has actually become the playmate of man" (p. 47). Describing the Christian response to such a possibility, Rahner entitles his third chapter "The Playing of the Church." The chapter richly illustrates the new kind of civic leisure in which, for example, Vergil's Tityrus, playing his pipe beneath the sheltering beech, has a Christian equivalent in this hymn by Notker of Saint-Gall:

> *Ecce sub vite*
> *amoena, Christe,*
> *ludet in pace*
> *omnis Ecclesia.*
>
> Lo, under the gentle
> vine, O Christ,
> the whole Church
> plays in peace.

(*Analecta Hymnica* [Leipzig, 1911], vol. 53, p. 96, quoted by Rahner, p. 51).

19. It is amusing to recall how the two Carthaginian martyrs, Perpetua and Felicitas, were greeted by four elders at the throne of God with the invitation, "Ite et ludite." See Rahner's discussion, *Man at Play*, p. 61, citing "Passio SS. Felicitatis et Perpetuae," *Ausgewählte Märtyrerakten* (Tübingen, 1929), pp. 40–41.

20. Tertullian, *De Corona* 13 (*P.L.*, vol. 2, col. 96).

21. Georges Florovsky, "Empire and Desert, Antinomies of Christian History," *Greek Orthodox Theological Review* 3 (1957): 146. My interpretation of the genesis of Eastern monasticism owes much to this concise and perceptive article. See also Thomas Merton's introduction to his selections from the *Verba Seniorum: The Wisdom of the Desert* (Norfolk, Conn., 1960). Like Berdyaev, says Merton, the anchorites believed there could be no such thing as a Christian state (p. 4).

22. Florovsky, "Empire and Desert," p. 158.

23. John Henry Newman, *Historical Sketches* (London, 1899), vol. 2, p. 385.

24. Hannah Arendt offers a searching critique of how the Christian pursuit of "goodness" enforced an even more private focus than the classical pursuit of wisdom in the *bios theōrētikos* (*The Human Condition*, pp. 65–69). That this is, paradoxically, itself

a new kind of civic dignity is implicit but not developed in her discussion; for example, "It is as though the early Christians—at least Paul, who after all was a Roman citizen—consciously shaped their concept of immortality after the Roman model, substituting individual life for the political life of the body politic" (pp. 287–88).

25. Athanasius, *Vita Antonii, P.G.*, vol. 26, col. 865 A–B. The phrase provides the title for the useful study by Derwas J. Chitty, *The Desert a City: An Introduction to the Study of Egyptian and Palestinian Monasticism under the Christian Empire* (Oxford, 1966).

26. Bernard, *Epistolae, P.L.*, vol. 182, col. 169 B–C. I quote the translation of the Reverend Bruno Scott James, *St. Bernard of Clairvaux Seen through His Selected Letters* (Chicago, 1953), pp. 72–73. The scriptural references are to Ephesians 2:19, Philippians 3:20, and Galatians 4:25–26. Cf. Bernard's equation of the religious life with Jerusalem, *Super Cantica* 55. 2, *P.L.*, vol. 183, col. 1045. These and other motifs (including the assimilations of the classical *locus amoenus*) are explored by Jean Leclercq, C.S.B., "The Heavenly Jerusalem," *The Love of Learning and the Desire for God* (New York, 1961), pp. 66–70; the entire work is relevant to the concern of this chapter.

27. Justin Martyr, *Cohortatio ad Graecos* 293, *P.G.*, vol. 6. He then quotes *Odyssey* 7. 114–26.

28. Thomas Merton, *The Silent Life* (New York, 1959), p. 145. Mircea Eliade, in discussing "The Yearning for Paradise in Primitive Tradition," finds an analogy in the ecstatic recovery of paradise in the experience of primitive shamans and Christian contemplatives (*Daedalus* 88 [1959]: 255–67); see especially his remarks about the paradisal symbolism of the monastery garden (p. 262).

29. Jacques La Carrière, *Men Possessed by God* (Garden City, 1964), pp. 191–92. La Carrière illustrates this thesis (p. 177) with the detail of a fresco of paradise from the monastery of Coutloumousi on Mount Athos. Chitty makes the same point with regard to the way in which Anthony's withdrawal reportedly returned him to "natural," Adam-like perfection (*The Desert a City*, p. 4). Cf. Athanasius, *Vita Antonii*, col. 865 A.

30. *Vita Antonii*, p. 50.

31. See Chitty, *The Desert a City*, p. 141.

32. Evagrius Ponticus, *Practica ad Anatolium, P.G.*, vol. 40, col. 1249 B. Cf. *P.L.*, vol. 73, col. 1018.

33. Jerome, *Epistolae* 43, "Ad Marcellam," *P.L.*, vol. 22, col. 479. I was led to this and the next reference by Kenneth E. Kirk's magisterial survey, *The Vision of God: The Christian Doctrine of the Summum Bonum* (New York, 1966). I employ his translations on pp. 172–73. What Kirk terms the "naturalism" of these passages should perhaps rather be seen at the imaginative (or spiritual) transformation of external conditions, which, described more realistically, could be as uninviting as Jerome's earlier description of his retreat: "I dwelt in the desert in the vast solitude which gives the hermit his savage home, parched by the burning sun. . . . Tears and groans were every day my portion" (*Epistolae* 22. 7, noted by Kirk, p. 176).

34. Basil, *Epistolae* 14, *P.G.*, vol. 32, col. 276.

35. Gregory Nazianzen, *Epistolae* 5, *P.G.*, vol. 37, cols. 24–28.

36. James's introduction to his translation of Bernard (see n. 26, above) refers to the tradition of a valley of wormwood becoming a valley of light (p. 2).

37. "To Saint Ailred," Abbot of Rievaulx, *P.L.*, vol. 195, col. 502. The letter appears as an introduction, by a certain Gervase, to Saint Ailred's *Speculum Charitatis*. According to James, however, Dom André Wilmart has proved conclusively that the writer is Saint Bernard of Clairvaux; see Bruno Scott James, "L'Instigateur du Speculum Charitatis d'Aelred Abbé de Rievaulx," *Revue d'Ascétique et de Mystique* (October, 1933).

38. "To Saint Ailred," col. 502.

39. Bernard, "Ad Magistrum Henricum Murdoch," *Epistolae* 106, *P.L.*, vol. 82, cols. 241–42.

40. See Kirk, Lecture 4, "Rigorism," part 1, "The Beginnings of Monasticism"; part 2, "Monasticism and the Vision of God," for a summary of these tendencies, with examples (Kirk, *The Vision of God*, pp. 174–206).

41. Kirk (ibid., p. 191) cites J. O. Hanney, *Spirit and Origin of Christian Monasticism*, pp. 115–17. The original reference can be found in *Historia Lausiaca, De Vitis Patrum*, bks. 8, 31, *P.L.*, vol. 73, cols. 1132–33.

42. Cf. the second epigraph of Pieper's book: "Have leisure and know that I am God," Psalm 45:11 (misprinted as 65 [lxv] in his English editions, it is Psalm 46:10 in the Authorized Version) (Josef Pieper, *Leisure: The Basis of Culture*, trans. Alexander Dru [New York, 1954]). The usual translation is "Be still." The Vulgate gives *vacate* for the first verb; yet, significantly, the Septuagint employs

the Greek root *scholē* that was so central to our first consideration of Hellenic leisure: *scholasate*. The instruction became an axiom of mystical epistemology according to Joseph Bernhart, *Die philosophische Mystik des Mittelalters* (Munich, 1922), p. 83.

43. Quoted by Cuthbert Butler, *Benedictine Monachism* (Cambridge, 1961), pp. 94–95. Butler's classic history and interpretation have influenced the following pages greatly. The original, Cassian, *Collations* 24, can be found in *P.G.*, vol. 49, cols. 1287–88, 1293.

44. See Cuthbert Butler, *Western Mysticism* (New York, 1923), pp. 5–6, 180–81.

45. Kirk, *The Vision of God*, p. 271.

46. See above, p. 300, n. 11. For the influential review of the tradition which applied this paradox to the biblical account of the loss of Eden, see Arthur O. Lovejoy, "Milton and the Paradox of the Fortunate Fall," *Essays in the History of Ideas* (New York, 1955), pp. 277–95.

47. See the discussion by Merton, *The Silent Life*, pp. 146–47.

48. Gregory, *Moralia* 28. 33, translated in Butler, *Western Mysticism*, pp. 221–22. The original can be found in *P.L.*, vol. 76, col. 467.

49. Here, and in later instances, quotation marks around "shepherd" or "pastoral" are meant to indicate the active connotations of these words in contrast to such older meanings as I have previously described.

50. Augustine, *Sermones* 105. 2, *P.L.*, vol. 38, col. 618.

51. Augustine, *De Civitate Dei* 6 (ed. William Chase Greene [Cambridge, 1960], vol. 19, col. 204; my translation); cf. Butler, *Western Mysticism*, p. 207. Kirk cites the discussion of the active life to illustrate Augustine's "true worldliness" (*The Vision of God*, p. 334, n. 1).

52. Erich Auerbach, *Dante: Poet of the Secular World*, trans. Ralph Manheim (Chicago, 1961), p. 17. Cf. Helen Waddell: "Augustine had the civic conscience: the sack of Rome sent him to his book of reconstruction, a city that had foundations, whose builder and maker is God, but a city that could be built on the rubble of the Empire" (Waddell, introduction to *The Desert Fathers* [New York, 1936], p. 18). The topic is similarly discussed by Kirk in *The Vision of God*, pp. 330–34.

53. Butler, *Benedictine Monachism*, p. 8. See also Christopher Dawson's "St. Augustine and His Age," in *St. Augustine: Essays on His Age, Life, and Thought*, by M. C. D'Arcy et al. (New York,

1957), pp. 13–77, esp. "The Dying World," pp. 13–39, and the discussion of Augustine's resistance to the "antisecular" Christianity of the African sects, pp. 53–58.

54. Newman, *Historical Sketches*, vol. 2, p. 410.

55. Ibid., pp. 407–9.

56. Justin McCann, *Saint Benedict* (New York, 1937), chaps. 4 and 5.

57. Benedict, *The Rule (Regula Monachorum)*, chap. 48, ed. and trans. Justin McCann (Westminster, Md., 1952), p. 111. Idleness here must be understood in its medieval sense as *acedia*, meaning not sloth but what Chaucer's Parson calls "the anguish of troubled herte," meaning something like the modern existentialist's despairing "sickness unto death." This is why the medieval mind, as Pieper points out, linked idleness with restlessness, sloth with the incapacity for leisure (Pieper, *Leisure: The Basis of Culture*, p. 48). For a brief and interesting survey of the vice's evolution as "melancholy" and "spleen" see Aldous Huxley, "Accidie," *Essays New and Old* (London, 1927).

58. Benedict, *The Rule*, p. 110. Cf. the difference from the view in Cassian, p. 176, above.

59. Monastic literary culture is the general subject of Leclercq's book, *The Love of Learning and the Desire for God*; see esp. pp. 20, 28–30, 45–61. For a concise account of missionary activities from England to Hungary see Butler, *Benedictine Monachism*, pp. 314–17.

60. Gregory, *Epistulae* 1. 5, *P.L.*, vol. 77, col. 440.

61. Gregory, *Liber Regulae Pastoralis* 1. 5 (*Pastoral Care*, trans. Henry Davis, S.J. [Westminster, Md., 1950], p. 31).

62. A. B. Giamatti, *The Earthly Paradise and the Renaissance Epic* (Princeton, 1969), pp. 116–18. My reading of Dante's earthly paradise attempts to describe an equally subtle complexity in the poetic texture of passages which on the doctrinal level (as Giamatti and Sayers, above, properly insist) directs the reader to higher values.

63. This and later references to the *Purgatorio* are to the Italian text and translation in the edition of John D. Sinclair (London, 1948).

64. Dorothy Sayers, *The Comedy of Dante Alighieri . . . Purgatory* (Baltimore, 1960), pp. 293–94.

65. Dante, *Monarchy*, ed. and trans. Donald Nicholl (New York, 1954), p. 92. Cf. John S. Carroll, *Prisoners of Hope* (London, 1906), p. 374.

66. *Monarchy*, p. 93. For the best account of the poet's commitment to the secular city see Charles Till Davis, *Dante and the Idea of Rome* (Oxford, 1957), pp. 1–40.

67. *Monarchy*, p. 93.

68. Auerbach, *Dante: Poet of the Secular World*, pp. 19–23. Cf. the same author's essay, "Figura," in his *Scenes from the Drama of European Literature* (New York, 1959), pp. 70–71.

69. Reality here is even more luminous than the dream. As Ruskin pointed out in his *Modern Painters*, the dreams not only anticipate the figures met the next day but are limited in contrast to them: "Leah took delight in her own labour; but Matilda—'in operibus *manuum Tuarum'—in God's labour*: Rachel in the sight of her own face; Beatrice in the sight of *God's face.*"

70. I quote the more familiar Revised Standard Version. In the Vulgate it is Psalm 91.

71. On the Christian interpretation of Vergil's "messianic" eclogue cf. *Purgatorio* 22. 70–71.

72. Erich Auerbach, *Mimesis: The Representation of Reality in Western Literature*, trans. Willard R. Trask (Princeton, 1953), p. 272. The quotation is from *Essais* 2. 3.

73. Butler, *Benedictine Monachism*, pp. 299–300.

74. Ibid., pp. 295–96.

75. Ibid., p. 360.

76. See the discussion of the last sermons on the canticles in Butler, *Western Mysticism*, pp. 160–67, esp. 165–66.

77. Ibid., p. 360.

78. For a very thorough account of the influence of the *Mystical Theology* in the Middle Ages and the Renaissance see the conclusion of Walther Volker, *Kontemplation und Ekstase bei Pseudo-Dionysius Areopagita* (Wiesbaden, 1958), pp. 218–63.

79. See pp. 194–96, above. In the essay appended to his translation John Frederick Nims notes the poet's debt to the pastorals of Garcilaso and the romantic diction of the troubadours (Nims, *The Poems of Saint John of the Cross* [New York, 1959], p. 121).

80. To the traditional interpretation of the Song of Solomon as an allegory of God's love for the soul, John of the Cross in two

commentaries adds a most precise interpretation of virtually every image in his poem. These commentaries are useful, and are quoted below, but one suspects that the image's power to communicate this kind of experience depends on its appeal to less cerebral faculties. The commentaries, along with a useful introduction, are in Saint John of the Cross, *Works*, vol. 2, translated and edited by E. Allison Peers, from the critical edition of P. Silverio de Santa Teresa, C.D. (London, 1947), hereafter cited as Peers.

81. Nims, *The Poems of Saint John*, p. 123.

82. This and subsequent references to *The Spiritual Canticle* are to the text (Codex of Sanlúcar de Barrameda) and poetic translation of John Frederick Nims in the same volume as the essay cited above. In this instance a more literal translation of *vestidos*, "clothed," would more convincingly illustrate the parallel with "the lilies of the field."

83. Peers, pp. 346–47. This commentary is from the second redaction.

84. This commentary is from the first redaction, Peers, p. 141. The original, of course, is the Song of Solomon 5:1.

85. Michael Drayton, "The Muses Elizium," lines 97–104, in *Poems*, ed. John Buxton (Cambridge, Mass., 1953), p. 206.

86. C. S. Lewis, *The Allegory of Love* (New York, 1959), p. 4. To emphasize the affinity of "courtly love" poetry with the Renaissance revival of pastoral poetry is not, of course, to deny analogous themes already present in the inherited classical models.

87. Guillaume de Lorris and Jean de Meun, *Le Roman de la Rose*, ed. Ernest Langlois (Paris, 1920), vol. 2, p. 30 (ll. 566–74), p. 33 (ll. 631–41). I quote the English translation by Harry W. Robbins in the volume edited by Charles W. Dunn (New York, 1962), section 3, ll. 30–35, 73–83, in his arrangement of the lines. In the lengthy moral section added by Jean de Meun we have, of course, the reassertion of the traditional image of Christian civic leisure in the *champ joli* of the heavenly paradise. Lewis takes pains to instruct the reader in how Guillaume's garden lacks the validity of the final one (p. 151); cf. Giamatti, *The Earthly Paradise*, pp. 60–67 (see n. 62, above).

88. Johan Huizinga, "The Idyllic Vision of Life," in his *The Waning of the Middle Ages* (Garden City, n.d.; first published 1924), p. 135.

89. Harry Berger, Jr., "A Secret Discipline," in *Form and Convention in the Poetry of Edmund Spenser,* ed. William Nelson (New York, 1961), p. 74.

90. The following discussion owes a great debt to the study by Hans Baron, "Cicero and the Roman Civic Spirit in the Middle Ages and Early Renaissance," *Bulletin of the John Rylands Library* 12 (1938): 72–97. In the terms of this book, the rediscovery of Cicero heralded the reassertion of civic leisure. For Cicero's reluctance to retire, see *The Letters to Atticus,* ed. and trans. E. O. Winstedt (London, 1925), vol. 3, pp. 196–257, esp. letters 10 (p. 212), 14 (p. 222), and 15 (pp. 222–24). One might also recall how Cicero praises the remarks of Scipio which Cato records: he was never less idle than when he had nothing to do, and never less lonely than when he was alone. An admirable sentiment, according to Cicero, which shows that "even in leisure hours his thoughts were occupied with public business" (*in otio de negotio cogitare*) (Marcus Tullius Cicero, *De Officiis,* ed. Walter Miller [London, 1958], pp. 270–71). Describing his own imposed retirement, Cicero opposes it to the voluntary withdrawal of Scipio (p. 271). Moreover, he insists, "I am not letting this solitude, which necessity and not my will imposes on me, find me idle" (p. 273). These issues are amplified in Hans Baron's *The Crisis of the Early Italian Renaissance,* rev. ed. (Princeton, 1966). For a different view, see Jerrold E. Siegel, " 'Civic Humanism' or Ciceronian Rhetoric? The Culture of Petrarch and Bruni," *Past and Present* 36 (1967): 21–37.

91. Baron, "Cicero," p. 79.

92. To defend the active life, Albertano da Brescia in 1238 first invoked the *De Officiis* against the traditional figures of Rachel and Mary. See Baron, "Cicero," p. 83.

93. Leonardo Bruni Aretino, "Cicero Novus," *Humanistisch-philosophische Schriften,* ed. Hans Baron (Leipzig, 1928), pp. 114 ff. Cited by Baron, "Cicero," p. 91.

94. Baron, *Crisis of the Early Italian Renaissance,* vol. 1, p. 363.

95. Thomas M. Greene, *The Descent from Heaven* (New Haven, 1963), p. 14. Torquato Tasso, *Discorsi del Poema Eroico* in *Prose,* ed. by E. Mazzali (Naples, 1959), p. 727, cited and translated by Greene, p. 14. Greene stresses the resonance of the final *maravigliose* as an instance of epic awe and what we have previously discussed as civic "glory."

96. Thomas M. Greene, "The Flexibility of the Self in Renaissance Literature," in *The Disciplines of Criticism: Essays in Literary Theory, Interpretation, and History*, ed. Peter Demetz, Thomas Greene, and Lowry Nelson, Jr. (New Haven, 1968), p. 250.

97. A discourse by that name attributed to Bernard is in *P.L.*, vol. 184, cols. 1212–14, part of the much longer *Liber de Modo Bene Vivendi ad Sororem*, cols. 1194–1306. See also Bernard's poem *De Contemptu Mundi* (ibid., cols. 1313–16). I owe these parallels to William James Hirten, whose edition of Thomas Paynell's sixteenth-century English translation of the treatise by Erasmus contains a useful introduction to the tradition (*De Contemptu Mundi* [Gainesville, 1967]). References to Erasmus are to the *Opera Omnia*, ed. Frobenius (Basle, 1540). *De Contemptu Mundi* is in volume 5, hereafter cited by page references in the text. The translations are my own. See also *Eclogues* 9. 39–43.

98. For a discussion of that chapter and the larger question of his ambivalent view of monasticism, see Hirten's introduction, pp. xxx–xl.

99. Erasmus, *Antibarbarorum Liber*, *Opera*, vol. 9, pp. 1430–31. For an interesting discussion of the implications of this and the next two notes, see William Harrison Woodward's ample introduction to his edition of various texts grouped under the general heading *Desiderius Erasmus concerning the Aim and Method of Education* (New York, 1964), p. 141. Woodward's references, however, are to an eighteenth-century edition.

100. Erasmus, *De Pueris Statim ac Liberaliter Instituendis*, *Opera*, vol. 1, p. 425. Cf. Woodward, *Desiderius Erasmus*, p. 187.

101. Erasmus, *Opera*, vol. 3, pp. 878–79. Cf. Woodward, p. 65.

102. References to the *Colloquia Familiaria*, cited in the text hereafter by page number, are to the original Latin in *Opera*, vol. 1, pp. 526–756. I employ the translation of Craig R. Thompson, *The Colloquies of Erasmus* (Chicago, 1965). I have, however, added such scriptural and other references as the 1540 edition provides; on occasion I have silently corrected misprints in the scriptural allusions in the 1540 edition.

103. Thompson, *The Colloquies of Erasmus*, p. 128.

104. See bk. 1, chap. 52, passim. This and subsequent references in the text to the *Gargantua* are to the Thélème section in the Pléiade edition, François Rabelais, *Oeuvres Complètes*, ed. Jacques Boulenger and Lucien Scheler (Paris, 1955), pp. 147–60. The En-

glish translation is that of J. M. Cohen, *The Histories of Gargantua and Pantagruel* (Baltimore, 1969).

105. Thomas M. Greene, *Rabelais: A Study in Comic Courage* (Englewood Cliffs, 1970), p. 51.

106. Leonardo Bruni, "Life of Dante," *The Early Lives of Dante*, trans. Philip H. Wicksteed (London, 1904), pp. 19–20.

107. Giovanni Boccaccio, "Life of Dante," ibid., pp. 24, 29.

108. Baron, "Cicero," pp. 90–91.

109. Francesco Petrarca, "Familiarum Rerum Libri," 25 (XXIV, 3), ed. Enrico Bianchi, in *Prose*, ed. Guido Martellotti et al. (Milan and Naples, n.d.), p. 1024; my translation. Subsequent references to other prose works of Petrarch are to this volume.

110. Francesco Petrarca, *De Vita Solitaria*, p. 434. Subsequent page references to this work are in the text.

111. "Familiarium Rerum Libri," 4 (IV, 1) (p. 840).

112. Jacob Zeitlin, introduction to his translation of Petrarch's *Life of Solitude* (Urbana, 1924), p. 71. This is also the theme of Salvatore Quasimodo's brief essay, *Petrarca e il Sentimento della Solitudine* (Milan, 1959).

113. The translation quoted is that of Jacob Zeitlin, cited in the preceding note.

114. Renato Poggioli, "The Pastoral of the Self," *Daedalus* 88 (1959): 686–99.

115. Ernest Hatch Wilkins, *Life of Petrarch* (Chicago, 1961), p. 36.

116. Zeitlin, introduction to Petrarch's *Life of Solitude*, p. 55.

117. Charles Trinkaus, "Petrarch's Views on the Individual and His Society," *Osiris* 11 (1954): 197.

118. Pliny, *Letters* 1. 3. 6–7, trans. William Melmoth, revised by W. M. L. Hutchinson (Cambridge, Mass., 1961). The correspondent is Caninius Rufus, not "Cornelius," as Montaigne has it.

119. Auerbach, *Mimesis*, p. 272.

120. Sclafert, *L'Ame religieuse de Montaigne*, p. 281.

121. Herbert Lüthy, "Montaigne, or the Art of Being Truthful," *Encounter* 1 (1953): 37.

122. Pierre Villey, *Les Sources et l'évolution des Essais de Montaigne*, 2d rev. ed. (Paris, 1933), pp. 38–66.

123. Donald Frame, *Montaigne's Discovery of Man*. See esp. chap. 6, "The Discovery of Others," pp. 1580–86.

124. A. B. Giamatti, "Proteus Unbound: Some Versions of the Sea-God in the Renaissance," in *The Disciplines of Criticism,* ed. Demetz et al., p. 441.

125. Frame, *Montaigne's Discovery of Man,* p. 44.

126. Frame, *Montaigne: A Biography,* chap. 7; cf. *Essais* 2. 6 (T., p. 414; F., p. 269).

127. Hugo Friedrich, *Montaigne* (Bern, 1949) (see p. 30 for his account of Montaigne's "evolution"); Philip P. Hallie, *The Scar of Montaigne* (Middletown, 1966).

128. Imbrie Buffam, *Studies in the Baroque, from Montaigne to Rotrou* (New Haven, 1957), p. 23.

129. Charles Feidelson, *Symbolism and American Literature* (Chicago, 1952), pp. 187, 189.

130. Ralph Waldo Emerson, "Montaigne, or the Skeptic," *Representative Men* (Boston, 1883), p. 160; cf. Emerson's *Journals* (Boston, 1914), vol. 5, p. 420.

131. See Auerbach, *Mimesis,* p. 273.

132. Frank Kermode, introduction to Shakespeare's *Winter's Tale* (New York, 1963), p. xxxv.

133. Ernst Cassirer, *The Question of Jean-Jacques Rousseau,* trans. and ed. Peter Gay (New York, 1954), p. 125.

134. See William F. Bottiglia, "Candide's Garden," *PMLA* 66 (1951): 718–33, esp. 727.

135. Villey, *Les Sources et l'évolution,* vol. 2, p. 135.

136. Jacques Perret, *Horace,* trans. Bertha Humez (New York, 1964), p. 115.

137. Georges Poulet, *Studies in Human Time,* trans. Elliott Coleman (New York, 1964), p. 48.

INDEX

DATE DUE	BORROWER'S NAME	ROOM NUMBER

PRINTED IN U.S.A.
GAYLORD